Soul care

Also by Peter Atkins:

Soul Time: Building a Relationship with God

Soul care

FACING LIFE WITH GOD

Peter Atkins

Chalice Press
St. Louis, Missouri

Cover design: Lynne Condellone
Cover photo: © Photodisc
Interior design: Elizabeth Wright
Art direction: Elizabeth Wright

This book is printed on acid-free, recycled paper.

Visit Chalice Press on the World Wide Web at
www.chalicepress.com

10 9 8 7 6 5 4 3 2 1 01 02 03 04

Library of Congress Cataloging–in–Publication Data

Atkins, Peter, 1936–
Soul care : facing life with God / Peter Atkins.
p. cm.
Includes bibliographical references and index.
ISBN 0-8272-3449-X
1. Self-acceptance–Religious aspects–Christianity I. Title.
BV4598.24 .A88 2001
248.4–dc21

00–010824

Printed in the United States of America

This book is dedicated to
my friend and colleague
in the teaching of pastoral theology,
the Reverend Dr. Philip Culbertson.

Contents

Acknowledgments

The contents of this book have arisen out of the experience of giving and receiving pastoral care over many years of ministry as both a pastor and a teacher. Those of us who minister to others are aware of how much our lives are enriched by those we try to serve. Each incident in the life of another, be it one of joy or one of struggle, helps prepare us for the vicissitudes and victories in our own lives. I therefore acknowledge with gratitude all those people who have helped me to see life as a whole and have revealed how the God of love can sustain and support us on all of life's occasions.

The research and writing of authors worldwide in the field of pastoral care have opened for us insights into ourselves and the situations we face in life. I acknowledge the help I have received over my years of teaching from such authors. For this book I am grateful particularly to those writing from experience in the area of coping with disability and to those in the hospice movement, who have taught us so much about facing up to death.

During the writing of this book, I have had to focus my thoughts on some tough issues, and what I write is in part a message to myself as well as to you, my reader. Only the inspiration of the Holy Spirit can add depth to our musings and courage to our dreams.

In the practicality of getting the words shaped into readable form, I acknowledge the assistance of some good friends in the task of proofreading, of Jon L. Berquist and his team at Chalice Press for the editorial work and the adaptation of language to their market, and to my wife, Rosemary, whose constant encouragement, love, and support enable my work and delight my leisure.

Finally, I acknowledge you, my reader, for this book is written to act as your partner in the task of looking after yourself with the help of God. The text provides for your input, reflection, and prayer so that together we can discover how you, with the support of God and your community, can respond to life's challenges and live the way of love.

Introduction

Using This Book

You may have picked up this book to read because you sense that you are in need of some pastoral care for a particular situation. Obviously, no author can cover the whole range of situations we encounter in life, but I have tried to comment in one chapter or another on the most common. If this is your situation, I suggest that you look at the Index at the back of the book to examine the detailed list of topics and turn to the one that concerns you. After looking at that one, you might find that you want to read more generally and cover the whole chapter. The book can remain in your library as a future reference for different occasions.

On the other hand, you may want to reflect more fully on the totality of life's situations, and thus be prepared to look after yourself more adequately when a particular issue arises. If this applies to you, I suggest that you read the book through in the order that I have set out. Different chapters touch life's ups and downs, and the variety should keep you balanced in your outlook on life.

Others of you may be students in the field of pastoral care and may add this book to your libraries to give practical ideas on how to look after yourselves and others in the vicissitudes of life. The list of books in the Bibliography will give you the titles of some other books that specialize on particular topics. I urge you to read a selection of these to give you a fuller perspective on pastoral care. My personal experience and that of others ground this book in the real world of human life, but it is also important for students to have a depth of knowledge on particular topics so that they are equipped to offer quality pastoral care.

God's Care for Us

As you care for yourself, I believe that the Spirit of God will uphold and guide you in facing the opportunities and difficulties in life. I pray that my words may be springboards for the Spirit's work. My hope is that what I have written will cause you to search deeply in your soul for a true response to your particular situation. I have written this book in an intimate, person-to-person style, as if you and I were sitting down together facing the situations before you. In this way I hope to allow you to engage the Spirit's voice. I have indicated places where I think that it would be helpful for you to pause and reflect before reading further. I have also included prayer outlines at various points. You may choose to use my prayers or express your prayers in your own words. This way of writing is not a device. It arises from my conviction and experience that God's spirit is always in action as we read, think, and pray.

You will also find biblical quotations. These help to ground my advice in the words of scripture. You may recall other biblical passages that confirm or enlarge what I say. Take time to look up these passages for yourself and return to my text when you feel ready to move on.

In writing this book I am building on the foundation of the relationship with God that I outlined in a previous volume titled *Soul Time.*[1] If you have not read that book, you may wish to find a copy and measure your faith experience against what I have written there. *Soul Time* expresses my belief that our relationship with God is one of partnership and interdependence. I do not believe that we should try to hand everything over to God and expect God to do our work for us. In both our prayers and our living we have to do our part, guided, upheld, and strengthened by God's spirit.

Gaining Knowledge

I also believe that to give ourselves proper care, we have to become knowledgeable and skilled to make the most of our opportunities in life. I trust that this book will help you achieve this aim and inspire you to think and learn more about the human condition and the way that we work in body, mind, and spirit.

I have used a variety of authorities as the framework for my writing. In the field of pastoral care the experts are numerous and the variety of opinion is profound. By referring to these authorities, I am not suggesting that they alone are the experts. However, their research has added to the pool of knowledge, and for that we are thankful. Some of the books to which I refer may not be available locally. If that is the case for you, I suggest that you use your community library to locate alternative books covering the same topics. The goal is to enable you to go more deeply into a topic when you need to know more for a particular situation.

---

[1]Peter Atkins, *Soul Time* (St. Louis: Chalice Press, 2000).

Topics Covered in This Book

Take a look again at the Contents page. You will see that I have chosen ten topics to illustrate in more detail the principles of how you can look after yourself with God's help.

I begin with the principle of love and how it operates and then set this against the various routine stages through which we might pass in a full life. As we reflect on chapter 1, we can begin to build up a set of routine responses by which we can care for ourselves in these various stages of life.

The essence of being human is the ability to make choices and come to decisions. To make wise choices we need to reach a level of maturity. Some choices are major–the choice of a marriage partner or the choice of a career. Some are minor–the choice of a home, a vacation, or a car. Whatever the choice before us, there are some basic principles involved in coming to a decision. Chapter 2 covers these and deals in detail with the two major choices mentioned above.

In chapter 3 we face the reality that not all of life is joyful or easy. We all have our despondent moments when we wonder about the value and meaning of life. A loss in some form or another is a common cause for such despondency. In writing this chapter I was very conscious of the difference between despondency and the medical condition of depression. The latter must be treated by a doctor, and my hope is that any so affected will feel encouraged to seek help. But in our despondent moments there are ways to help ourselves, and these are examined in this chapter.

We turn in chapter 4 from times of feeling down to occasions when we are riding high. I seek to help you make the most of your times of celebration. I have a great desire to see people in the twenty-first century learn to celebrate the high points of life, not allowing them to slip by unnoticed. You will find in this chapter a range of times for such celebrations with some suggestions as to how they may be highlighted.

As we grow in life, new responsibilities come our way, or we create them. I have always found inspiration in the book of Nehemiah to provide a pattern of positive actions to take when faced with a new responsibility–perhaps parenthood, a work task, or a community role. In chapter 5 I set out the teaching from scripture that can help us establish a pattern by which we can take up our new responsibilities.

I experienced some hesitation in writing chapter 6, in which I search for ways to care for oneself when living with a disability. However, my admiration for the many courageous examples I found made me want to share my experiences and my research. The increasing visibility of those with disabilities is good for us all. In the end, I found this chapter promoted real growth and learning in my own approach to life, and hope it may do the same for you.

Leisure is both a joy and an essential for modern living, and I knew that I ought to include it among the ten topics. The nature of the Sabbath, vacations, and socialization through leisure are all topics covered in chapter 7. It emphasizes that care for the body is as vital to life with God as care for the soul.

Ethical questions of truth and justice are so much a part of the Christian response to life that I felt they should have a place in this book. We are called to tell the truth and act for justice, and our responses put major pressures on us. How we might look after ourselves in such stress is the subject of chapters 8 and 9. The ethical questions might seem rather vague, but the issues that arise from them, which we face day-to-day, are very practical, and I concentrate on these.

Chapter 10 looks at the ways we can care for ourselves at the conclusion of our earthly life. Much research has been done on the common reactions to the news of impending death. I have tried to share this research with you in the context of my own experience as a pastor and priest. Death is an emotional subject, but it is a part of our living experience. It should never be the subject of silence. I aimed to write in a sensitive way that would release emotions rather than stir them. My hope is that the dying will find new faith for the journey to resurrection.

I have ended the book with a short Conclusion in which I try to draw the threads together and, in table form, reiterate the essential ways that we can all find care for ourselves in the various situations of life.

A Christian Perspective

My prayer is that you might enjoy reading this book and find it useful in advancing your care of yourself with the help of God. I write as a Christian out of a personal faith in Jesus Christ, who is my stay and guide. It is not necessary for you to share my faith, but I do ask you to respect it. It gives life and color to what I write. If you respect my convictions, I am certain that you will be able to make sense of this book and use it, whatever faith position you hold.

Go well on your journey.
Seize your opportunities.
Enhance your relationships.
Comfort your sorrows.
Laugh at your joys.
Celebrate your triumphs.
Enter into your resurrection.
And God will be with you.

1

Looking after Yourself in the Routines of Life

Most of life is routine. That may sound dull to you but don't be put off by such a statement. Without routine most of us would collapse. Think of breathing, for example. Inhaling and exhaling breath is an essential routine for the body. It is so natural that we only notice it when we stop to think about it. If we concentrated all our thoughts on the action of breathing, we would be so occupied that we would have little mental energy left for the more exciting things in life. In times of stress we should take notice of our patterns of breathing–but otherwise just do it! Take a few deep breaths now, and then let your lungs continue their routine to give you life.

The Image of the Triangle

We need routine in our lives as a framework on which we can build that which is significant for us. This framework should be well constructed so that we can make the most of the lives that are gifts from God in partnership with humanity. How can we construct this sort of framework? Imagine a triangle standing upright. Each side equally supports the whole structure. Use this as a parable with God, yourself, and others as the three sides of the triangle. To maintain the triangle in its proper shape, we need each side to be strong. Likewise, in our lives we need to receive love and care from God, self, and others and, in turn, give love and care back to God, self, and others.

This is the working out of the commandment that Jesus gave his disciples:[1]

Love the Lord your God...love your neighbor as yourself.

If you weaken any side of the triangle, you weaken the whole. If you do not live with an equal emphasis of love, you distort the whole of life.

Some people struggle with such a statement. They note the order in Jesus' commandment: God first, others second, and ourselves last. They say that any other order promotes selfishness, which they say is the greatest of sins. It can be, but it is more often true that the greatest sin for such people is the hatred and denial of self. If we hold to the belief that God delights in creation, to hate self is to tell God that we are not worthy of our creation and the care that is God's gift to us. That surely is a sin. We also know that those who hate themselves are more likely to pass on that hatred to others, and that is a sin. On the other hand, if we keep the balance among love of self, love of others, and love of God, we will be fulfilling God's purpose for life and offering our thanks to God in the lives we lead as well as in the words we say.

Caring for the Body

Looking after yourself with God's help includes caring for your body, mind, and spirit. In recent years an entire industry has arisen to help us care for our bodies. On the waterfront road near my house in Auckland, hundreds of people rise with the sun to keep fit by walking, running, swimming, jogging, and cycling. In gymnasiums throughout the city, people push their bodies to the limit to keep them active and healthy. Some people even have personal trainers to establish the best routine for the body. As a walker, I find it good to reflect on the amount of walking that Jesus and the disciples did to keep themselves fit. They fasted and feasted, they slept and woke, they toiled and rested, all according to their bodies' needs. Most Christians take care of their bodies as a gift of God to be used and kept fit for God's glory. Caring for ourselves with God's help will certainly mean establishing a routine to keep our bodies fit.

Caring for the Mind

The mind is a part of the body, but it is so vital to our full functioning that Jesus gave it its own emphasis. In the "age of information" we can be tempted to let our minds become slack and

---

[1]Matthew 22:37, 39.

allow our feelings to dominate our responses to events or opinions. We need to train our minds to link feelings with logic and logic with feelings. To achieve this, we must exercise the mind, stretching it in both directions at once. We will ask ourselves what the facts are behind a situation or opinion, and what the feelings are of those concerned. Try such an approach for a moment about an item of news that you have read or heard today. Now reverse the order—feelings first and facts second—about another item of news. You will probably find that you have a preference for the order in which you look at an issue, so it is vital to work for a balanced approach.

Caring for our mind in the routine situations of life will mean that we keep it exercised and active in the search for material. With so much "information" about, we can allow our mental processes to become lazy, simply absorbing the material fed into them. Minds, too, can become obese with junk intake. Christians must follow Jesus' pattern of wrestling with the question Why? as well as What? and How? We will look at all sides of the issue to discover more of the truth. We will seek to understand from the other person's point of view. We will look for the larger picture. We will consider the context and the culture. We will seek to enlarge our minds.

It is for this reason that Christians over the centuries have trusted God enough to be engaged in research, pushing the boundaries of knowledge and seeking to integrate this into an understanding that enlarges our belief and trust in both God and one another. Such knowledge is for the good of all and not for our own aggrandizement or profit. I know that this is a noble ideal, but it is a response to the saying of Christ, "The truth will make you free."

To care for yourself with God's help will mean exercising the mind regularly with an established routine. Your mind will be stimulated by imagination as well as fact, by music as well as the media. You can explore through art as well as word; through theater, opera, and ballet as well as books and newspapers. The Internet will allow an explosion of information, but we must give our eyes opportunities for inner reflection as well as outward response. Take a few moments now to outline a routine to care for your mind.

Caring for the Spirit

Our spirits need nourishing as well. Many people currently recognize this but struggle with the concept that God must be involved in their spiritual development. Surely, human beings have "grown up" and can control their own destinies. As we will see later in this chapter, to be "grown up" is to recognize interdependence–that is, we cannot exist on our own power and must learn to receive and give equally. To care for our spirits will entail receiving from God and others to enlarge our souls, as well as exercising our souls in the disciplines of the spirit. In *Soul Time,* my first book in this series, I set out how each of us can grow in our relationships with God and others for the health and happiness of our souls. If we truly care for ourselves, we will make the effort to develop our spirits at a pace equal to that of our bodies and minds. The three are so intertwined in our makeup that each affects the others–for good or ill. For example, some of the effects of the loss of a limb can be compensated for by a healthy mind and spirit so that the person can go on with a well-rounded life. Yet the opposite can also be true when depression of the spirit can cause the collapse of the body.

In keeping our spirits healthy, we need to pay attention to how we worship, how we pray, how we forgive, how we care for others and ourselves, and how we let God's will affect our lives. If you feel that you need help in establishing a routine for such work, I invite you to locate a copy of *Soul Time* or a similar book. Pause now and record for yourself the routine you will follow to build the solid foundation for your spirit so that you can face all of life's situations.

The Routine Development of Life

In caring for ourselves we will become aware of the various stages through which we move during a lifetime. Research in recent years has given us insight into what major developments take place at each stage and how these developments build up a framework of competencies with which we respond to the events in our lives. There are developments of body, mind, and spirit. This research has produced a variety of "markers" for each stage that correspond to chronological age brackets. Observation tells us that these are average age markers, for some people "grow" at different rates than others. Some people look "old" at sixty, and others look "young" at eighty. Despite these cautions, the general information about the developmental stages can help us gain a large measure of self-understanding.

I have chosen to use a pattern set out by Erik Erikson that he summarized in one of his later books, *The Life Cycle Completed.*[2] Erikson had spent many years looking closely at the characteristics of

[2]Erik Erikson, *The Life Cycle Completed* (New York: W. W. Norton, 1982).

people in various stages of the life cycle from the cradle to the grave. He noted what positive developments take place at each stage. Our own observations will probably affirm his insights and give us examples from our own and others' experiences. What we also know is that it is possible to make up for some of the deficiencies in our development at a later stage if we are surrounded and supported by love and wisdom. As we pass through these stages, we are interdependent, needing others to help us acquire the relevant competencies. Sometimes key people let us down, but others can compensate either at that time or later. To give a physical example, we usually have a number of people who can help us stand on our feet and take our first steps. Parents and siblings are mostly responsible for this, but the circle is widened by a mixture of grandparents, aunts and uncles, cousins, friends, and neighbors. Such a wider group can help us with mental and spiritual competencies as well. It is good to use the image of the triangle again—our development involves God, others, and self, with strong interplay between the so-called separate roles.

The Eight Stages of Life

What follows is the list of the eight stages noted by Erikson. Look at it carefully and try to recall examples from your own experience.

Erikson's own understanding is that, to some extent, we are in all of the stages all the time, but that in the age stated we are focused on

Age Range	Stage	Main Development	Question Asked
0–2 years	Infancy	Trust	Whom can I trust?
2–3 years	Early Childhood	Willpower	What should I do?
3–5 years	Play Age	Purpose	What are my goals?
6–12 years	School Age	Competency	How can I achieve my goals?
12–18 years	Adolescence	Fidelity	Can I be trusted?
19–35 years	Young Adulthood	Love	How do I give/receive love?
35–65 years	Adulthood	Care	How do I care for others?
65 onward	Old Age	Wisdom	How can I pass on my knowledge and experience?

the development of a particular competency that is critical for our future well-being. The good news is that, with love and God's help, we can make up past deficiencies and heal the hurts. Achieving this will require an openness on our part and a willingness to revisit some painful memories. Because this is a short, general book, I should point out that you probably need trained help to make such a recovery. My aim is to lay a good foundation so that you find the confidence to seek help from those who offer such a ministry. In the Bibliography you will find a list of books that should be able to point you in the right direction.

Our self-understanding is enhanced as we look in more detail at these routine developments through which we pass. With such knowledge we can give ourselves the care we need and note if we seem to be weak in any competency. We are then in a better position to work at making up the deficiency, recalling that God's love for us will give us the strength to face the issues and seek the help we need.

Infancy and Trust

In infancy we are dependent on others for our development. They do nearly everything for us except take over our personality, as any parent knows. If we were to paint a picture of touch, we would probably choose the tiny finger of an infant clinging to the bigger finger of an adult. It is a sign of trust in the adult, who must provide what is required for growth—food, warmth, cleanliness, and most of all love, which to an infant is expressed by touch. Of course, what we need as infants, we go on needing throughout our lives. As we develop we learn to provide for our own basic needs and work cooperatively to make such provisions for food, shelter, cleanliness, and love. Basic to our being is the need for touch to express love. Hugs are the "in thing" for good reason! In an age of sexual freedom, touch has a confused connotation—there is good touch and bad touch, as every child soon learns. Yet in our fear about bad touch we must not deprive our bodies of the positive values of good touch.

Touch and trust are closely connected. To touch puts us in a proper relationship with others, and we also want a sense of touch from God. That is why "blessing" was so often an activity of Jesus, and the church has entrusted this ministry to certain representatives to act in God's name in giving a blessing. Holding hands with Jesus is often a necessary image for people to capture if they want to restore trust in God that has broken down either because they distanced themselves from God or because they hold a false view about a distant God. My guess is that most people with an undeveloped ability to trust God and others were "kept at a distance" as tiny infants. This may have been caused by rejection from parents or significant others, or by poverty, crisis, or other pressures that caused the infant to be deprived of sufficient time or care. Some people are able to recover later and develop an ability to trust because of the depth of love experienced from others and from God at a later date.

Ask yourself the question, Whom do I trust? Make a list and give thanks to God for the gifts of all these people. If you are older than forty, the list may be quite long, but it will also reveal your need to forgive some people whom you wish you were able to put on the list but cannot. Such forgiveness is important and will free you to focus on the many who did help you develop a sense of trust.

Early Childhood and the Ability to Make Choices

In early childhood we begin to develop the capacity to choose in relation to others. If we have learned the basic quality of trust, we will know that our limited experience as a child can be enlarged by the trust that we have in the knowledge and experience of others. Our first inclination is to try to experience everything for ourselves. We quickly learn that we do not have the physical ability to do what we would like. We are too small to see over the crowd, so we accept with delight the lift on to the shoulders of a trusted adult. The second year can be an age of frustration because our vocabulary is not wide enough to make clear our wants, and our legs and arms are not sufficiently coordinated to give us full mobility. Out of this frustration we can enter a struggle of wills. Yes and no come to equal a battle rather than a discovery of possibilities. If the young child is dominated and controlled, the ability to choose is restricted, and the conscience is left undeveloped. Making mistakes should be a positive experience of discovering a proper way, not a negative experience of punishment. With the best of support, this age group also develops the competence of cooperation, not competition, in learning to ask for help, which empowers rather than takes power away. If we are spoiled because those around us say yes without regard to their own needs and feelings, we do not learn the art of saying yes and no in the proper places. If we learn to trust others and see no as a positive response to an unhelpful or impossible request, we will be able to handle no in the future as a sign of love, not of hate or rejection.

Ask yourself what yes and no mean for you now. Do you still see yes as an affirmation of love and no as a sign of rejection? You see the point I am making. You may have to replay the record of your childhood in the light of your answer and come to some new conclusions in your care for yourself with God's help. God's yes and no are always for our good.

The Age of Play and Setting Goals

In the age of play you rehearse many of life's future situations. You learn to cook with play dough; you dress up for grand occasions; you draw or color your first pictures and share them as gifts to parents and grandparents; you play at building a home or sewing a garment; you build castles and demolish obstacles; you enter into deep conversation and share opinions in confidence; you kiss your first friend of the opposite gender; you play at weddings and funerals. The boundary between imagination and reality is rightly blurred, as play and life are one and the same event. This is why we must never sacrifice play for education in this age group.

In the age of play we learn to set goals for living and to accumulate the energy and skill required to face them. Between the ages of three and five we learn three basic skills:

- Language–to say what we mean
- Movement–to go where we want to go
- Imagination–to perceive what is possible even before we can achieve it

As the child moves toward five years old, he or she can grow in confidence in others and in self. This confidence is not arrogance, because there is an awareness of the limitations of the possible. It is the confidence that our dreams can be achieved once we have learned the skills to bring them to pass. Our inner confidence is based on the trust that we have developed in others, on the choices of what is beneficial to us and to others, and on a power that is greater than ours that will help us to achieve our goals. This play age is an essential platform for our sense of vision and expectancy. If we do not try out our play wings, we will never become the angels that we dream we are. It is no wonder that we feel close to heaven at this age and that the adventure of life fills us with excitement rather than fear. It is an age when we can learn to pray. We have the very skills that prayer requires–language, movement, and imagination. In our prayers we see the vision of what might be and what should be and do not throw these thoughts out as impossible or impractical. We have learned the stimulus of energy and the revitalization of rest. How appropriate this is for prayer and reflection.

Give thanks to God for your dreams and playful imagination and feel your confidence arise again as you share your request for help from others to make the play "fun" as well as real. As adults we may need to revive this sense of "fun and games" and the delight that imagination can bring.

School Age and the Acquisition of Skills

Going off to school is a major landmark in life for parents and children. It can mark a new sense of independence for both. Parents gain a new understanding of the skills of their child and how these will develop within the community as well as the family. Children have to repeat the learning of their development to date: trusting in a new set of adults and peers, making choices for themselves and others, hearing yes and no in a new context, and redefining their goals and dreams. The skills of cooperation, conflict resolution, language, movement, and imagination are all tested, and a whole range of competencies is introduced–interpretation, explanation, articulation, numeracy, and coordinated movement. These skills may be acquired in a competitive and judgmental framework. The ability of critical assessment is begun, and often the basis of such assessment is unclear. The child asks whether love equals affirmation and if mistakes cause damnation or become the building blocks for future achievement. These are critical questions for future behavior. Is it better to have tried and failed or to attempt little and be safe from possible scolding? The need for love and courage is never more pressing, and the experience of forgiveness can be either a release from guilt or a reservation as a future threat. The struggle for the school-aged child is between feelings ranging from competency to inferiority and failure. Many parents have endured the agonies of their children in this period when so many other adults are involved–all with their own limitations in full maturity. In this process many parents have relived their own agonies and the damage that was done in their early years at school.

For those who are supported by genuine love and hope, this school age stage can end with the flowering of great promise. The body and mind reach a platform of stability that is creative and agile. The child can search for answers to his or her questions and find what is satisfying and stimulating. Adults are growing down in size as the child grows upward. Adults can even admit that they are fallible. Life is full of hope, and most things should become possible to achieve tomorrow if not today.

Remember your days of hope with joy and recall your school reports with a smile. What did they teach you about your attitude toward life, and how accurate were their predictions? Offer your feelings to Jesus and feel his understanding arm around your shoulders as you experience the range of emotions from these memories of your early youth.

Adolescence and the Struggle to Be Trusted

Just as life begins to seem so coordinated, adolescence throws challenge and confusion at us. Having become accustomed to our bodies, they go through radical changes that shake our confidence. We feel awkward and often external to our bodies. We can experience the sense of standing outside our bodies and our feelings. Our moods can swing wildly, and our clothes never seem to fit our bodies or our pockets. Young people of this age feel that the roots of everything have been or should be torn up. It is like being age two again. We do not know if we can trust ourselves, others, or God. We are constantly in a battle of wills–What should we do? What should we be allowed to do? Why can't we do what we want to do? Most of all, Can I trust myself–my body, my mind, and my soul–to act properly? I feel that I hurt myself and others, and most of the time I do not know why. The good I would do I seldom do, and feelings of guilt abound. Will I grow up to be the new me that is emerging, and will I like that person? Will anyone else like that person? The problem for most adolescents is that they feel they cannot rely on things anymore. The confidence of late childhood evaporates, and introspection has no fixed reference point. If I believed in God before, I am not certain anymore. I desperately want to be accepted for who I am, but even I do not know who I am or what I will become. My friends are important to me, but they are changing all the time as well. My parents and elders are important to me, but I am struggling to be their equal, and it feels as if competition is part of the struggle of formation. Sometimes my grandparents understand and love me the most, but they are going through life changes also–aging in a different way, losing their power as I gain mine.

As the pendulum stops its violent swinging, many young people in their late teens look for a savior and role model. The scriptures have many examples of those who, in the midst of struggle, discover God–from Jacob, to Jeremiah, Paul, and young Mark. God can be a new point of reference and our guide as we cross the stormy seas.

Like Paul with his feelings of guilt, when the adolescent calls for a Savior, Jesus is there in his own strength and vision, with hope and realism combined. As we trust this Jesus to be Savior and Lord freeing us for service, so we can learn to trust ourselves again. The commitment of youth can be the foundation for a life of service. At the end of this stage we need to be loved and to be taught how to love. We are ready to move on to young adulthood.

Young Adulthood and the Ability to Give and Receive Love

Erikson names the stage from the end of the teens to the middle thirties young adulthood. It is the age of discovery and responsibility. It is the time of intimacy and the age of true love. Hugging, touching, and kissing all give and share affirmation. Even parents are appreciated when they give affirmation with appropriate touching. The discovery of love is about its mutuality. It feels good to turn the "I" into "we." Having overcome our insecurities, we can reach out in love and humbly receive love. It can be an age of acceptance for the secure and of fragility for the insecure who still retain the hurts of adolescence. In modern society this age has difficulty in deciding the priorities of love. Love of status and money are alluring when compared with the sacrifices often involved in love of the other in a deep relationship. Love of sport and travel also may take priority over love of a possible family.

The discovery of love is also about the difference between sexual and nonsexual love. The experience of many relationships of different types—but all on the basis of equality as an adult—takes time to sort out. Yet this differentiation is essential and accumulative. I gradually work out the answer to the key question: How do I give and receive love? I do this through a range of relationships—parents, siblings, friends, partner, maybe spouse. I learn to see them as people, not objects, capable of entering a mutual relationship of affirmation and cooperation. I learn to discard as well as accumulate, and that can be a painful lesson.

There is also the discovery of God. I discover that God has grown up as I have grown up. I no longer think like a child, for I now appreciate the complexity of life's situations. I can seek forgiveness in order to move on to the future as well as to heal the past. I can take affirmation and criticism, understanding the role of each for my good. In God I discover the ultimate about loving and look for others who can reflect that love to me, and to whom I in turn can give my love. I know that joy and ecstasy are possible, but they carry with them responsibility. I am ready and equipped to give something back to life.

If you are a young adult, see how many points you can relate to in the above description. Make a list of the times you have experienced the mutuality of true love. If you are older, try to remember the times of affirmation that you received as a young adult and reflect on why they were so helpful for your growth.

Adulthood and the Ability to Care for Others

Erikson observes that adulthood is the longest span of life for most people, lasting approximately thirty years. It is the time when we make the highest contributions to life. It may be through raising the next generation. It may be through significant work for society. It may be through community building. It may be through caring for the generation ahead of us. The focus of our skills is on how we are able to care for others–whoever those others may be. It is never an easy time, because people want to succeed at what they are doing for others. For example, adults feel responsible for raising the next generation well. This is tough work and is demanding of our physical and spiritual resources. Many adults feel squeezed between two generations–their children on the one hand and their parents on the other. They often feel "drained" of love and, in their busyness on all fronts, find it hard to stop and receive love from their own generation. Often the demands of the day shut out time for God in either public or private worship.

In their expected maturity, adults often are reluctant to admit their own needs. These can be highlighted by the actions of others for whom they care. Even though they may be aware of the gaps within themselves, the pressure from others is to be fully competent. It is a difficult stage when we are expected to be givers of love and advice at the very moment when we know we have a need for love and knowledge. This is the age when many adults find that their growth in relationship with God has become stuck. The child asks the parent about God and the Bible, and the parent comes up with a few mumbled words or dismissive phrases. It seems easier to avoid the question than to admit that we have no idea of the true answer. Some repeat their childhood attempts at the answer and soon realize that it satisfies neither themselves nor their children. Advice about a lifetime process of learning seems to be simpler to give to others than to apply to oneself.

In contrast, growing adults learn both from their new experiences and from those who seek their help—be it peers or children. Each question is a new opportunity to explore the situation afresh. To sustain such output requires a strong routine drawing on the resources of the body, mind, and spirit. This provides a central core of support that enables re-examination of the past and a constant review of the present. Regular times are set aside for reflection amid activity. An annual stocktaking is essential to both business and one's personal life. Most people in this age group find retreats valuable and want reading materials that keep them on their toes, ready for the race through life and the spiritual race with the saints of God.

The most vital ingredient in soul care at this stage is the affirmation of love. It enables the healing of the hurts suffered by us and those for whom we care. It recharges our batteries with the love we need to show to others, and allows us to forgive and be forgiven. It allows us to absorb the little losses that prepare us for greater losses—the death of a parent, the departure of a child, the loss of a job, or the realization that age is catching up with us.

Pause now and reaffirm God's love for you—whatever age you are. Then name two or three other people to whom you will give affirmation in a special way, acknowledging that God loves them as well as you do. If you are younger than this age group, recognize this group's needs and choose a person of this age who needs to receive your love. If you are older, share with a person in this age bracket your understanding of their difficult position of being the "meat in the sandwich" between the demands of the younger and the older group.

Old Age and the Quest to Pass on Wisdom to Others

Erikson honors the old with the responsibility of sharing wisdom with others—old and young alike. From sixty-five onward the question arises, How do I pass on knowledge and experience? The How is as important as the What, for the younger generation will not appreciate being told, "This is how you should do that." When withdrawing from taking full responsibility for everything, the older person is able to offer a range of experiences to be considered: "Have you thought of this way?" or "You might like to take my experience into account as you make your decision." These are the expressions of wisdom rather than dictatorship.

An older person often has time for reflection, rocking backward and forward, mulling over the issues. Impetuosity should be replaced by patience, but not complacency. One of the joys for older people is sharing their stories with their grandchildren's generation, who are more interested in the "old times" because they know that the previous generation's learning must be reapplied to the new conditions. It is therefore less threatening than talking to their children's generation, who may have a harder time hearing them. The younger people also feel that they can share their new experiences with the old because they are new to them, and there is mutual excitement at the new discoveries.

Age requires us to come to terms with diminishing powers. This can lead to despair or release. Despair traps us into grieving for what is lost. Release sets us free from the responsibility of keeping up when it is not our place to be in the position of power any longer. Age is a time when we can lighten the load that we carry forward. We can forgive the hurts we have received, and we can seek forgiveness for the hurts we've inflicted that still burden others. We can be loved for who we are, not for what we have done.

As we get older we ask, Who will remember me and for what? We do not want to leave behind a message of power, but a message of love. We want to share our experiences so that others do not have to climb over broken glass to reach the right door. We want to tell of the reliability of the God who stood with us throughout the passage of time and the passions of life. Above all, we can use our imaginations again to dream of the future in God's keeping. In a way, we return to our infancy by learning to trust and to play, knowing that we will need the help of others to make life livable.

What older people find is that the power of prayer does not diminish if they know how to replace despair with trust. In their dependency on trust they learn to commit themselves and others in prayer to God, releasing them into the hands of the God who loves us all in this life and beyond. There is a lovely phrase for the end of this stage of life, a time when "I let myself go into the Hands that never let go."[3]

In this stage of life our daily routines should support us with their familiarity and their sense of continuity. There is a sense in which we are "handing over" and "letting go." To do this well we need to receive love from God and from others. Our wisdom leads us to seek what we know to be true and to refine what life has to offer to those things that are essential. Then we will be content in the hands of our God.

---

[3]From Matthew Linn, Dennis Linn, and Sheila Fabricant, *Healing the Eight Stages of Life* (New York/Mahwah: Paulist Press, 1988).

Routines and Stages

This summary of life's stages can help us see the framework in which life is to be lived. The care we need for each stage differs, but the basic requirements do not. We need to find ways to be loved and loving; to use each experience as a stepping-stone to a closer relationship with God and those around us; to ground ourselves in a faith that can face mystery without fading and that grows through a deep trust in the ultimate purposes of God; and to offer all our lives to God in prayer. Out of this routine we will find ways, according to our current stages, to care for our bodies, minds, and spirits. Each stage demands a new way of carrying out this routine, but the essential principles remain the same.

Reflect now on what you have learned about yourself in this chapter and then offer this prayer or one in your own words.

Loving God, throughout our lives you care for us
with full understanding of our humanity.
Help us to learn to trust you, to choose the best that is possible,
to use all the talents you have given to us,
to love ourselves and those around us,
and to discover true wisdom from the experiences we face.
Then we will find ways each day to honor and serve you
with the strength of the Spirit you breathe into us.
In the name of our Savior, Jesus Christ, we pray. Amen.

2

Looking after Yourself in Times of Decision Making

It is a part of human nature to make choices. In the last chapter I noted that in the second phase of life we learn to exercise the "will." It takes many years to feel confident in assuming responsibility for our choices, especially when we have to admit that we sometimes make poor ones. Gradually we learn that if we make a poor decision, we must admit it and go on to make another decision that will have a better outcome.

Making decisions is so much a part of life that in routine matters we hardly notice the process by which we come to a decision. It becomes automatic. That is fine if we have developed a good process of decision making, but if we have a disastrous pattern, all our decisions are likely to be poor. For this reason I believe that we need help to check out our decision-making process from time to time and, with God's help, see that it is the best possible. I hope this chapter will help many of you achieve this.

Learning to Make Choices

Many people with some knowledge of the Bible remember the choice that Adam and Eve faced in the garden of Eden.[1] As the story is told, we are eager to see whether the woman will choose to eat the fruit of the forbidden tree, even when she is able to choose the fruit from any other tree in the garden. Those of us with children know

[1]Genesis 3.

only too well parallel situations. They have many toys to play with, and we warn them not to play with the precious ornament on the bookcase. Somehow the child's fascination is to do just what the parent has said not to do. It is as if the piece on the bookcase has a magnet in it drawing the child's fingers into temptation. Children are, of course, testing the boundaries of "will" and learn many lessons the hard way. Making choices is difficult for us all, but we must learn to do so, for it is an essential activity in life. The garden of Eden story highlights the fact that God holds humanity accountable for its choices, and also that as we gain wisdom, we learn that there are boundaries that need to be in place to strengthen the process of decision making.

A Decision-Making Process

Reflect for a moment on the things that you do when you are faced with making a decision or choice of any type. You might like to check your list against the following pattern, which I have set out under eleven headings.

A Sense of Trust

If you are a Christian, your sense of trust in God and in others will be the foundation for your process. Others may have developed a trust in their own judgment and in the judgment of others. The groups start from different points, but much of the rest of the process is similar.

As Christians we may express this trust in God in a prayer at the beginning of the process, at the end, or at various stages on the way. Somewhere in the process we want to acknowledge before God that we trust God to help us make the best possible choice and to give us guidance as we come to our decision. Some Christians go further and want to make God responsible for the choice itself. In the garden of Eden story they blame God for putting the tree of wisdom in the center of the garden in the first place. No doubt they blame the parent for leaving the ornament on the shelf within reach of the child. However, when we say that we trust God, a more balanced Christian approach is not to make God responsible for our choices, but to know that God has given us as human beings the capacity to make good choices. Our task is to live up to the trust that God has in us. We are partners with God, not puppets of God. The choices are our responsibility, but our trust in God gives us the confidence to face the issues and accumulate the wisdom of scripture and communal experience to help us make the best choice. Such a sense of trust gives us a calm mind and a heightened sensitivity, thus enabling us to make better decisions.

Clarification of the Facts

With such a sense of assurance, we are able to look clearly at the facts on which we will base the decision. Our minds gather the relevant information and ask the right questions. We are not sidetracked by things that are irrelevant to this particular decision, nor are we confused by too much information. It is often helpful to write a list of the questions you need answered and later write a list of pros and cons for each possible decision. If your personality has a preference other than lists, use a period of silent thought to see the issues from as many angles as possible.

Sensitivity to Feelings

Facts and feelings must always be balanced. Your preference may be to put feelings before facts or facts before feelings. The order does not matter as long as you include both in your decision-making process. Certainly, in establishing our choices we need to take feelings into account. We can ask, What do I feel about the choices? and then go on to the vital question, How will my choice affect the feelings of others? Some people explain that they make their decisions on the basis of "hunches." This is a way of saying that they have deep feelings about an issue and that this, combined with their intuition, overrides all other factors in coming to a decision. There is nothing wrong with hunches, but it would be less than satisfactory to ignore everything else in the process and decide on that basis alone. Hunches should be balanced out by facts, the feelings of others, the advice of friends, the word of God in scripture, and the Christian community. From my experience, there is much more to good decision making than following hunches.

Advice from Others

Fortunately for us, we do not live in isolation. We live in some form of community, especially if we are Christian. Because of this, we have the opportunity to listen to the advice of others in making our decisions. As we take on such advice, we must remember that it is still our decision. Anyone offering advice is not responsible for the decision; it is ours to make and ours to act on. Yet the advice can be helpful because others can sometimes see what we have overlooked, and others can confirm for us the accuracy and importance of any particular factor. Many adults need to outgrow resentments that they acquired as young people when they felt oppressed by the "advice" of others. Such advice may have come in the form of a command or threat: "Do this or else!" With that sort of experience it is often hard as an adult to seek advice from others, because you fear a repetition of the past. However, it is vital to our maturity to seek advice and to take it into consideration in our decision-making process.

Pause for a moment now and identify some people whose advice you would value and, if necessary, acknowledge and wave good-bye to those people and times when you were not allowed to take responsibility for your choices. You may find it appropriate to let your heart forgive the people concerned and see them in a new light from now on.

The advice of trusted others allows you to tap into a range of experiences. This may help you see opportunities and disasters that may have arisen from your kind of decision, without your having to undergo these experiences yourself. I don't think that I have to break a leg myself to decide that it is stupid to jump off a ladder from three meters above the ground. It is said that you learn from experience, but experience can be that of others and not just your own.

Following the Way of Love

The advice of others, if they are Christians, may well include their interpretation of the Christian ethic and experience of scripture. We can take time to reflect on the way of love that Jesus taught by word and example and see how it impacts our decisions. On the whole, Jesus did not lay down laws to govern each situation. Rather, by word and example Jesus established the principles of love that would serve as the basis of our decision making. Some Christians, when faced with a choice, will ask themselves: What would Jesus have done in this situation? Of course, we can never give an exact answer to that question, but we can be certain that the answer would follow the principle of love. Such a principle does not mean that we take the "soft" option. The way of love calls for courage and determination. It often means standing up for justice and truth out of love for ourselves and others. The way of love always seeks the best possible for all those involved in a decision. Following the way of love, we never treat other people as outsiders or as if they were of little value. In all our decisions we should give full respect to everyone who may be affected. In seeking the good for others, we also seek the best for ourselves. That is how Jesus lived, and that was the basis of his teaching.

Looking at the Consequences

We can never be certain how things will work out in the future, but that should not stop us from looking at the consequences of our decision as far as is possible. If someone decides to take a job in an office with air conditioning, the consequences may be that they become vulnerable to sinus trouble. Such consequences may govern the choice of job for that person. In all other respects it might be a good choice of employment, but the consequences for that person's health would make it an unwise choice. To move to a new town at a particular point in the schooling of one's child might have such adverse consequences for them that the best decision might be not to move.

The consequences of our choices are important. Some we can see as positive, and this adds weight to other factors in the choice. Choosing a change in career may give a parent more time to spend with a child at a vital point in her or his development. The financial sacrifice may have longer-term benefits for all. When we look at the consequences of a decision, we want to forecast the outcomes not only as they affect us but also as they affect others who will have to live with our decision.

Incorporating Moral Principles

When we make decisions, our conscience raises a code of moral principles that we have built up over a lifetime. Most of our decisions are connected to others that have gone before or that will follow later. For some people, this becomes a pattern of behavior, and it resonates so strongly in them that anything that is decided contrary to this pattern calls forth the comment, "They are acting out of character." We say, "Mary would never do that," with a tone of disbelief at the facts presented. Such a code of principles or a "developed conscience" can save us a lot of energy in the decision making process. We can quickly sum up the options and say yes or no to that type of activity. We have only to work on the details, not on the principles.

For example, some people choose not to be involved in any form of gambling, so each time they see a betting opportunity of any sort, they pass it by. They do not need to decide whether their finances can "afford" a gamble. They have already decided on a principle, and that governs all such decisions. In another example, some people have decided that they will always answer the telephone if they are in the house. They do not have to decide each time it rings whether the moment is right or not for them to answer the phone. Others have decided that during meals they will put on the answering machine and all callers can wait, whether the call is urgent or not.

If we have such principles, it is important from time to time that we check them out in accordance with the full process and confirm that they still stand. Otherwise, we can find ourselves in a bigoted position that overlooks important new factors.

Working with Boundaries

A further step in our decision-making process is to see whether or not there are absolute boundaries in place. These are so basic to our behavior that we will not cross them in any circumstance. Some Christians feel comfortable only when such boundaries are in place and look to their church community to reinforce the boundaries for them. These boundaries are there to prevent people from being hurt if at all possible. The Ten Commandments are seen by some Christians as such a boundary. They feel secure in being able to check all decisions against the commandments, and if a boundary would be crossed by making a decision, that choice is not possible. For some, killing is a clear boundary, and it is always murder. Armed warfare and capital punishment can never be a choice, because each has the consequence of killing another person, and that is always wrong. In the same way, using the name of God or Jesus as a swear word is an impossible choice for some, no matter what size brick falls on the foot. The marital bond is so sacred that any relationship outside it is forbidden in any circumstance.

Such rigid boundaries can lead to a certain "hardness of heart" as well as safe behavior. This has given rise to the criticism of hard boundaries and a cry for greater freedom in responding to the needs of the moment. The consequences of this freedom can now be seen in the danger it has posed to many people suffering from broken relationships. So the call for firmer boundaries is growing louder again. The truth is that for boundaries to work well, they have to be chosen rather than imposed. A good process of decision making, including the acceptance of boundaries, works toward forming a mature person—and that is God's will for us all.

Dreams

Some people dismiss dreams as pictures to be forgotten as soon as they wake up to their responsibilities. Others point to the place of dreams in the scriptures as strongly influencing good decisions. The second chapter of Matthew's gospel mentions dreams as key factors in the decision of the wise men not to go back to Herod[2] and in the

---

[2]Matthew 2:12.

decision of Joseph to take Mary and the newly born Jesus to Egypt to escape Herod's reign of terror.[3] What psychologists tell us is that for some people the process of decision making is worked through while they rest, and the decision is often prefigured in a dream. We can therefore use the material in our dreams to help us make decisions, but with the caution that we should match the dream against the other factors we have listed and adequately test each in the balance. We then choose with the whole picture in view.

Our dreams also can be an expression of our fears, and in the light of day we may feel more confident. Other factors may help us see that our fears should not hold us back and, in the end, the consequences will be positive for us and for others. It is possible that our dreams will highlight factors that we have suppressed in the cold light of day, and these too should be carefully considered before reaching the final decision.

Weighing the Factors

At this point in the process, which might only take a couple of minutes for a routine decision, we find ourselves weighing the factors that we want to take into account. This is often the difficult part when the outcomes of the choice seem to be finely balanced between positive and negative. Sometimes the positives are for us and the negatives for others, and we feel torn apart by the process. If this is the case, we may decide that we have to involve the others who are affected by the decision and indicate that the responsibility for the decision is a joint one. We may want to reach this decision by consensus. The others may agree that we should go ahead with the decision despite the downside for them. This is often the case when adult children ask their parents for their support in a decision to take a job requiring a move to another part of the country or globe. The parents can see that in similar circumstances they would choose to move, and so they encourage their children to do so despite the losses for themselves. At other times adult children choose to be near an aging parent even though such a decision is difficult for their career paths or circle of friends.

When we have weighed all the factors and reached the decision, we need to learn again to trust God and our own ability to make decisions. As Christians we express this in two practical ways.

---

[3]Matthew 2:13.

Prayer and Reflection

Through prayer and reflection we make a final check on our decision by holding it silently in the presence of God and checking each step out with Jesus. In most cases we "hear" the affirmation that if that is what we think is best, we should act on it. God shows us that we are trusted. In a few cases we may "hear" God caution us or remind us of a boundary. We may also be cautioned about the way we carry out the decision. The danger ahead may lie in the way we do something rather than in the choice itself. The reminder of the boundary may be a way of helping us call to mind the effect of our decision on the wider community. We may be free to make the choice, and it may be a "good" one for us, but its effects on the standards and values of the community may be negative. We may also need the reminder that some choices are necessary for the sake of the community, even though they are painful for us. Christ's choice of the cross was necessary for the salvation of the world—even though it cost him his own life. I am sure that Jesus was "happy" in the choice that he made because of the joy and freedom that it brought through forgiveness. The same may apply to some of our choices after we have reflected in prayer.

Our concluding prayer will always ask for God's grace and spirit to help us carry out the decision well and, if necessary, to recognize that it was not the best decision possible. We must always have the humility to revisit a decision when the outcomes are not what we expected or if they prove harmful to us or others. The worst thing for a Christian to do is to stubbornly persist with a wrong decision in the false belief that somehow it is "God's will."

A Note on "God's Will"

This is a good point for a short discussion on the meaning of the phrase "God's will." It can be used as a cover for our lack of responsibility for a decision or for what I consider to be a false belief that God makes all decisions on our behalf and that we have only to discover God's will and fulfill it.

I think that the only way to discover God's will is to use the sort of process that I have just outlined. There can be no definitive answer to what the will of God is in a particular instance without the input of humanity. This is the nature of our partnership with God. The parent's will for a child can never be absolute without a denial of the love that respects the child and his or her part in the decision. Otherwise "will" becomes control without nurture, and that is not the nature of love. The child must be trusted to participate fully in the decision in accordance with his or her capabilities and age. Of course, the child must give due weight to the experienced advice of the parent. When this is given in love, it will be fully respected, if not immediately, then at the point when the consequences become obvious.

So it is with God. To be the human beings we are created to be, we must learn to make decisions and take responsibility for them. Out of love and respect we will listen to the advice of God as revealed by Jesus Christ in Holy Scripture and in the inspiration of the Holy Spirit. Once we have done this, we add the facts, feelings, and all other aspects of decision making and come to a conclusion. If we share this with God in prayer and reflection, the decision should be God's will and our responsibility. We may be frightened by this level of trust placed in us, but our faith and trust in God will overcome such fears.

God's will can never be solely discovered from the word of God in scripture or in the experience of the church, because the word must always be applied to the new context of the decision that lies before us. Jesus models this principle. Jesus keeps the Sabbath as an important opportunity for the whole community to rest and worship together. On the other hand, he will "break" the rule about the Sabbath in order to heal a man in great need. The principle as a whole must be weighed, balanced, and then applied to the context. The closer we live in the spirit of Christ, the more we can trust ourselves to reach the best decision. A heavy weight of responsibility lies on our shoulders, but we are never alone. The Spirit and the community of Christians support and help to shape our decisions.

Sample Prayers

Here are some outlines of prayers that you might like to use as a guide for prayer in the process of decision making.

Before the Start of the Decision-Making Process

Gracious God, you trust us to be mature people,
making decisions for ourselves and others.
Give us clarity of thinking,
sensitivity to the feelings of others and ourselves,
a listening ear to your word,
and a courageous heart in the face of pain.

Guide us as we go through the decision-making process,
and help us to weigh the choice in the balance of your love.
This we ask with Christ, our Savior and our Guide. Amen.

At the End of the Decision-Making Process

God, the good Shepherd, I thank you for your inspiration and
guidance as I have made my decision.
Give me your Holy Spirit to strengthen my courage and my love
as I carry out the choice I have made.
As I involve others, keep me sensitive to their feelings
so that together we can fulfill your purpose for our lives.
Gracious God, give me the skill to do the task well
and the insight to make the next decisions wisely,
for my trust is in you, my God, to empower me
in all that I do in your name. Amen.

Our Preferred Order for the Process

In making decisions, we typically establish a preferred order for considering each step in the process. This saves time, but take care not to overlook a step, especially for big decisions. We also know that it is easy for so-called small decisions to lead quickly to big ones; thus, it is not always possible to see at the time which decisions are big and which ones are small. However, I think we can identify some of the major decisions in life. You will probably be able to add to my list, but here are the ones that seem general:

- Choices of career/job/occupation/retirement
- Choices of relationships: friends/partners/spouses/children
- Choices of a place to live: country/community/type of housing
- Choices of leisure: sport/vacation/hobby/health program
- Choices of spending: major purchases/gifts to others/donations to charity

Some Examples of the Process in Practice

In the second part of this chapter I set out an example of how the process might work in relation to two particular choices.

Choice of a Career

Christians used to speak of this process as discovering their "vocation" on the grounds that they were responding to the call of God. The church authorities narrowed down the word *vocation* to the careers of certain groups in the community–clergy, doctors, and teachers. The church said that such people were called to a vocation, and other people "found a job." Such an idea is now rightly dismissed as implying that God shows partiality. The Christian community now speaks of all those baptized as having a ministry of love and service–either as laity or ordained members of the church. Part of this ministry is the work we do for the community and for our own fulfillment. With limited employment opportunities in today's restructured world, it is often difficult for a young person to make the right choice in preparing for a career or for a particular job in a chosen field of endeavor. In fact, most people need to carefully choose a career path, yet still remain flexible, ready to retrain and realign as work patterns change.

Using the Process

What follows is how the outlined process could work regarding the choice of a career.

1. We begin by acknowledging that we are trusted by God to make a contribution to the community and to fulfill the gifts that we have been given by the Creator.
2. We assemble all the facts that we can find about a particular career. We talk to those in such jobs. We will read the literature available. We list our own skills and preferences. We see whether the career calls for gifts and attitudes that match or do not match those we possess.
3. We examine how we would feel in a such a job and its environment, and whether we have the sensitivity required to work with others in such a career. For example, I could never be a miner because I am fearful about working in a confined space. On the other hand, I love working with people and responding to their requests.
4. Fortunately, when it comes to choosing a career, many experienced people are available to offer us advice,

including career advisers and human resource managers. From the experts we can discover our personality type and preferences in a variety of ways. We can visit work sites and even spend short periods of time in a work experience.

5. Christians will want to consider how the career would enable them to fulfill the "way of love." We have learned to respect and value the contributions of a wide range of people to the fabric of society. Most people carry out the "way of love" through their jobs in society, but Christians may still feel the call from God to give sacrificial service in a vocation, and see their careers in this light rather than simply as a job to earn a living. It would be sad if Christians failed to respond to such opportunities and challenges.
6. When making a choice of career, we need to be conscious of the consequences. If the career calls for a long period of training, can the costs be covered? If the career calls for stamina of body, are we physically capable of sustaining our bodies for such a task? If the chances of a job in that career are few and far between, do we think that we can become so skilled at the task that we will be chosen for the vacancy? We should look hard and long at the consequences of any decision.
7. Our moral principles may indicate that we would not be happy in a certain career. If we believe that there should only be a narrow gap between rich and poor, we would be foolish to pursue careers in the futures market in the financial sector. If we hold that all animals should live in their natural habitats, we would not be happy working in a zoo. If we hold strong principles of honesty and integrity, we may want to serve as accountants for a charitable trust. Our principles are likely to have a strong influence on the careers we choose.
8. Likewise, our established boundaries may rule out some careers that we believe may demand we cross such boundaries. Some people will not work in the gambling industry or the liquor industry. Others will not take up a career in advertising if it means that they must use sexuality and sales pressure to entice people to purchase goods. Others will not take up farming if it means the use of fertilizers or restriction of the freedom of animals. Our

boundaries narrow down our choices of career. We must ask ourselves, Would my conscience allow me to do that?

9. Dreams have a major influence for many people on the careers they choose to follow. In their dreams they picture themselves as successfully doing the work and wake up to the possibility that that could be their career. As I said earlier, it is important that we check out the dream against the rest of the decision-making process. Otherwise, we may realize a little too late that it was only a dream, and now we have to live with the reality. For those who want to dream while remaining awake, the use of imagination is a vital tool in trying to decide which career path to follow.
10. So we come to weighing all the factors and reaching a decision on the career we want to follow. This is often the hard part for younger persons, because at their age they have not fully discovered their own personalities and gifts, and their knowledge of the tasks to be done in the chosen career is rather limited. Young people need encouragement to make the best possible choices, knowing that there is always the opportunity (and nowadays often the necessity) to change directions in the light of experience and train for another career.
11. In making such a key choice, a Christian will spend much time in prayer and reflection. We will trust God to guide and support us. We will feel the encouragement of God and know the gifting of the Spirit to undertake the training and the tasks. If we have carried out the process well, there will be many occasions when we can thank God for the opportunities that have presented themselves to us while following the way of love.

Choosing a Marriage Partner

The second example of a major decision that faces most people, but certainly not all, is the choice of a marriage partner. There is a prevalent "Hollywood" idea that love is blind and humans have no choice in the matter of marriage. Love indeed is essential to marriage, but the consequences of the heart's ruling the mind are so obvious in our world of broken relationships that we would do well to heed the warning that this must not be so.

The first decision to be made is one of principle. Should we get married and give ourselves to another person of the opposite gender through a lifelong commitment? Can we give and receive love to such an extent that we can enter the deep relationship that is required in a marriage? Most people are helped to a positive decision on those questions by experiencing deep love from a particular person. Many people only look at the possibility of being married once they have met a person who they feel truly loves them. However, before the relationship proceeds further, it is important to clarify whether you are ready and willing in principle to be married. Many a heart would be saved much pain if that decision was clear from the outset. The process that we have established is a good one to enable such a decision.

Once the decision in principle has been clarified, there is a second decision to be made. Should you marry this person with all his or her unique and special qualities or lack of them? The decision is complicated, because it needs to be a mutual one for completion. Each of the persons entering the marriage must do so of free choice. So there are two decisions that can only be effective when they become one decision made with united respect and love.

In coming to such a decision it is often difficult to ascertain the facts and the consequences. The facts have to be disclosed, often by the other party. Each person has to know himself or herself sufficiently well to put the facts in front of the intended spouse. There must be a large measure of trust for this to happen, and this takes time to establish. The facts range from "What food do I like?" to "How do I leave the toothpaste in the morning after cleaning my teeth?" It is important to know how the person handles money and celebrates anniversaries. I often find it helpful when assisting a couple to prepare for a possible marriage to ask them to describe how each would want to celebrate their first Christmas together. The answers reveal the culture of the family, the place of faith, the importance of family relationships, readiness or lack of readiness to change and establish new patterns, and the ability to laugh at the continuing "child" in the other person. Such a question brings out a mixture of facts and consequences and is very revealing not only for me in knowing more fully the intended couple but also for them in getting to know one another.

It is also hard to define our feelings as we approach a decision about marriage. We do not always have an adequate vocabulary to communicate feelings. We can say we like something, but when asked why, we stumble around for the words to tell others (and maybe even ourselves) about the feelings we have. Often we end up frustrated, saying, "Well I just like it," which is only partially helpful. Despite all the public talk about sex and sexuality, many people find it hard to express their feelings about sexual matters. It can be the subject of much boasting and banter but little sensitivity and clarity.

When it comes to receiving advice from others, we may be confused about who is suitable to advise us. Even though they know us well, parents can be seen as too involved in the consequences to offer advice for the sake of the decision maker rather than for their own benefit. Friends are helpful on occasions but can also be rivals in the choice of partners. Most agencies seem to focus more on counseling those with marriage difficulties than on helping those trying to choose a marriage partner. If the intended couple are both Christians, the church community will hopefully provide people appointed and trained to give good advice. However, many couples think that they must already have made their decision to marry before approaching the church. What is needed in society and in Christian communities is an extension of "Relationship Advice Services." These should help the couple to individually and mutually reach the best decision, using a process similar to the one I have outlined. Many of the clergy have been trained and can offer good advice if the parties deciding on marriage will approach someone they trust early enough in the process.

When someone turns to the Word of God, the advice individual passages give about marriage can be rather confusing. At times scripture indicates that to follow the way of God we need to avoid, if at all possible, the entanglements of the marriage relationship.[4] It points to the one relationship that matters above all else, the relationship with God.[5] Other passages balance this viewpoint[6] by highlighting that you cannot enter fully into a relationship of love with God without experiencing what love is in a human relationship.[7] Marriage, and the family that it creates, usually provides the best experience of the qualities of love at their fullest: mutual affection, full respect, forgiveness given and received, practical care and support, sacrifice, and thanksgiving. In the first chapter of this book we noted the triangle of love in Jesus' commandment–love of God, love of others, love of self.[8] Within the marriage relationship we can find full expression for this triangle of love in a balanced way that brings joy and intimacy. Individual scripture verses can be taken out of context

[4]1 Corinthians 7:7, 8.

[5]Luke 14:26.

[6]Hebrews 13:4.

[7]1 John 4:7, 20.

[8]Matthew 22:37–39; John 13:34.

to distort this balance. The man can be mistakenly viewed as dominant, and the woman subordinate, in the process of love.[9] Taken as a whole, scripture shows the mutuality of true love.[10] Jesus declared that marriage can only be seen as a whole. Two persons are so united that they cannot be seen as separate.[11] Each will have distinctive gifts, but in love these are contributed freely to the whole. The Word of God calls each spouse to live toward the ideal vision of total love,[12] and, though it is not always reached, it is the goal for which we aim with God's help.[13]

When two people reflect on the big decision of marriage, one of the major considerations is the possible clash of principles and boundaries. Unity requires flexibility and growth. Everything must be viewed through two pairs of eyes. The question arises as to whether it is possible to retain the firm principles and boundaries that each has established separately. When one party to the decision is a Christian and the other is not so committed, can unity be maintained in the marriage? This is a dilemma that has troubled many. Some have decided to throw away their principles and boundaries so that they can love this spouse, only to find that the future decision-making process is one of constant confusion and sometimes conflict. Others hope that the other party will change and grow to accept the principles that they hold firmly. This is always a possibility, but there must be evidence of a desire and willingness to change for the risk to be rightly taken. When the marriage is blessed with children, any clash of boundaries and principles will be even more apparent. In advocating serious attention to these issues, I cannot offer a fixed rule, because there are so many examples of different outcomes. What I do know is that to hide from the difficult discussion about boundaries will only give rise to bitterness later. Each party must be prepared to reveal deeply held convictions and be ready to respond as to how they will respect, or not be able to respect, the principles of the other.

Marriage is all about dreams and reality. Without a dream, marriage is without romance. With a false dream, marriage is a nightmare. In our decisions about marriage, dreams must be cherished, but they must also be checked for reality. We should not marry a dreamed-up spouse, for the prince or princess will always show him- or

---

[9]Ephesians 5:22–24, 28; 1 Peter 3:1, 7; Colossians 3:18, 19.
[10]Colossians 3:14; Ephesians 5:33.
[11]Matthew 19:5–6; Mark 10:7–8.
[12]Titus 2:4.
[13]1 Corinthians 13:4–8a.

herself in real life. We can grow toward the hopes of others (even the hopes of God), but only if we are open to growth; only if we can accept and give love; and only if we work toward the best for each other and for the marriage. Love can perform miracles, but only with faith, and that is the precious quality in a person that can so easily wither if it is not rooted in the will of God.

Decisions about marriage are major ones for all concerned–the families as well as the couple, the community as well as the church. Because the family unit is the core of the developing society, every decision to marry has ramifications for a wide circle of people and, in the end, for society as a whole. The casualties of poor decisions are a burden on the fabric of society. The successes of good decisions strengthen the fabric of society. It is for this reason that I hope these short paragraphs will stimulate your thinking about the process of making such decisions. They may equip you to undertake your part in the process more adequately–in whatever part you are involved. The Bibliography will provide a sample of books that expand on this topic and allow us to exercise care for ourselves and others.

Summary

From these two examples I hope that you can see how it is possible to apply this process of making decisions to a wide range of issues that face us throughout life. You will want to establish your own order and way of working through this process, which is an essential part of your care for yourself and for others. Trust in God will make the process all the more effective. God will respond to your prayers with guidance and love.

3

Looking after Yourself in Despondent Moments

Despondency and Depression

All of us recognize that however smooth the outcomes of our decisions might be, life has its "downs" as well as "ups." That is the nature of human existence. From time to time we all have to face periods of despondency and look after ourselves in such times. In this chapter I could easily have used the word *depression* to describe this condition in the loose way that is employed in common speech. I have avoided this because I believe that depression is strictly a medical condition and that we must define our terms carefully. I am sure that there are some overlaps between despondency and depression and that the advice I give about the former may be beneficial to those faced with the latter. Yet depression as a medical condition should be handled with professional care by a fully trained person. Later in this chapter I outline the usual definitions of the depressed condition and firmly insist that those who consider themselves to be suffering from it take courage and quickly see a doctor. Thankfully, much can now be done to help those with this condition. However, most of us will just be despondent from time to time and, in such moments, need to know how best to take care of ourselves with the help of God, our families, and our friends.

The Outward Signs of Despondency

Can you describe how you look, act, and feel when you are despondent? From my observations and some personal experience, I would say:

- When a person is despondent, the body sags, the shoulders droop, the mouth turns down, the eyes look at the ground or out into space, walking is slow, and feet drag.
- Those despondent may lie in bed or sit slumped in a chair. They are negative in all they think and say and put others down. They sulk and maybe burst into tears. They let things get into a muddle and have little energy to respond to needs. They may undereat, overeat, try to drown their sorrows in drink, or sit vacantly in a chair smoking one cigarette after another. They either shut themselves away from all company or tell friends and strangers all about the bad things that have happened.
- Those despondent often feel as if someone has kicked them in the guts or hit them over the head. They believe that everyone and everything is working against them. They believe even God has deserted them and believe they are useless to God and to everyone else. They may even believe that it would be easier for all if they were dead. There seems little point in living on in this mess. Everyone else is blamed for the troubles, and therefore others should fix the problems.

A writer of an earlier generation put it this way: Despondent people

> take no interest in their work; their pleasures bore them; they do not believe in themselves; they detect wrong motives in others; the power of their will seems paralysed; they think slowly and heavily; they shun society; and the only thing they enjoy is to talk about their own condition, the rottenness of the weather or trade or the Government; they frequently express the wish they were dead, until they make others share their wish, for depression is one of the most infectious diseases of the soul.[1]

---

[1]Leslie D. Weatherhead, *Psychology and Life* (New York: Abingdon Press, 1935; reprint, London: Hudder and Stoughton, 1957), 221–22.

I wonder whether these descriptions match your own experiences of despondency? You will have your own vivid way of describing your feelings.

Causes of Despondency

We probably recognize despondency without too much difficulty, but it is also important to identify some of its causes. We need to know causes in order to tackle some of the underlying issues, thus beginning the road to recovery. Here are some of the possible causes of despondency:

1. *Negative messages from others* during our childhood and developing years, and/or similar messages from those with whom we now live and work. Such messages have told us so often that we can never do anything worthwhile that we have come to believe this about ourselves. This "disease" of running others down, especially children, can be passed on from one generation to the next, or one group of people to another. We probably tell others they are failures so that we look more effective by comparison. Feelings of inadequacy are taken out on others through words of condemnation. School reports often reinforce such attitudes, and we quite literally "learn" to be despondent. Reports highlight failures and inadequacies rather than basic, average achievements. School still seems to be set up for the brilliant to succeed and the rest of us to fail. Parents can wrongly reinforce this message as they wish for a "brilliant" child. Those children who have received some measure of praise either at home or at school will learn to rewrite the report in their minds. They may also have some interesting comments about teachers and parents in their heads. Those who never receive praise will fall into periods of despondency and keep hearing the negative messages throughout their lives. Adult life may confirm the experiences of childhood.
2. *Sense of a need for perfectionism,* leading to a false expectation that everything, including myself, should be perfect. This frequently is a cause of despondency. Human beings can never achieve 100 percent perfection, and the judgment of constant failure against this impossible measure will quickly wear us down. Such perfectionism

may be self-imposed, but more often it is the result of the threatened withdrawal of affection and love in words such as, "If you do not do everything with excellence, you cannot expect me to love you (or give you a reward)." The intended message may be: "Do try your best because we love you and want you to do well," but that is not how the inner ear receives the message. What is heard is: "The better you do, the more we will love you." Such messages create the drive toward perfectionism and the craving for love through success. This attitude is false, because true love accepts us as we are and encourages us to reach our *realistic* goals. The messages about perfectionism seem to be reinforced by the scriptural command, "Be perfect, therefore, as your heavenly Father is perfect."[2] Perfection is to fulfill the purpose for which we were created, just as God is perfect because God is bringing the universe, as a whole, to fulfillment. Such perfection is a goal we aim for, and all progress toward the goal is a delight to God. It is God's love for us as we are that gives us the confidence and the courage to aim for the goal. Too many people hear the verse say that God does not love us until we reach the goal. If that were the case, none of us would ever make it, and God would be cruel. The false sense of a need for perfectionism always digs a pit into which we fall despondently, and from which we can rise only when we correct the falsehood.

3. *Stress from emotional problems.* Stress can stir us onward with the adrenaline running, or stress can strike us down, sapping the energy we need to tackle the issues that caused the stress. We deal in two major ways with emotional problems or problems of relationship with self or others. Either we are able to sort things out and restore the relationship, or we accept the situation without changing it and learn to live with it the best we can. For example, we may love our enemies, but if they do not reciprocate, we cannot restore the relationship. We can, however, accept it in the sense that we fit our life pattern around the given situation, so that we do not spend all our energy worrying about it. We may, and probably should,

[2]Matthew 5:48.

revisit the issue from time to time to see if the relationship can be improved, but the breakdown does not cause us to break down by using up all the energy that is required to tackle the many other issues in life.

Stress can also cause despondency when we are facing too many emotional issues at one time. We can only cope with so many, and another one will be the straw that breaks the camel's back. Some people are unrealistic and take on more and more issues, as if that will bring them greater credit. This is the "martyr" complex that hopes to win fame and sympathy by being seen as carrying heavy burdens. True Christian martyrs are not created because they bring trouble on themselves, but because they accept, with the Spirit's courage and steadfastness, the troubles others have brought on them. Despondency *can* be self-inflicted, and we have to recognize this for our own well-being. Stress can also get out of control, and we need to find ways to bring ourselves out of near despair.

4. *Fatigue due to overwork.* In a parallel way, despondency can be caused by burnout, that is, physical fatigue over a long period of time leading to total loss of energy. In today's economic world this is a constant problem. Society seems to be driven by cost-cutting exercises that make some employees redundant and others overworked. This damages society and makes little economic sense. Employees cannot perform well when they are exhausted from overwork. Performance reviews would do well to look at the quality of the work as well as the quantity. The quality is just as much about the advancement of the person's life as it is about the quality of her or his "work." Work is there so that the creative and human skills of a person have an opportunity to contribute to the community as a whole. It is not there as a creator of profit for those who are already rich. A worn-out and negative society will soon bring down every member–rich and poor alike. We can all see this, but it is difficult to make the "system" recognize the truth.
5. *Profound disappointment.* It is quite natural that we should feel down when we have suffered a profound disappointment, especially if we have put a great deal of effort into something and then find it not supported or accepted.

An obvious example is a job application. We may have agonized over whether we should apply, used much energy in the interview process, and had our hopes raised by comments, only to find after weeks of being keyed up that we are rejected. The same may apply in buying or selling a house. It might even apply to a couple exploring the possibility of a marriage relationship, where one or both parties pull out. Such serious disappointments give us that "let down" feeling, and despondency can occur. It is important that we take particular care of ourselves at such times and do not project the negative onto the whole of life. It is unhelpful to keep repeating, "Nothing ever goes right for me," or else we will cease the journey to fulfill our goals in life.

6. *Jealousy of others' successes.* Always comparing ourselves with others can be a cause of despondency when the comparison is not in our favor. In disappointment it is easy to become jealous. If we are not picked for the team, we look at those who are, and in bitterness, tell ourselves that we are much better than they are, but of course no one recognizes this. On the other hand, we may tell ourselves that we will never be good enough to be picked for the team. Jealousy in despondency can be judgmental–of others and of ourselves. In the depths of our despondency we ignore our own talents and gifts, and we wish we had the gifts of others that led to their successes.

   The current measurement in society is money. This means that most people are jealous of the wealth of others and despondent about their own lack of money. This lack prevents them from displaying the signs of wealth that make them appear successful. In despondency of this type taking a gamble is an attractive escape route. As we know (but find it hard to acknowledge in despondent moments), gambling leads to further depths of despondency when we lose. The cycle is addictive. If you recognize this as your trouble, seek help. Later in this chapter I point to ways that you can do this, but the help you need is not only general but also that which is applicable to gambling addiction. Such assistance is there for you, so use it with God's grace.

7. *Weighed down with guilt.* Guilt that has not been healed by forgiveness will cause despondency. Like all emotional problems, it eats away at our conscience and saps our

energy. Most people dealing with guilt shut themselves away or strike out at others, thus shrinking the circle of the relationships available to help them. Turning in on oneself is an outward sign of this desperation. As with all emotional issues, we have to face the situation with help and find a resolution. The Christian faith deals realistically and graciously with guilt and offers us a clear path to find forgiveness. This lifts both guilt and despondency and opens the way for new hope and new life.

8. *The result of hormonal changes in our bodies.* There are occasions in all our lives when our bodies undergo major changes that affect the hormonal balance in our systems. Such changes are particularly pronounced in the teenage years as our bodies develop sexual powers, and later in middle age when these powers are in decline. Some would say that for women this "change of life" may be in the middle to late forties and for men in the early sixties, but every person experiences this differently. The process of childbirth also results in major hormonal changes for women, and for some this causes despondency or even medical depression. Medical professionals have tried various methods over the years to support our bodies during these adult changes. However, each person seems to be different, and this makes both society and the medical profession cautious about generalizations. I think that teenagers have the most difficulty in their times of despondency due to hormonal changes. They have lower levels of self-confidence to ask for help and less experience coping with the variety of moods through which we all pass. Each group needs help, which may include medical as well as spiritual assistance.
9. *The outcomes of sharp emotional swings.* At other times in our lives we are subject to sharp emotional swings. These are in response to events rather than bodily changes. Life has its peaks as well as its troughs. If we have not learned to handle such swings, the peaks can often be followed by the troughs of despondency. For some people a major religious experience can be followed by a period of doubt and despondency. But I am not advocating a flattening out of life to create a dull uniformity! What we need to do to take good care of ourselves at such times is to be aware of what is happening, not be frightened by it, and care for

ourselves with patience. We can learn to let ourselves down gently and to avoid chasing another high as an antidote for the despondency. Such behavior is as dangerous as the next "fix" for a drug addict.

10. *Physical illness.* This often drains our resources and leaves us "down." Influenza is not usually a life-threatening illness if treated carefully, but it leaves the patient seriously depleted of emotional and physical resources. During a recovery period from any illness we use up a lot of energy just getting well again. If another crisis engulfs us at such a moment, we may suffer all the signs of despondency. We need to develop a system of support for such occasions. Society is rather intolerant of those who have what is considered a "disposition" rather than a serious illness. "Carry on!" seems to be the slogan, but it is an unreasonable expectation for many people in the recovery phase. Our bodies tell us that it takes time to recover, and major decisions or responses to crises will have to wait until we have the energy to tackle them.
11. *Financial collapse.* In many societies "security" has been sacrificed to economic development. Few people are insulated from the chilly drafts of financial insecurity. However hard you work, the job or company may disappear, being no longer required in the new financial model. However wisely you invest, companies can fail and the shares prove worthless. Financial collapse can be the outcome of an accident or an unexpected medical cost. It is only natural that people curse their bad luck and feel "in the dumps." At the very moment of financial strain, when we need to be most resourceful, our inner systems for coping can collapse, and we have no energy to rearrange our lives. The shock leaves us paralyzed, and we find we cannot "buy" ourselves out of the situation. In our panic we can often make bad financial decisions and make matters worse. In such despondent moments we want help but often feel ashamed to ask for it.
12. *Other causes.* Accidents, grief, losses of many kinds, a sense of failure, or a host of other similar causes may give rise to despondency in a particular case. Pause a moment now and recall those causes that you can identify as resulting in periods of despondency from which you have since

recovered. Such an exercise will help you establish a system that will identify causes when you are in a time of despondency in the future. If you are feeling "down" at this moment and have consulted this section, turn to the next page now to that point where I have set out the actions you can take to give yourself the care you need.

A Note on Clinical and Genetic Depression

Clinical Depression

This is a medical condition in which the symptoms that I have described for despondency are much more severe and prolonged. The difference of degree may be stated as similar to that between a bruised foot and a broken leg. The first needs rest, care, and attention. The second needs medical treatment for recovery to take place. Clinical depression is caused by the inability of the body to produce those substances that stimulate positive feelings, thoughts, and energies. This serious malfunction requires medical treatment. The causes are complex, but ongoing research is revealing possible stimulants to restart the body's usual functions or substitutes to make up for the body's deficiencies. If you or your friends think that you may be clinically depressed, *see your medical adviser,* who will know the best sources of assistance available in your community.

Genetic Depression

The medical condition of those suffering from genetic depression is similar to that above, but the cause is a genetic deficiency. The causes of the condition have been brought to light by research that has led to a greater understanding of genetics. It is often a relief to people to find out that their depression does not arise from some "fault" on their part or from some known trauma. The genetic deficiency explains why there is no outward reason for the body to malfunction. Genetic depression may become more "acute" during times of hormonal changes or when the general energies of the body and mind are no longer strong enough to compensate for the symptoms of depression. Research continues in many fields of medical science and is revealing greater knowledge about this condition. Self-diagnosis is neither required nor helpful, and, as with all depression, *medical assistance is required.*

The wonderful news is that much help can be given to those who suffer from depressive conditions.

Actions to Care for Yourself in Times of Despondency

We have looked at the causes of despondency, and I have described some of its effects. As you read through the list, you perhaps realized that it is a common condition that affects us all from time to time. I hope that this information helps you to understand yourself to a greater extent and therefore has removed the fear that you cannot make sense of what is happening to you when you feel like this. The mysteries of the body, mind, and spirit are so great that we will never fully understand our conditions, but, for the most part, we are satisfied and less prone to panic if we have some clue as to what is going on. What are the things we can do to help our recovery? You may have worked out some for yourself as you have been reading. Here is the list of my suggestions, born out of my own experiences and others'.

Trust

Exercise the trust you have in God so that you can work patiently and firmly through the issues that lie behind your despondency. Rekindle your faith and allow others to share their faith and confidence with you. You may need to be carried by their faith for a time until your own grows firmer again. Remember that God trusts you to play your part in the recovery process. Open yourself up to receive God's grace. On the other hand, trusting God does not mean that you expect God to "take over" and do it all for you. That would lower your sense of self-worth even further. Exercise a proper trust in God and in your friends.

Physical Actions

Because we are dealing with issues that affect our personalities, we can take actions with our bodies that are also beneficial to our minds and souls.

Bodily exercise plays a vital role in recovery from despondency. The type of exercise depends on our general physical condition, but should always increase the amount of oxygen in the bloodstream. Breath is the source of life and therefore is the word in scripture that is used for the Spirit of God. Deep breathing, especially with a consciousness of God's gift of grace and new life, is a good way to start the exercise, and from there we should develop it as far as we can. If possible, go outside and walk, or be wheeled out by family or friends, and breathe deeply. We know from research how important sunshine and light are in the process of recovering from despondency.

Whole communities that have a tendency toward this condition have shown worse symptoms when deprived of light, especially sunshine. Those who work inside should take note of this and on breaks from work make a special effort to go outside into the natural light.

Having a good laugh is a great antidote to despondency. Laughing is not only a mental stimulus but also a physical one. It causes deep breathing, stimulation to the head and chest, and valuable movement to the whole body. People who know how to engender a good laugh are a wonderful tonic, and the clown has wide respect in any healthy community. Jesus could lift the crowds with his amusing stories and make his points with humor so that they were more readily accepted. The story of the log in the eye of the person trying to extract a speck of dust from the eye of another is a good example of what I mean.[3] Just imagine the picture and have a good laugh.

A good laugh is usually best as a communal event. Another physical action we can take to recover from despondency is seeking the company of others. Loneliness and despondency go together, so it is right to seek the company of others in such times and to speak and listen equally. We need to hear others' accounts of good times in life as well as expect them to listen with sympathy to our list of woes. Despondency can be an infectious disease unless the listening is mutual. Often walking together with friends in the fresh air in mutual conversation blows away some of the blues we feel.

Our ancestors were keenly aware that diet had an important influence on mood. They had special foods as "pick-me-ups." In our times we too are conscious of how vital diet is to good health. A poor diet leads to depletion of energy. A heavy diet leads to lethargy. This is all obvious, but too often we ignore our physical diet when we are considering troubles of the mind and spirit. When we are down, we need healthy food presented so that it whets our appetite. Much of this wholesome food is also economical. Family and friends play a vital part in keeping us on a good diet through encouragement and restraint. In despondency you may find that you want to eat a lot to compensate for emotional "starvation." Trust your friends to help you use diet to serve you, rather than enslave you.

Drink is an even greater issue in despondency. The temptation is to look to it to give us the stimulation that will lift us up. Caffeine and alcohol will certainly do this, but after the lift comes the greater fall.

---

[3]Luke 6:41.

Water is probably the best medicine, as it clears the body of toxins. Water, air, and exercise, taken together, will be the most effective aid to recovery. You may think that this sounds dull, but used well, they are the best "stimulants" for us.

Some people find that eliminating caffeine is the best way to improve their mental health. Caffeine is known to have a depressing effect on some people and to cause emotional stress in others. In despondent moments it is certainly worthwhile to see whether it helps to lessen or remove the intake of caffeine.

Alcoholic drinks can mask the problems that are causing despondency. As we will see shortly, our minds require help to concentrate and have the energy to deal with the issues that have caused the despondency, or to accept with patience and understanding the bodily and emotional changes that are the causes of our current state. Except as a brief antidote to shock, alcohol is unhelpful to the despondent person, even when it is considered an acceptable pleasure during the ordinary periods of life. If we or our friends suspect that we are misusing alcohol during times of despondency, we should again seek professional help. This help is readily available in most societies. The success of such programs is a reason for great thanksgiving.

In summary, take care of your body and "listen" to it. Sustain it with the most basic ingredients in the food and drink chains, and exercise it with care. You will be amazed at the way this improves your general condition, especially during despondent moments.

Mental Actions

In times of despondency the attention span is short, and it is easy to daydream or become sidetracked from the real issues. Many find it helpful to set aside a short period (say two or three minutes) to focus on the issues and then to relax. This period of time can be progressively increased as the recovery quickens. In this "period of concentration," focus on a particular question, decision, or action. At the end of the time, write down in note form everything that is useful, however small. It might be as straightforward as deciding to go for a short walk, or as complex as defining the reason for current feelings. In the end, the various pieces of the jigsaw puzzle will fit together. Following the period of concentration, say a prayer (see the heading below) and then let the matter rest for a while.

Gradually our minds allow us to organize the issues that are before us. This will not give an immediate answer to all our questions or solve all the problems, but it will provide a framework to deal with things step-by-step. Some people by their natural preferences keep adding ideas and issues to the pile rather than working in an ordered way. If this is so, be careful to add positive as well as negative ideas.

As the mind gains energy, it will find it easier to work out priorities and to "stock-take." Not everything can or must be done at once, so it is valuable to draw up a short list of things to do first. As you attend to these in whole or in part, you will receive the encouragement to deal with more. In stocktaking, see that you balance the positives and negatives. I have heard a good theory that states there should only be as many negatives on a list as there are positives until trust and confidence return. Ask a friend to help you make this assessment.

As your mind makes progress, see that you note what has been achieved and give thanks for that. Thanksgiving comes from the realization that all of life is a gift, and that we receive much from others, including God, to make our lives fuller. The absence of simple thanksgiving is often a root cause of despondency. At these times we fail to note the good things about ourselves, and we often fail to encourage and support others as we forget to give them thanks for the things they do for us. Thanksgiving helps us to acknowledge the interdependence of human existence. From this we are encouraged to look for help from those with special talents and skills in the complexities of modern life. As we face the issues that cause our despondency, we may find that such specialists are gathered in organizations with special purposes. For example, there are groups that give budgetary advice or emergency aid to those who care for persons with rare diseases or conditions. Often a local organization can link us to the professional agency we need. We should not feel shy about seeking such help. The community has set up these agencies to be of assistance, and it is best for the whole community when those who need help seek it. When we have recovered, we may be in a better position to offer our particular talents to the community for the benefit of others. The church community can model this interdependence, offering care to those in need and offering opportunities for those who have something to give. In this mutuality is a cause for thanksgiving.

The mind, like the body, needs the right amount of stimulus through activity to spur it on to recover from times of despondency. Consider reading a book, seeing a good film or play, attending a concert, or participating in a sporting event. Staring blankly into space will not improve your condition. Friends can help motivate you to such activity. I encourage you to respond positively to their invitations and not say that you are too tired or dispirited. It will require effort on your part and some insistence on theirs, but the benefits will be mutual.

With some or all of this mental stimulation, your mind should be better equipped to identify the possible causes of your despondency. In doing this, you may find the following questions helpful in eliminating and identifying causes:

1. Can I identify as a cause any of the twelve causes mentioned earlier in this chapter?
2. Can I give more specific detail under one or more of the headings?
3. If not, is my despondency a disguise for deeper feelings, such as
   - looking for sympathy,
   - seeking appreciation,
   - covering low self-esteem,
   - repeating childhood behavior,
   - uncovering some buried loss or hurt?

It is not easy for us to see all the issues for ourselves, and this is where the trusted friend or skilled expert can help us. It is a common experience that we stop our ears from hearing the truth when we are told it. However, if we uncover the truth for ourselves with the help and support of others, we are more likely to be able to make the necessary changes or accept the situation. What is most important for us to know is that there is some traceable cause for our despondent feelings, and that we can and should identify it. At that point there are many ways that we can receive help.

Spiritual Actions

Up to this point I have been hinting at the spiritual actions we can take in conjunction with physical and mental actions. Now it is time to give full weight to this aspect of recovery.

We started with a reference to our trust in God, and that is how it should be. I did not record this as "faith" in God, because many people, when they are despondent, tell me that they have "lost their faith." By this they mean that they are uncertain about the content of their faith and indeed whether they have the energy and spirit to say yes to God. Even in this uncertainty we can hang on to our anchor of trust—unless we have been deprived of this development so far in our lives. If that is the case, I ask you to reread chapter 1 and see what I said there. Otherwise, we can draw on the deep reserve of trust that we have built up and proceed to act *as if we could believe in God,* even when we are not certain about that.

Once we have taken this step, we can open ourselves up to pray. In our simple prayer we ask for God's help to create in us a willingness to receive support from others, to listen to their encouragement and praise, and to learn from their critical comments. This openness is vital in light of our shut-in feelings of being trapped by circumstances. Such a prayer expresses our longings as well as our hopes that others will bring us support.

Our prayers also lead into thanksgiving. We back up our mental process of stocktaking with thanksgiving for the gifts that we have received—from God and, by the grace of God, from others. Such prayers of thanksgiving in all their simplicity are a major stimulus to regaining a balanced outlook on life. The positives begin to be placed alongside the negatives, and the balance of life is seen as it is—a series of events that affects us but does not give us our ultimate value. That comes from God and is incarnate in the affirmation of others. The act of spiritual thanksgiving makes this possible, as I have explained in greater detail in *Soul Time.*[4]

When we see life in its wholeness, we are in better shape to face up to the spiritual activity of forgiveness. It is impossible to carry the burden of guilt for long before it causes emotional collapse complete with despondent moments. The good news is that the burden of such guilt can be lifted so that we can tackle our responsibilities in letting go of pain or in relieving pain that we have caused others. Note carefully the order of forgiveness: Our forgiveness flows first from the total generosity of God as put into action by Christ, thus allowing us the freedom to take our part in the forgiveness process.

Through the action of forgiveness—of oneself and of others—we gain a new spiritual understanding of the cross of Christ. We can see pain as something to be accepted as a contribution to the greater good. We can see pain as the motivation for tackling the underlying causes of evil. We can see pain as a glory to be offered to God, not as

---

[4]Atkins, *Soul Time,* 133–46.

oppression to shut us off from God. We can see Christ's suffering on the cross as the pledge of God's total involvement in the world—its hard times as well as its good times. Through the cross we discover that we can never be separated from the love of God, and in that love we take support for the journey of recovery.

Such an understanding of the cross gives us new spiritual courage to face life in all its circumstances. On the road to recovery we may have to "rest in the grave" while we gather our energies and spiritual resources, but even there we will have a new spirit of hope that we will rise again. This hope is a key ingredient in recovery. It makes the dead tree of winter blossom in a new spring. Hope is the inspiration for a love that lifts us from despair, because it believes that love can overcome all obstacles.

As hope returns, we are ready for a realistic spiritual assessment of our own special gifts and qualities. We put these alongside our mental stock-taking of our talents. We see what we can offer and what is not in us to offer others. We have overcome perfectionism and jealousy and entered the mutuality of community. We know that we do not have to earn God's love for us, nor can we earn the love of others. Love is a gift that we give and receive.

Out of this spiritual mutuality we develop our gift for listening well, to God and others, as they seek to help us out of our despondency and set us on the path of positive living. As we listen we realize that we do not always have to be right to be of value. Our value is in who we are rather than what we do. Of course, our contribution to the whole is important, but success does not lie in being perfect or being better than others or always doing things for others so that we are exhausted. Success lies in being fully ourselves whatever the outward circumstances in life. We all know stories of prisoners of war who shine with a radiance that the horrific circumstances cannot extinguish. We have all heard of long-term hospital patients who, despite utter weakness and immobility, remain whole in their inner person. In our moments of despondency, our true glory is in being willing to receive the gifts of love and grace from God and others until we are ready again to move forward. It sounds humbling, and it is, but it also makes the best spiritual sense.

A Biblical Example

Jeremiah's Experiences of God in Times of Despondency

One of the best examples of handling despondency to be found in scripture is in the book of the prophet Jeremiah. He is known as a great spokesperson for God in the First Testament. His difficulty was that no one heeded his warnings. None changed their ways. The enslavement of the people of God became inevitable in the political chaos, the self-aggrandizement of the leaders, the divisions within society, and the infighting among ordinary people. Jeremiah could see this and spoke out, but no one listened. Worse still, the wicked grew stronger, and some of the disasters were avoided by good luck and external forces. In the face of this, the prophet turned in prayer to God and laid this complaint in his bitter despondency:

> Woe is me, my mother, that you ever bore me,
> a man of strife and contention to the whole land!
> I have not lent, nor have I borrowed, yet all of them curse me.[5]
>
> Why is my pain unceasing,
> my wound incurable,
> refusing to be healed?
> Truly, you are to me like a deceitful brook,
> like waters that fail.[6]

The Lord replies to these complaints:

> If you turn back (to me), I will take you back,
> and you shall stand before me.
> If you utter what is precious,
> and not what is worthless,
> you shall serve as my mouth.
> It is they who will turn to you,
> not you who will turn to them.
> And I will make you to this people
> a fortified wall of bronze;
> they will fight against you,
> but they shall not prevail over you,
> for I am with you
> to save you and deliver you, says the LORD.[7]

What do we learn from this passage?

- God listens and responds to our prayers spoken "out of the depths." God can take our complaints without dismissing us as weak and useless.

---

[5]Jeremiah 15:10.
[6]Jeremiah 15:18.
[7]Jeremiah 15:19, 20.

- God trusts us to take courage and use the talents we have.
- God equips us with the strength to overcome difficulty and danger.
- God has already acted to save and deliver us, not from outward difficulties–Jeremiah had lots of that treatment–but from inner collapse.

In our times of despondency, such a message is what we most need to hear. This is the message that God has for us when we are despondent even as Jeremiah was in his day.

Pause now and read the last two verses again. Take to your heart the affirmation that your life is precious to God. Here is a prayer you may use at this point.

God, I trust you.
Open my heart to receive your trust of me.
Light the candle of hope in my time of darkness;
Lighten my mind to perceive the causes of my despondency;
Lighten my load through the help of friends.
Give me courage and patience until I am strong enough for a new start.
Then let your Spirit enliven my life,
and fill it with love
for you,
for others,
and for myself.
With Christ, my Savior, I pray. Amen.

4

Looking after Yourself at Celebration Time

Celebrations

Celebrations are part of community life in every culture and are essential to the well-being of each individual. In this chapter I want to share with you some of the reasons why we should celebrate, some of the occasions suitable for celebrations, some of the best ways we can celebrate, some of the outcomes, and some of the cautions we should heed in our times of celebration. All this is set against the background, for a Christian, of the example of the feasting Christ and the encouragement of the Spirit of God to show forth joy in our lives.

Why Celebrate?

Remembrance

We celebrate because we want to highlight and capture for the future something that is of vital importance to our personal, family, or communal life. A celebration is a marker by which we remember and hold dear a key event. This may be an achievement, a new life in the birth of a child, a victory in sport, a farewell to a family member, an eightieth birthday, or even a funeral when a long life is remembered and celebrated.

Thanksgiving

We celebrate because we want to give thanks. Thanksgiving is an important part of life because it acknowledges the contributions of people to what has been achieved. We give thanks to God. We give thanks to one another. We give thanks for the gifts in ourselves that make the achievement possible. For example, a parent at the birth of a child will mark the occasion with a time of thanksgiving. Such delight and joy does not have to be conjured up. It pours out naturally. We see wonder and happiness shining in the faces of the proud parents. On their lips are words of thanksgiving. Parents express their thanks to each other–the man especially to the woman. They thank those who assisted with the birth process. Most parents in their hearts want to thank something greater, the source of life itself: God if they so believe, good fortune if they cannot name their sense of "mystery." What I have experienced and observed is that all this thanksgiving flows naturally. What is your experience?

(I am, of course, aware of the contrasting feelings when the birth does not go well or if it is not possible for you to have a child. If this is your experience, pause now and feel God's tenderness and love as you care for yourself amid the memories of pain. Having acknowledged your hurts, you may also want to celebrate their healing.)

Much of life is a reason to be thankful, and we want to express this in celebration at special moments. Sometimes we do not take enough notice of the "smaller" occasions for thanksgiving and miss the opportunities to mark them appropriately. We will look at such occasions later in this chapter.

Joy

Life is often hard, and Christians acknowledge this. The major symbol of the Christian faith is a cross, and this keeps us realistic about life. Yet in the midst of this realism the Christian has also been given the spirit of joy. In Saint Paul's list of the fruits of the Holy Spirit, joy comes in second place only to love.[1] When you read the epistles and the Acts of the Apostles, you can see this constantly demonstrated in the lives of the followers of Jesus Christ.

It is a shame that Christians in more recent years have been known more for the no they have uttered than the yes to life that early Christians showed. Christian joy is not froth and bubble, but a deep joy that gives a positive outlook on life and a spring in the step for the journey ahead. There is an affirming yes to God and life.

---

[1]Galatians 5:22.

This joy is not "turned on" to cover up unhappiness. This joy shares the purpose of God that life should be good, creative, and communal. We rejoice in the faith that God has in us; in the forgiveness that we are offered through the cross; in the future of life beyond the grave; in the trust that others have in us and we in them. We rejoice not in an easy life, but in the opportunities to live life to the fullest. This sort of joy cannot be taken away from us. It is the wonderful wellspring that flow's over into celebration.

Gifts

Gifts and celebrations go together. Ask any child about that! We mark our celebrations with gifts. Our celebrations themselves mark our "gifts." What we have received from one another and from God is a basic reason for celebration. A funeral celebrates the "gifts" of a person, but it is a pity that so often we miss the opportunity to celebrate while the person is alive. There was good sense in the earlier custom of a presentation celebration after twenty-five or thirty-five years, when employees were honored for their gifts by the firm that benefited from their labors. The opening celebration of an artistic exhibition honors the artists as well as promoting their works for sale.

Some parents and grandparents realize the importance of marking the gifts of a young person during the school years. This should not be seen as a reward or payoff for some special effort, but as a celebration of the developing gifts of the young person. We celebrate who they are and what they have to contribute to their community—from the family to the nation.

Balance

Another reason that we need to celebrate is to make sure that there is balance in our lives. As individuals we need to have variety to make our lives whole. Too much of one type of activity distorts one's outlook on life. We need joyful occasions to balance our times of strain and sadness. We are helped by having celebrations to mark the conclusion of long periods of hard work. As a community we need celebrations to give us time to meet one another without the pressures of decision making or problem solving.

Celebrations help to balance our activities and provide the rhythm to our existence that mirrors the changing seasons of creation. In agriculture there are seed time and harvest, drought and rain, cold and heat, as nature goes through the routine of activity, rest, and re-creation. The flowers of summer are a celebration of life, which leads to the seeds that are the source of continuity for creation. Likewise, our times of celebration capture the energies of the past, give us joy in the present, and prepare us for the future. Celebration links our lives together and gives balance to the whole.

Occasions for Celebrations

While pointing out the reasons that we should celebrate, I have referred to occasions on which we might celebrate. You may have thought of some additional examples. Check them against the list that follows and see how many overlap.

Anniversaries

The annual cycle of nature prompted our ancestors to see that a year was a good measure for life. Each year brings a remembrance of past events. The first few anniversaries of a major happening are full of sharp memories, so people naturally gather to keep the anniversary. We have seen this happen in communities following a major tragedy or, more happily, to remember the conclusion of a war. As the years pass, other events tend to overlay that remembrance, and it passes by noticed only by a few. It is often revived after twenty-five or even fifty years. It is important for us, young and old, to participate in these community anniversaries so that we gain a proper historical perspective on life.

In our personal lives anniversary celebrations are equally important. Birthdays, marriage anniversaries, and the annual remembrance of the death of a loved one are all occasions to be marked by appropriate celebrations. It is good to see adult birthdays given equal place to those that children enjoy. The establishment of a birthday ritual is a key way to affirm the place of each person in the family. Some birthdays will be a time for special honor. These could be the first birthday of adulthood (at 12, 18, or 21 years of age, according to the culture), the birthday to mark mature responsibility (35 or 40), senior status at 60 or 65, or the birthdays of honor at 80, 90, and 100. All these are occasions of rejoicing, giving thanks, sharing memories, and affirming gifts.

Think back on your own anniversaries and what they meant for you. Which ones passed without celebration, to your regret? It is even possible to plan a "catch-up" anniversary party.

Major Achievements

Celebrations marking a major achievement have the powerful effect of letting a wide circle of people share in the rejoicing that a task has been done well. America shared its triumph of the moon landing when the successful team returned to a celebration. Through the media it became an international event, so that the space walk was not just for the person or the nation but "one giant leap for mankind." Through the celebration of the achievement, we all came to feel we had a share in its glory.

On a personal level, we often feel undervalued when a major achievement is not recognized by an appropriate celebration. Even in a small matter such as the construction of a building, the "shout"[2] when the foundation is laid, another when the building is topped, and a final one at the opening, is important for all those involved.

Think of major achievements in your life and how these have (or have not) been celebrated. For the future, I encourage you to plan an appropriate celebration to mark important achievements for yourself and those for whom you care.

Marriages

For many people a marriage is the most important celebration of a lifetime. The guests are carefully chosen by the couple and the parents. It is a celebration of both the couple's commitment and the pride of the parents. The list of the toasts tells us who is honored. In the marriage of a couple with children from previous marriages, the children may well find an honored place in the marriage celebration.

The level of expense relative to the financial wealth of those involved shows the value that most people place on the marriage celebration in a society where money is the measure of most things. Christians, in contrast, should witness to the value and priority they give to love, care, and thanksgiving over material wealth. The celebrations are most enhanced by the participation of the greatest number of people in a practical way. By this they offer their most important gifts–themselves. I am sad to see floral arranging contracted out to people with no emotional connection to the wedding when others would be only too glad to give of their talents. Their participation demonstrates how celebrations not only involve community but create community. The shared work and shared contributions all help us to feel part of the celebration.

Marriage is primarily the celebration of the love and lifelong commitment of a man and a woman. The way the couple "celebrates" the marriage will have a lasting effect on the quality of the marriage

[2]This is a celebration given on site to the planners and workers by the owners or builders.

itself. The preparations, the service or ceremony, the feast, and the honeymoon are all part of the overall celebration of love in marriage. All need to be given due weight. It is a good test to ask these questions about each part of the celebration:

- In what way does this activity contribute to the celebration as a whole?
- How does this part highlight the love between the couple that is at the heart of the whole celebration?

Some activities and expenses may be removed in light of this test and be replaced by others to fulfill the true purpose of the celebration.

Birth of Children

I noted earlier that the birth of a child is a major event in the life of every person, every family, and every community. Normally it is a cause for joyful celebration. In a few instances, it is the cause of a sad celebration, which is just as important to mark the event and keep us in proper relationship to it. The joyful event, like a marriage, comes in a series of occasions: as soon as the child is born; when the child is welcomed by the family for the first time; and when the child is welcomed by the community. For Christians, this latter occasion may be associated with the baptism or dedication of the child into the Christian journey or the blessing of the child by a minister of the church. Consider for a moment the way your church affirms the value of a child to the God of all creation and the commitment of the Christian community to share its faith with the child. For Christians this celebration involves the whole church community, as well as the wider circle of family and friends.

Each part of the celebration contributes to the whole. The first welcome of the child by the parent(s) and any siblings is a wonderful opportunity for affirming the newly born. This celebration establishes the rightful place of the child in the family circle. Each member of the family, young and old, should have the opportunity to welcome and affirm the child. Though a major responsibility for all in the family, the child at the same time holds the potential to contribute much to the family, bringing his or her special gifts. Affirmation by each sibling is especially important as the newly born may otherwise be seen as a rival for affection.

The celebration of mother's safe delivery and her new role in the first few years of the child's life is one that should receive due emphasis. Many cultures have special ceremonies for this occasion. The mother is duly honored for her key role and, in response, has the opportunity for giving thanks–to God, to those who helped with the delivery, and to her husband and family for their support. Many service books have special prayers for such occasions.[3]

The welcome of the child into the community is the third step in the process. This is the gathering of the wider family and friends who mark the occasion with prayers, good wishes, and often with symbolic gifts. The notice of the birth in the local newspaper also allows the community as a whole to rejoice. Parents should decide whether this celebration takes place at the same time as any religious ceremony or on a separate occasion. However arranged, each part should stand in its own right and have an equal but different part to play in the whole process of celebration.

Pause now to reflect on what I have written and see how it fits into your own experience. If you are expecting the birth of a child or it has just occurred, you might like to share your thoughts with your spouse and family. If you feel that your child missed out on some part of the process, you might like to consider what occasion of celebration would be the best substitute for what she or he missed. As far as baptism is concerned, this is appropriate at any age, and your local church community will help you and your child make suitable decisions.

Rites of Passage

Social scientists give this name to those celebrations that mark the turning points in our development as people. The rites can mark the time the child takes a seat at the family table; first goes to primary school; loses the first of his or her baby teeth; paints the first picture or writes the first letter; wins a game of sport; learns to swim; reaches puberty; goes to secondary school; has the first formal social occasion; or graduates.

The celebration of these rites of passage is important not only for the developing child or young adult, but also for the entire family. The celebration is an opportunity to express joy and affirm the value and participation of the child in the life of the community. The way we celebrate will be in proportion to the occasion, and expense should never be the criterion of its value. What should be remembered is the value of love mutually expressed, not the amount of money spent.

---

[3]Cf. "Thanksgiving for the Gift of a Child," in *A New Zealand Prayer Book/He Karakia Mihinare o Aotearoa* (London: Collins, 1989).

Rites of passage do not end with childhood or teenage years, but these are firm foundations. Taking up the first job is a rite of passage. So is engagement, the conception of a child, promotion in a career, retirement, being a first-time grandparent, and relinquishing responsibility for family leadership to the next generation. All rites of passage deserve a celebration, especially when we need courage and strength for the next step. Going to school, responding to puberty, and beginning new responsibilities are all times when we need a celebration to launch us into the future by rejoicing in the new status we have and the gifts we bring to it.

A New Home

The physical place for a home is so important for human beings that we should mark moving into a new home with celebration. Homes are places of memory and security, and if they fail us in this respect, it only highlights all the more our expectations of what they should be. The celebration of a new home helps us share our joy with others, particularly our neighbors and friends. It helps us "bond" to our new surroundings. Ideally, we have articles that we transfer from one home to the next, and this provides a sense of grateful continuity. Even if the place is the first home of our own, we will gift it with symbols of our most precious memories–a photograph, an ornament, an heirloom.

Our celebration is a pledge to our community that we will contribute to it and a sign of thanksgiving that we have this safe haven for our emotions. Many Christians ask for God's blessing on their homes with prayers and invite the minister to bless it room by room. This is an important action signifying that we seek to find God present in all we do and are in our homes. We recognize a home as the place where love, forgiveness, care, and support are most required as we live in close personal relationships.

The celebration of a new home is also a time for the sense of neighborhood to be affirmed with joy. In an age when we all fear violence within our communities, the importance of neighborhood is vital to overall well-being. The celebration gives the neighborhood a sense of joy and forges the bonds between those who look to one another for mutual support.

Leave-takings

Departures as well as arrivals are occasions of celebration. Life is a series of comings and goings. In our mobile, fragile society, this is especially true. Leaving home is as great a reason for celebration as setting up a new home. If we do not complete our "business" at one place well, we often get into tangles. We need to say good-bye positively to family when we first move out to take up a place of our own. We need to celebrate with thanksgiving our departures from home and district before we move on. We need to mark our leave-taking from our workplace or community organizations. It is never good to just slide away or let others drift off into the unknown. Farewells should be just that–a time of celebration when we express our hopes that the one leaving will fare (do) well in his or her future. Most businesses and organizations are good at such celebrations and have developed standard rituals for them. The person is thanked for their "gifts," supported with good wishes, and given the opportunity to respond by expressing their own feelings. Tears may be shed amid the laughter, and gifts are exchanged. Schools also often have such occasions for departing pupils.

We need to establish similar rituals in our homes and in our church communities. In a Christian home the departure will be a celebration, a time of sharing and of prayer. The same should be true of our church communities, but often this only happens for key laity and staff. In our mobile society, it should happen more frequently for all those leaving the congregation (as it should for those arriving). The scriptures regularly record such celebrations of departure, from Christ's ascension to Paul's departure from Ephesus.[4]

A Prayer for Those Leaving Home

Jesus, you left your home in Nazareth to begin your ministry of teaching and care.
Be with us in our celebration as we say farewell to ________, leaving home today.
We give thanks for his/her gifts and all that has been contributed to our family life. We ask you to bless ________ with courage and strength, patience and faith
as a new part of life's journey begins. Keep us close to you and to one another
so that, bound in your love, we may only be separated by distance.
God, we trust you for our future, and we trust one another through your Spirit,
now and always. Amen.

[4]Luke 24:50–53; Acts 20:36–38.

Funerals

A funeral is a particular form of departure celebration. It is a time of mixed emotions. We are sad because we are left behind, but rejoice in the remembrance and resurrection of the person who has died. This ambivalence can lead to the confusion of emotions. We can either be too sad or too full of celebration. We need the opportunity to express both emotions fully. The best form of funeral service gives us time to celebrate the life of the person who has died and all our love and affection for him or her, and then a time to mark the departure with an appropriate level of sadness. The age and the circumstances of the deceased will cause a variation in the balance of the two emotions. What I personally find confusing is when the service is not sure which type of celebration is happening, and a switch is rapidly made between the types, or they are muddled together.

The funeral, by celebrating the past, also prepares us for the future–resurrection of the dead and comfort and strength for the bereaved in their newfound loneliness. A Christian funeral service provides this framework and gathers the community around the family, affirming with thanksgiving the gifts from God that the deceased exercised, assuring us through scripture and the Word of hope for the future, and entrusting the living and the dead into God's care. There will be a time for laughter and a time for tears, and we will carry forward a firm memory of the occasion as we come to terms with a new pattern of life.

Christian Celebration

Our Christian community will provide us with many different occasions for corporate celebration. Worship always fulfills the reasons we celebrate. Jesus left his disciples a command to hold a "feast" that would provide a regular occasion to celebrate with and in Christ.

The festivals of the church also provide a different type of celebration. The great festivals of Easter, Christmas, Epiphany, and Ascension are supported by lesser festivals of saints and holy days of remembrance. Solemn preparation and joyful festivals are balanced in the church's year. Lent and Advent are times to acknowledge our dependence on God and our need for repentance. These are followed by Easter and Christmas as the times to rejoice in God's loving power made manifest in Jesus Christ.

This public worship mirrors the opportunities we have in our personal lives for restriction and celebration, for feasting and fasting, for stock-taking and letting go. This matches the rhythm of life and helps us to live in balanced harmony with ourselves and all creation.

How Can We Celebrate?

We have looked at the occasions for celebrations; now it is time to consider the best ways to celebrate. The following is a list of suggestions that you can match against your own experiences. Celebrations and culture are so intertwined that when it comes to methods of celebration, I can only share some general headings and give personal examples. I invite you to adapt them to fit into your own context and culture.

Using Rituals

Celebration is best supported by ritual. By this I mean a set framework that is well recognized and can be used again and again. A ritual is a pattern of words and actions that helps us to express our feelings and emotions. An example of a simple ritual is the greeting of a person who visits your home. We know the ritual so well that we hardly ever think about it until we move from one culture to another. Then we notice the particular way in which that culture carries out the ritual, the set words and actions. Pause here and work out step-by-step how you welcome someone. When you think about it, most ritual has a history. The handshake was done with an open hand to show that the visitor was not carrying a weapon to attack the host. You may greet with an embrace or a kiss as a sign of affection and love. The appropriate ritual for greeting varies depending on the relationship between the greeter and the one being welcomed. Then there are set words to say by way of affirmation, invitation, and relationship. The ritual ends with the incorporation of the visitor into the home/family/community so that the bonding is complete.

Similarly, a ritual should be (and usually is) established for different types of celebrations. The ritual regularly recalls the reasons for the celebration, the key people in the celebration, and the wider community established. It provides a place for words and speeches, for gifts and symbols, and for appropriate food and drink.

Having a ritual as a framework for the celebration makes it easier on the emotions (we know roughly what will happen), makes participation flow (we know when and how we can make a contribution), and makes it easier to bring suitable gifts, thus saving us from embarrassment.

Embracing Community

Celebrations call communities together, and every member is embraced as having a part to play in the celebration. All are participants rather than spectators. We may be closer to or farther from the main action, but we still form a part of the celebration. On our own there is no real celebration, for joy is an emotion that wants to be shared. It is interesting to note that most Christians have a custom that the service of Holy Communion should never be celebrated by one person on his or her own. It is a three-way celebration between God, neighbor, and self. This is a good model for all celebrations.

The community provides us with the support we need to put the celebration into perspective for the whole of life. In the community are those who can empathize with our joy or sadness and who release the appropriate emotions as a support for our own. We can embrace one another in the closeness of our feelings.

Feasting and Toasting

Food and drink are part of the ritual of celebration. They are the symbols of shared community. They also provide opportunities for specialized symbols for particular celebrations. No birthday celebration would be complete without a birthday cake. No welcome to a new child complete without a toast. No Thanksgiving dinner complete without a turkey. No Christmas celebration complete without Christmas cookies or a Christmas pudding. No doubt you can think of the "right" food to go with each celebration in your own culture.

The food not only adds a festive tone to the celebration but also gives the community a focus for the interchange of its feelings. The family table is representative of unity and solidarity. An empty place at the table is a poignant reminder of the gap that has been left. Food is not an end in itself, but a means to achieve the purpose of rejoicing in community, of sharing more than bread.

Drink has been traditionally associated with feasting. It adds that special lift and increases sociability. It is even said to help indigestion after feasting.[5] The drink is not an end in itself but is a means of affirming the words of honor and best wishes. It is something special for a special occasion. The Fijian culture has a particular drink called "kava" that is used to honor guests and create community as it is served from a shared bowl. Strict rituals accompany its use. The same

[5] 1 Timothy 5:23.

is true of wine in many societies where a bottle is only brought out on a special occasion of celebration.

Sharing the Spirit

When people come together in celebration, they share a certain *joie de vivre* (joy of living). We laugh and joke; we sing and clap. For a Christian this is the spirit of joy that is a gift of God to those who are open to the presence of God in their lives. Paul advises the Christians in Rome that "the kingdom of God is not food and drink but righteousness and peace and joy in the Holy Spirit."[6] We can give thanks in prayer or spoken word for this gift that enables true celebration.

Such a sharing of the spirit of joy creates the bonds of fellowship, which is another outcome of the Spirit's presence. In a group, everyone responds to the person who adds zest to the conversation. We say that they make a party "come alive." The best of such people are not showing off or seeking attention for themselves, but enkindling sparks of joy to light up the whole group. Nearly every family and community has such a person. Ask yourself whether this is your role or who has this gift in your community.

Honoring the Occasion

Another essential task at a celebration is to express words of praise and honor on behalf of those present. At a wedding anniversary dinner, husband and wife may tell how much they appreciate and honor each other. At a larger gathering, chosen representatives speak for the group or the subgroup. When such speeches are done well, the celebration is deemed a success. Some people are endowed with such a gift and need to be invited to fulfill this role. They may ask to be supplied with information and stories from other members of the group so that they can speak for all and not simply for themselves. They need time to prepare, and the invitation to speak should not be sprung on them at the last moment. Their skills at speaking will add much to the quality of the celebrations.

Giving a Blessing

The conclusion of a celebration is a key moment. It needs to be a high point, or the celebration will fizzle out. The ending is so vital to

---

[6]Romans 14:17.

the overall success that careful thought should be given to it beforehand. One positive way to conclude is for a representative to offer thanks and give a "blessing" for the future. For Christians, this will be in the form of a prayer. If it is believed that a prayer would embarrass those present, the spokesperson can present the blessing in words that wish everyone God's guidance and help in their future lives. Such an action binds together the past, the present, and the future in a positive way.

Some people have a song of blessing, and others say a prayer as a corporate action. Words of thanks precede the prayer or good wishes. These honor all who have contributed to the celebration, the hosts, and God as the giver of all life and joy. With such words, no one feels awkward that there is no public acknowledgment made to those who have worked hard toward the success of the function. If the conclusion is done well, everyone leaves on a positive note, and the planning has been most worthwhile.

The Outcomes of Celebration

Bonding

The most important outcome of any celebration is a new sense of bonding with those who have shared it. A celebration may honor an individual who is the focus of attention, but it touches everyone present. In a family gathering, we reaffirm the place of each member and strengthen the ties that bind us together in love. If the celebration is a community one, the group is identified again and emerges stronger. The interrelationships are empowered, and the whole unit moves forward as one. Celebrations are times to renew friendships and, in many cases, give individuals the opportunities to explore deeper relationships with those to whom they are especially attracted.

Perspective on Life

A celebration brings a new perspective on life. Many celebrations are about new beginnings or affirming important qualities in people. For this reason they give us positive feelings about ourselves. Celebrations connect the past to the future through the present. A ten-year-old child at an eightieth birthday party sees her or his own life in perspective and links history with a known person. The affirmations given to those we honor help us to reassess our priorities in life. Celebrations are times of pride and in this way encourage self-esteem—either in individuals or in the group.

Thanksgiving

Celebrations are times when thanksgiving is expressed, and this results in an understanding of the key role that thanksgiving has in the life of a healthy person. We no longer feel that we can take people for granted, or that others take us for granted. Mutual recognition for the variety of gifts is made through thanksgiving. If you are a Christian, your thanks will also be to God, increasing your faith and the place that you give God in your life.

God Shares All of Life

The final outcome of celebration is that we recognize that God shares the whole of our lives–the times of joy and of sadness, the extraordinary events, and the routine events. This helps us develop a rounded view of God that gives balance to our lives. When the celebration is one of remembrance, we can look back and trace the part that God had in the journey. When the celebration responds to the present, we can observe how the spirit of joy and unity creates a loving fellowship. When the celebration looks forward to the future, we can pray in faith for God's guidance and blessing.

The Feasting Christ

Our memories of Jesus Christ may not include Jesus' celebrating frequently with his friends. Yet the various gospels all give a picture of the feasting Christ. Luke particularly highlights this activity of Jesus. First is the time when Jesus, as a boy of twelve, goes up to Jerusalem for the festival.[7] This is a special celebration for any Jewish boy and marks the beginning of adult responsibilities. Luke records that Jesus readily responded in his later ministry to the invitation to a feast.[8] Levi found that there was more to a celebration than eating and drinking. It could be life transforming. Obviously, Jesus had quite a reputation as a partygoer, and the strictly puritanical did not think that this was appropriate. Of Jesus the crowd says, "Look, a glutton and a drunkard, a friend of tax collectors and sinners!"[9] There are those today who would no doubt criticize him for being too free and life affirming. Does this color your attitude to celebrations?

---

[7]Luke 2:41.
[8]Luke 5:29.
[9]Luke 7:34.

Luke's gospel records Jesus as challenging those giving a feast to check on the guest list. Is the party only for the "in" group, or do we extend our hearts and our communities by inviting the "outsider"?[10] This issue is highlighted in the story of the return of the prodigal son. His forgiveness and affirmation is sealed by a feast, but the elder brother refuses to join the party.[11]

There is also the final feast that Jesus shares with his disciples before his death.[12] This celebration seals the bonds of love between Jesus and the disciples and prepares them all for the trials ahead. After the resurrection, the feasting is resumed.[13] Finally, the end times are pictured as a great feast when all will be gathered to share at the heavenly table as the sign that the kingdom of God is fulfilled.[14]

Does this picture of the feasting Christ help you to give him a special place at your own celebrations?

Exercising Caution at Celebration Times

We need to note some cautions as we celebrate. Some of these are the advice of scripture, and others are a "must" because of dangers in modern society. Here is a list for you to consider:

- The fellowship is more important than the quantity of food and drink accompanying the celebration. Fussing over food only heightens tension and spoils the joy.

- Our celebrations should model inclusiveness. All invited are equally welcomed and honored. At a special celebration, one or two people might be given pride of place but not in such a way that others feel excluded.

- In our feasting we should never overlook the needs of the poor. At every celebration we remember those in need. This may take the form of an invitation to a lonely person in the street or a donation of food or money in a symbolic way.

- Loosened emotions at a celebration must not be allowed to run riot. We need to restrain gossip, jealousy, and unwelcomed sexual behavior. Those responsible for the celebration should set boundaries and by example and action see that the company observes them.

---

[10]Luke 14:13.
[11]Luke 15:25–32.
[12]Luke 22:7–23.
[13]Lukc 24:36–43.
[14]Luke 14:15–24.

- Young people in the developmental stage of life need help and guidance on how to enter into times of celebration and how to handle their emotions. With good role models to follow and help in setting and keeping boundaries, young people will soon learn the art of good participation.
- Alcoholic drinks must be limited and alternatives provided. No celebration is comfortable when people drink too much. It cannot end well if there is any likelihood that dangerous driving and the risk of accident or death will follow. The organizers are responsible for seeing that people are only offered what is safe.
- People should be able to conclude the celebration positively so that there will be no hangover or let-down feeling afterward. Christian joy is not artificial, so it is an ongoing state of living. Such joy comes from good fellowship, firm bonding, thanksgiving, and encouragement for the future.

None of these cautions will "spoil the party." They will make it safe for people to celebrate with joy. This is all part of looking after ourselves well in our times of celebration.

Summary

Think back now over the points that we have covered in this chapter. We have seen the importance of celebrations for a balanced life. We have discovered some ways in which we can celebrate important occasions. We have taken notice of the scriptures as they picture the feasting Christ whose spirit we invite to our celebrations. We have reminded ourselves of the due cautions we should exercise.

Now it is time for planning and action. What celebrations should you be preparing for in the months ahead? Who should share the planning with you? How can you see that people are invited to exercise their gifts to enhance the celebration? How can you set things up so that the cautions are given due weight? How can you acknowledge God's part in the celebration and feel the presence of the feasting Christ?

In your planning and your celebrating, may God bless you with joy.

5

Looking after Yourself with New Responsibilities

Taking up New Tasks

I remember the feelings I had when I realized my new responsibilities on taking up the role of bishop in the Anglican Church in New Zealand. The feeling of affirmation on being elected was soon followed by feelings of panic. My head was full of questions as I faced the task that was before me:

- How could anyone do such a complex job?
- Where were the role models?
- Who would support me in the loneliness of decision making?
- Who would be jealous and oppose any new plans?
- How would I find out what had to be done?
- What priorities should be set?
- What long-term plan of action would be best, and how could this be formulated?
- What ethical principles did I have in place to guide my actions?
- How could a consensus be reached when there were so many conflicting points of view?
- How does one cope with the inevitable opposition and "difficult characters"?

- What part would God play in equipping me for the various tasks?
- What talents did I possess, and what new ones would I have to acquire?
- Who would provide guidance and teaching in the new ways required?
- What effect would the new responsibilities have on my home life?
- What did God expect of me?
- What did people expect of me?
- Was I worthy of the call of God and of the church, and how could I retain a due sense of humility in exercising my new responsibilities?

What a long list of questions tumbled through my mind. All of them seemed exceedingly pressing in light of my new responsibilities and the high expectations of those who had chosen me for the task.

Time to Prepare

Thankfully, I had an understanding group of people around me who said that I should take the opportunity to prepare for the new task and then gave me time to reflect. I went away to the neighboring country of Australia and picked the brains of many there–bishops, financial managers, legal advisers, bishop's secretaries, laity in management positions, clergy, and children. I asked my questions, processed the answers, listened, and watched. Finally, I spent ten days with a religious order praying, listening to the word of God, and compiling a report I titled *Called to Be a Bishop in the Church of God.* It was a wonderful time, and I thank God and those concerned for preparing me as well as possible.

I have shared this personal account because I am convinced that it contains the core of the way we might approach caring for ourselves when we are faced with new tasks–whether it is our first job, parenting our first child, or being chosen for leadership in our work, our community, or an organization within it. The thrill of affirmation is always balanced by the butterflies in the stomach over the weightiness of the responsibility.

A Biblical Example

One of the best examples in the Bible of how to face new tasks can be found in the book of Nehemiah in the First Testament. This book comes from the postexilic period of the history of God's people. At that time, some of the people had returned from exile, but many more had stayed behind in the various centers, holding important positions. Representatives of those who had returned to Jerusalem brought a report to Nehemiah in Susa, the capital of the Persian Empire. The visitors bemoaned the low morale of the leaders and people in Jerusalem and blamed this on the state of the wall and gates there. They were lying in ruin just as they had been since the sacking of the city so many years ago. What was needed was strong leadership that could restore morale, gather resources from those with power, lead by personal example, stand up to opposition, and complete the task of rebuilding so that people could live in pride and security. This was a reconstruction task demanding great skills of leadership, tact, and energy.

Nehemiah heard the report as a call from God and the people, and volunteered for the job. The first eight chapters of the book provide an excellent study into the way we can take up new responsibilities. I encourage you to read it for yourself in your Bible and make a few notes as you proceed.

Essential Steps in Carrying Out a Task

You might like to compare your notes against this list of essential steps to be taken in carrying out a task.

Good Preparation and Reflection

Before taking up the responsibility, it is best to do some preparation and take time to reflect on the issues. It is unwise to rush into a new job or task. There is a major benefit in reflecting on our gifts and talents and the things that we have to offer this particular situation. If it is possible, ask many questions of those who chose you for the task. In light of their answers, come to a sober assessment of your own strengths and weaknesses. What are your gifts and gaps? What special attributes do you bring to this responsibility? Calculate how it may help you grow and develop as a person by gaining new attitudes and skills.

The other part of the preparation is an assessment of the people involved with you in this situation. What are their needs, and what have they to offer? People are the key resource for any task, but they need financial and practical resources to enable them to do the work. Without these, all human efforts will ultimately fail. We need to assess this before we assume responsibility if at all possible. Even with the responsibility of parenthood, the couple should know that they have love for each other, are committed to the role of parents, and have the financial resources for the addition of a child into the family.

The final part of our preparation is prayer. Nehemiah asked for God's blessing and prayed: "Give success to your servant today."[1] It is right for Christians to look for God's empowerment to do the task, but not to ask God to do the impossible. God has made us responsible human beings with gifts and talents. If we and those who advise us are convinced that this is a responsibility we can fulfill, we can expect God to empower our actions and bring forth in us the Spirit's gifts to enhance our performance.

Identify Helpers and Opponents

No one can do any major task alone. We live in a corporate world, and we work in the company of people. So an essential task in assuming a new responsibility is to identify those who will assist us with the work. If the task, for example, is buying a house, we pick out the most knowledgeable people in various fields of specialty skills–salesperson, lawyer, engineer, surveyor, bank manager, and some tradespeople for repairs. In a new job, we quickly assess who is willing to provide assistance and who is reluctant to offer their services. If you ask the wrong people for help, you will soon discover that they have only negative advice. Obviously, the best helpers are those who have the resources you need to complete the task successfully.

It is often the case that we can only fulfill our new responsibility if we have the support of those who hold the power. You will need to recruit such support without making yourself so dependent on it that you have no room for your own level of action. Nehemiah won the support of his employer and gained leave for himself and the necessary resources for the task. When we take up a role in a community organization, we often have to hold discussions with our full-time employer to gain the flexibility to do both tasks well. Sometimes we can even invite our employer to give material aid to the community task for which we have accepted responsibility.

When it is obvious that we will encounter opposition in the new task, we should try to discover the reason. We can ask: "Did the opposition want the job themselves? Do they lack affirmation for the tasks they already do? Is there a gender issue so that they feel angry that my gender was chosen? Do they see my appointment as taking away power from their position?" If you can identify the motivation

[1]Nehemiah 1:11.

behind the opposition, you can more easily work out the best approach. You need to ask yourself whether you can heal a hurt or give some reassurance so that there is more of a chance that they will support you. If the opposition cannot be overcome in this way, you will need to be firm and strong and make it clear that they will not be able to control the way you do the task.

On-the-spot Inspection

Nehemiah's story illustrates well the advantage of seeing the situation for yourself.[2] He goes about his on-the-spot inspection with wise secrecy. In seeing for himself, he ensures that no one pulls the wool over his eyes. We, too, on first entering our new role need to have the opportunity to find out the true situation. We will want to talk directly to those involved. We will not wish others to give their interpretations of the situation or to filter the facts. As we take a look for ourselves at the nature of the task before us, we need to examine any difficulties and assess what has to be done immediately. There will be time later for full planning and implementation, but some things must be done as soon as possible. This gives confidence to others and makes it obvious that we are people of action.

Our inspection will help us learn the history of the situation that we are inheriting. Most tasks have a past as well as a future. In our firsthand inspection, we may be able to learn why things are as they are and what has contributed to any difficulties. Talking on the spot often gives us a fuller perspective of the situation than we can gain from a distance.

Planning and Goal Setting

Nehemiah was obviously a leader who had a clear vision of his goals. Once he had seen the situation for himself, he was ready to work out a plan that involved all his resources and took note of the main points of opposition. The time spent in planning and recruiting others to share the work is vital to long-term success. God's spirit of guidance is a key element in our planning. As we formulate our plans, we try to look at things with the eyes of the Creator and be in tune with God's long-term purpose for the whole of creation.

There are two levels of planning–setting short-term goals and then long-term objectives. Both should be coordinated to go hand in

[2]Nehemiah 2:11–16.

hand. Nehemiah knew that the short-term goal was the rebuilding of the city walls so that the city was safe from actual and threatened attack. Without that security the people could not plan for their lives or for their community. His longer-term objective was to create a community that would witness to God and live in obedience to God's laws. We can learn well from this approach so that our short-term plans fit adequately into our longer-term objectives, given the experience that the goals will have to be adapted to the emerging circumstances.

Our plans have to be made in conjunction with those who are to carry them out with us. Leadership requires us to be out in front but never to lose touch with those who empower our leadership through their support. If our planning involves as many people as possible, those people will share more readily in carrying out the plan. Any who do not feel involved may spoil the plan out of ignorance or out of spite. People want to see how their part fits into the whole.

By breaking down the plan into manageable sections, Nehemiah inspired the groups and their leaders to reach the goal. Step-by-step achievable objectives are always best when there are large numbers of people involved.

Meeting and Coping with Opposition

One of the hardest parts of taking up a new responsibility is meeting and coping with the opposition. This sometimes comes from unexpected quarters, but if we have carried out our assessment well at the beginning, we will be more prepared when opposition arises. Nehemiah experienced all the main ways that opposition is shown. First, he found that his enemies tried to discredit his ability to do the task. This subtle style of opposition hopes to undermine confidence to such an extent that the prophecy of failure becomes self-fulfilling. To meet such opposition we need dedication and courage. We need not let ridicule undermine the true assessment of our qualities or, because of our desperation, push us into arrogance or dominance.

Nehemiah also experienced the next level of opposition—strongly negative actions. The opposition was not only presented in words but in actions that had to be countered. In chapter 4 we note how Nehemiah dealt with opposition by taking counteractions to make sure that his plan succeeded. The wall of the city was not yet half built when the opponents, realizing that their cause would be lost if they did not act quickly, began to threaten attack. In coping with this active opposition, he had to strengthen the hearts of those carrying out the practical details of the plan. At the same time, decisions had to be made as to the measures that would be used if the attack happened. Strong, courageous, and wise actions with a certain amount of bravado made it possible for the task to be concluded successfully.[3] In the end, as usually happens, the opposition backed down.

The qualities of endurance, determination, and hard work are the best weapons against opposition. We rely on the love and support of God and God's people, and this keeps us realistic, hopeful, humble, and cared for at a time when it is hard to measure one's own performance.

If you are facing opposition at this time and what I have written or you have read in scripture is especially pertinent, pause now and enfold yourself in the love of God through prayer. As you conclude your prayer, identify some special family member or friend with whom you can share your situation who will give you support and guidance.

Dealing with Problems That Arise through Stress

Stress and hard work cause problems for those around you as well as for yourself. It is important that you are sensitive to these problems and use your pastoral skills to relieve the stress in others. Nehemiah was well aware of the lateral stress felt within the community. Often, interpersonal relationships come under pressure during times of danger and hard work. People tend to take it out on those around them when things are tough. Parents have to watch this particular issue so that they do not make life hard for their children after coming home from difficult situations at work or in the community. We should not show undue anger when a child "disobeys" our commands, when our anger really is with adults who will not obey our decisions at work or in an organization.

Nehemiah applies his ethical principles to the community under stress. The principles promote his longer-term objective of building up a good community. He declares that there must be

- No extortion
- No slavery
- No becoming rich at the expense of the poor

All such actions would undermine the interpersonal relationships that are at the heart of the community. Later in this chapter I look

---

[3]Nehemiah 6:15.

more closely at a fuller set of ethical principles to guide our actions in a new task. What is important to notice at this point is that stress within the community can bring out the worst human behavior, and leadership must set boundaries to curb greed, dominance, and lack of care for neighbor.

Modeling a Pattern of Behavior

When you assume new responsibilities, you will find that your basic pattern of behavior will be tested. What you do will show others the person you are. As a leader you will be measuring the behavior of others; yet at the same time they will subject you to equal scrutiny.

In the story of Nehemiah, his quality of leadership provides a model for the other leaders. He sets a standard of behavior that he can expect others to follow. Jesus, as the best model for us all, knows that teaching is not only done in words but also by example. What Jesus tells us to do, he models for us. What he shows through his life, death, and resurrection is explained and instilled through his teaching.

Our ethical behavior sets standards for those around us in our families, at work, and in the organizations we serve. If the model is good, our inner qualities should be mirrored in those who are sharing the task. For Nehemiah such qualities included a certain amount of cunning, as well as courage. Matthew's gospel records Jesus as praising a similar combination of qualities: "See, I am sending you out like sheep into the midst of wolves; so be wise as serpents and innocent as doves."[4]

There is a refreshing realism here about the problems of leadership. The serpents are wise because they know how to take appropriate action in the face of the enemy. They either back away or choose the best point of attack. We, too, need this sort of prudence. We also need the courage to maintain our chosen course of direction when others feel like giving up in the face of difficulties. Combined with this quality, we need the innocence of doves that has no spite or guile when faced by opposition.

Celebrating the Achievement with Joy

The outcome of doing a task well should be not only improvement in material things but also improvement in the ethical behavior of the

---

[4]Matthew 10:16.

community as a whole. If this goal is reached, it brings great satisfaction to the leadership. There will be a general lift in the spirit of the community, and everyone will want to be involved in a better way of living together. Chapter 8 of Nehemiah's record shows that the whole community participated in setting a new code of conduct. The outcome of Nehemiah's work was that the people gained new confidence and dedicated themselves to living in harmony and prosperity with their neighbors. When such a goal is reached, it is time to celebrate.

As we saw in the last chapter of this book, a celebration is a fitting climax to such an achievement. In the story of Nehemiah the people share a feast of joy, marking what has been done and sharing in the sense of pride for their part in the success. The corporate celebration affirms both leadership and participation.

These steps, clearly shown in the account of the work of Nehemiah, are a good guide for our own paths when we take up new responsibilities. Check back now and see where you have taken similar steps in one of the areas for which you have responsibility.

Qualities to Match Responsibility

As we have followed his account, we have been able to note the special qualities Nehemiah possessed that made it possible for him to reach his goals. Here is my list. I encourage you to look at it and work toward attaining similar qualities as you undertake new tasks and do them well.

Nehemiah was

- Dedicated to the task
- Intelligent and insightful
- Sympathetic to the needs of others
- Cooperative in working with others
- Realistic and hopeful
- Hardworking
- Strong in the face of opposition
- Determined to achieve his goals
- Principled in the methods he employed
- Willing to be a model for others

- Cunning and courageous
- Wise in planning
- Active and full of initiative
- Inclusive of all groups of people
- Faithful in prayer
- Trusting in God

These qualities can be acquired by training, as well as through the gifts we have inherited. We will have gaps in our abilities, but fortunately there are many ways in which we can receive help to fill in these gaps. Our society is conscious of the need for ongoing training and for the provision of support for those with various types of responsibilities. Our education does not stop when we leave college. Further training is widely available.

As you care for yourself, identify your weaknesses from the above list, highlight particularly important gaps, then seek out those who can assist you. In our workplaces, employers usually provide opportunities for their staffs to gain further skills and even personal development. The topics covered include interpersonal relationships, self-confidence, inner motivation, and self-assessment. Sadly, some community groups are not so aware of the need to equip those who are asked to do various tasks. Often people are thrown into the "deep end" and expected to do a good job without proper training or support. The difficulties of working in a voluntary society are well known, especially since all members seem to reserve the right to opt out if they dislike any decision made by the group. Any leader of such a group must be skilled in motivation and group dynamics if she or he is to help a voluntary organization achieve its objectives.

If you are asked to accept such a task, look to the wider community to provide you with the training you need. Sometimes it may be possible to suggest that the whole group share in such training, which will lift the level of participation and skill. This will also help spread the financial cost among group members rather than its falling on you alone.

Many church communities are now aware of the need to provide training and support for their members and leaders. There is training for parents with a new child, youth preparing for their first work opportunities, leaders of various groups in church and community, and those undertaking care within their families or communities. Each responsibility demands its own skills, but there are enough basic issues for training to be done in groups.

Those taking up new responsibilities should look for ongoing support from a wise adviser. For your own care, identify such a person and build a relationship with the person before you reach a major crisis. The support includes affirmation and listening as you make assessments of the situations and how you can best respond. The adviser will not solve your problems for you, but will help you work out ways of facing and overcoming the difficulties and challenges.

Ethical Boundaries and Signposts

Earlier I referred to the need for a set of ethical principles to guide our actions in the task we have taken up. Most Christians are aware of the Ten Commandments and Jesus' summary of the law. They try hard to apply these to the various situations they face.

Many find it easier to apply the summary of the law of love–love God, love your neighbor, and love yourself–in personal situations than in corporate positions. It is not easy to answer the question, Who is my neighbor? when you are a managing director of a public company or a trade union official. Is it the board of directors, the shareholders, the managers, the employees, those who supply the company, or those who use the output of the company? Yes, it is all these groups and more, and often love of one may mean a lower priority for another. Or to take another example: How do you, as an engineer in a factory making weapons, love God? Should you quit your job or stay and try to influence the political system to see that such weapons are kept in reserve to maintain the peace? The summary of the law is good, but its application is often very difficult.

In light of these difficulties, some groups or professions have listed an ethical code of practice that deals with their particular issues. I know that there is a code of practice for doctors, nurses, teachers, airline pilots, and travel agents. I do not know whether there is one for politicians. If you are in a profession or organization with a code of practice, it would be good to look at it again and reflect on how it helps you act in your new responsibility.

I believe that there are common ethical principles that we can apply to most of our responsibilities, whether these are great or small. Being a Christian colors what I say, but these ethical principles probably have wide community support.

Basic Ethical Principles for Those Holding Responsibility

Duty of Care

We have a duty to care for the welfare of others as well as for ourselves. Such a duty of care promotes well-being, healthy living, full participation in the setting and achievement of goals, and a recognition of the value of both the group and each person.

Any decision that is made is for the benefit of the widest group possible. Conversely, favoritism of any sort is avoided. Nothing is done to set one section of people against another. Attempts to divide and rule are resisted.

Our duty of care extends to ensuring that everyone takes time out for leisure, rest, and recreation, and that no one is overburdened by work or responsibility.

Our duty of care includes care for the environment, as well as people. Our actions enhance the natural world in which we live and give it the best opportunity to flourish in its own right. Such a duty of care is particularly relevant to those gaining production from natural resources, but it also applies to our responsibilities at home and in our communities.

Duty of Safeguard

Our actions should promote the safety of all those for whom we are responsible. We do our utmost to prevent and reduce accidents, including the removal of or protection from dangerous equipment and health hazards. Every parent has this duty, as well as managers and employers. Obviously, it is difficult to foresee some accidents, but keeping an eye out for such hazards is the least we can do. For those responsible for employees, the prevention of accidents may seem costly in terms of the time set aside for training and the provision of extra equipment and protection materials, but a responsible employer will regard this cost as essential for business. If an employee sees a hazard, his or her duty is to point out the danger and push for a remedy.

The community has put many regulations into place to help safeguard its members, and we all have a duty to comply with the regulations gladly. In my own society, failure to fulfill the regulations has led to toddlers' drowning in unfenced swimming pools and severe head injuries to cyclists who have not worn safety helmets. Such accidents affect not only the injured person and the family but also those who carry the guilt of failing to comply with the duty of safeguard through obeying the regulations. In such cases, repentance and forgiveness are the only opportunities for healing both the grief and guilt.

Again, it is appropriate to point out the duty of safeguard of the environment, as well as people. From the destruction of forests to the effect of greenhouse gases, there are many examples in our time of the failure of the community and individuals to fulfill their duties of safeguard of the whole created order.

Duty of Service

The purpose of taking up any responsibility should be service to others. We often see the opposite happen when new responsibility equals the opportunity for self-aggrandizement. In the end this attitude is self-defeating. Other people will withdraw their support and those whom we manipulate (be they children, employees, employers, or partners) will turn against us in hatred.

Responsibility always calls for service that seeks the good of all before pride or profit for oneself. To serve others is to promote the common good. It does not mean that we should become a doormat on which everyone else is permitted to wipe their feet. We should never allow anyone to walk all over us. The reverse is also true–we should not trample on others.

Jesus is the model of how to combine service and responsibility. Jesus is clear about his goals–to inaugurate and embody the rule of God. Through Jesus the Servant, Christians are caught up in the new life and energy of God and, in turn, accept the role of servant gladly.

Our duty of service will be that of an enabler. We will see that others, as well as ourselves, grow into their full potential and are given every opportunity to use the gifts and talents that God has given them. New parents easily recognize such a responsibility. Good employers include this in their duties. Those in leadership in the community see this as an opportunity for full participation in the goals of the organization concerned.

Inclusiveness

One of the principles guiding our actions should be an attitude of inclusiveness. We should aim to include as many people as possible in what we are doing. One of the temptations in getting a job done is to do as much as possible oneself. Some say that it is easier and more efficient, achieves better results, and saves arguments. Then the person alone can receive the credit or blame. Such an attitude ignores the fact that life is lived in community and that we need one another for survival. If we do not work together, in the end we will fight one another.

Our principle of inclusiveness does not allow us to exclude people on the grounds of their age, gender, religion, race, or culture. We obviously have to consider the individual's capacity to share in the task at hand, but that will be the only criterion we use. On a worldwide basis, ethnic groups are becoming more exclusive and are stressing the differences between people rather than the common nature of humanity. This makes the principle of inclusiveness even more difficult to put into practice. With this background, Christians will want to highlight more clearly the inclusive nature of God's love and our links with one another as members of the human family.

Improving and Enhancing Relationships

In doing a task it can be helpful to examine whether the goals and the means of achieving them will enhance the relationships of all those involved. If the Christian ethical principle is love, every opportunity should be seized to enhance the quality of the relationships that occur through the task.

Unfortunately, some people see the task itself as more important than the quality of relationships achieved through the task. If reaching the goals means that we build up conflicts between people and deprive them of affirmation as participants, the goals are not worth the cost. This principle is especially true in any voluntary organization. Sometimes it is necessary to weigh the value of a task to one group of people over another. The building of a child-care facility may benefit young children and their parents, but at the same time cause disturbances for older neighbors through constant daytime noise and increased car traffic and parking problems.

Can you think of similar examples from your experience in which actions that enhanced relationships within one group of people at the same time damaged relationships within another group? Also ask yourself when you are doing a task if you concentrate more on the job to be done than on the feelings of the group that is involved.

Justice and Fairness

The previous principle leads us to consider the ethical imperative for justice and fairness. Justice aims to remove bias, prejudice, and all actions that might give unfair advantage to ourselves or those whom we favor. The symbol of justice is the scales that are held in balance.

In reality, balance is hard to achieve, but we must do all in our power to aim for this goal.

Fairness does not always match equality. The story Jesus told about the owner of a vineyard who paid the same wage to those who worked different periods of time–some a full day and others only for the last hour or so–always raises the question of equality and fairness.[5] The generosity of God goes beyond our sense of fairness but is in accordance with the true meaning of the concept. This takes into consideration the needs of those involved rather than what each deserves. Justice is about promoting the good and seeing that people have what is required for full lives. Justice includes protecting the weak from exploitation and being an advocate for those who cannot speak for themselves.

Truth and Honesty

In undertaking our responsibilities, we should match our actions against the principles of truth and honesty. The public has little respect for those who are dishonest, because they have a basic feeling that no one should gain advantage by lying about the facts of a situation. Trust is built on full disclosure, even when the facts are unpalatable. We appreciate the doctor who tells us of the severity of the operation even though it makes us afraid of the pain. If the situation is not fully disclosed, we are frightened that even worse things are hidden from us. It is also true that if it is not necessary for us to know the information because we are not affected by it, it is unhelpful to be loaded with "the truth."

One of the hardest decisions that many parents have to make is how much of the truth about situations to reveal to their young children. Do we share details of *every* danger that could possibly happen, thereby risking an overload of fear that may stifle a growing trust in other people? The "stranger danger" program has been important to warn young children of the risks of accepting kindness from unknown adults. On the other hand, some children have become so frightened that all adults are seen as potential threats. Another example is the warnings given to travelers about the dangers of theft and violence in other countries. If taken too far–however accurate the facts–no one will venture farther than the front door.

Truth is a matter of setting the facts in a wider context so that we are able to see as much of the whole picture as possible. This is one

[5]Matthew 20:1–16.

of our responsibilities toward others that we exercise in whatever tasks we undertake in life.

Honoring God and Revealing Christ

Many people, whether Christian or not, may subscribe to the first seven principles that I have outlined. This last one is one that Christians want to follow as part of their commitment to their faith. They should seek in all they do to honor God and reveal Jesus Christ to those who do not know him.

Parents may see this as one of their duties in the nurturing of their children. Christian doctors in the course of their healing work may want to reveal the gift of healing from Christ that makes their work possible. Christians in business often see their work as an opportunity to honor the Creator God and to witness to the impact of Christ on their lives.

The truth is that our faith affects our conduct to such an extent that it witnesses to what we believe, whether we intend it to or not. People who believe that they alone matter in the world will make that belief very clear in the ways they behave. Those whose lives are modeled on Christ and are empowered by the Holy Spirit show their faith clearly to others. This is the "silent" witness we all give to our beliefs.

Some people see it as their Christian duty to turn this silent witness into spoken proclamation of the gospel. Christians should be ready to give witness to the work of Christ in their lives. Some will do this in response to an inquiry from another person. They will give an explanation of the way their faith influences their work. Others may feel that this type of witness is too passive and want to be active in proclaiming the gospel at every opportunity. Our personality probably determines whether we feel confident in using one method or the other. Both honor God, and when the witness is given in a way that is appropriate, it is more readily received and heard.

Pause now and reflect on these eight principles and how they match the ones that you use as working guidelines for your actions. Try to have a firm set of such guidelines in place so that you have a system in operation on a regular basis. Use this prayer to help you focus on the principles.

Gracious God, you have given us the narrow way
as the path by which to follow your commandments.
We pray for wisdom to see the truth,

for fellowship to include others in our tasks,
for strength to serve you in our care of others,
for gifts to equip us for the work we do,
and for words to tell how Jesus is the model for our lives.
May the guidance of your Spirit help us to make the right choices,
and the power of your Spirit enable us to carry them out with sensitivity and love.
We make this prayer in the name of Christ, the Servant. Amen.

Exercising Authority

I want to conclude this chapter with a short note on the care that we need to take with ourselves as we exercise authority. We all receive power when we are given a task to do. We may think that this power is so small that it does not affect others or ourselves. Our power is usually greater than we imagine. For this reason all of us need to be aware of how to handle power and how we can use it for the good of all.

First we need to be fully aware of the power we have. We can test this by asking who will be affected by the way we carry out tasks. Take, for example, teachers. They have the powers of possessing knowledge, of being able to demand work and effort from those whom they are teaching, of setting goals and standards, and, greatest of all, of being a model for the learners. Look at your own situation and draw the parallels. This will help you understand what power you have and how it affects the people on whose behalf you exercise that power.

I like to think of power as a gift given to me by God and the community. It is never mine by "right" but is granted to me "on trust" for the benefit of all. We need power to make things happen, but we cannot exercise it for our own glory without damaging others.

The current philosophy in our society is one that promotes a competitive spirit. Competition is said to create efficiency, to cut out inflated profits, and to keep everyone on their toes. The trap in this argument is that competition sets one group of people against another so that the object of power is to "beat" other people. We are then polarized into winner and losers, and power is concentrated in the hands of fewer and fewer people.

Cooperation is always a better way of using power. I use my power in a way that is complementary to your power. We build rather than break down. This should make for a happier community of winners.

As we look after ourselves in carrying out our responsibilities, it is good to feel that we are cooperating to maximize the power to build up the community as a whole. My success becomes our success, and more and more people feel that they have contributed. Then if I misuse my power out of ignorance or even deliberately, others may be more ready to forgive and rebuild because we are jointly accountable. It is not solely my responsibility. If we use power in this way, we are less likely to be corrupted by it. Sharing and contributing power for the common good are useful brakes on accumulating power for self.

Reflect now and think of the powers with which you have been gifted, and how you use them. Thank God for these gifts and for the people who allow you to exercise power on their behalf.

Generous God, you endow us with gifts so that we can fulfill your purpose.
We thank you for the opportunities you give us to undertake new responsibilities.
Make us aware of the ways our power affects the lives of others,
so that we can work together with them for the good of all.
Make us strong in leadership and humble in acknowledging the source of our power.
Then we will follow in the steps of our leader,
Jesus Christ our Lord. Amen.

6

Looking after Yourself in Times of Disability

A Right to Write

This is not an easy chapter for me to write because I have not been severely disabled at any time in my life. Some of those who are disabled may feel that I therefore should not have included this chapter in the book. On the other hand, to leave it out would be even worse. First, that would show that I failed to value the contributions of people with a variety of disabilities to our corporate life. I would have fallen into the greatest sin toward those with disabilities–making them invisible. I cannot do that. Second, it would indicate that the "normal" condition of health is to be totally free of disabilities. This is against all the evidence if we take total life span into account. Most of us at one time or another suffer a disability, whether it is of a temporary or permanent nature. So I consider the inclusion of this chapter a must.

My personal experiences of disability, though limited, are of being unable to walk for a time because of an injury to a leg; of watching as my eyes, through the process of aging, grow dim and are not able to see fully even with glasses; of having a painful knee that on occasion restricts my ability to drive. I recognize that these "impairments" are minute compared with the disabilities that some of those whom I know and admire have lived with. However, my losses give me the beginnings of insight into some of the issues. In addition, I prepared for the writing of this chapter with careful research into the recent literature. I also consciously and prayerfully recalled my experiences with those with disabilities to whom I have ministered over the years and who, in turn, have ministered to me out of their vulnerability. I suggest that before you read on, you, too, recall those occasions when you have been disabled and how you felt and acted. Also recall those people you have known who have shown you how to live well with a disability.

Various Types of Disablement

Because it is important to distinguish between degrees of disablement, attempts have been made to find suitable words to define the general categories.[1] Three terms are employed: impairment, disability, and participation restriction.

Impairment is used when the condition means a loss of a body function to such an extent that one is restricted in making use of a sense organ (eyes, ears, smell, taste) or a limb (arm or leg), but the condition is not so restricting that one loses the use of it to a major extent. For example, restricted sight is an impairment, but blindness is a disability.

Disability is the word generally used for a loss that affects the ability to be mobile without being dependent on other helpers or mechanical means. As we will see later, modern technology and developed physical methods have been devised to compensate as much as is possible for this loss of mobility. The guide dog, wheelchair, hoists, and lifts are obvious examples, but these cannot take away the disability, only help the person to live more fully with it.

Long-term disability is used to indicate a disability that remains with a person in contrast to one that is of a temporary nature. Long-term disabilities have a different effect on the emotional and physical health of a person, because the state is one they must face over many years without the expectation that the "norm" will return. This is illustrated in the difference between a leg that has been broken and one that has been amputated. Long-term disability can result from an accident, the sudden onset of a medical condition, or a genetic condition that deprives a person of the use of a body part, either from birth or progressively sometime later.

---

[1]As defined by the World Health Organization and adopted by the World Council of Churches. For further details see Jessie Van Dongen-Garrad, *Invisible Barriers* (London: SPCK, 1983), 10–13. The term *handicap* was used in earlier WHO and WCC documents, but WHO now replaces it with *participation restriction.*

Participation restriction denotes a social disadvantage that results from an impairment or a disability, or from a social barrier that could be overcome. Lack of mobility is a handicap resulting from the impairment of a broken leg or the disability of blindness.[2] The inability to enter into community conversation is a handicap for the deaf. In any of these cases, there are both physical restrictions and social restrictions involved.

The lines between these definitions may often be blurred, as impairment can become disability and then long-term disability, but the general definitions do help us to understand the degrees of disablement. Whatever the condition, the real fear that accompanies the loss of a body function is the fear of isolation and dependency. If I cannot do anything for myself and I am shut away in a room on my own, I may find it hard to retain a sense of being a person of value and worth who can confidently enter into meaningful relationships with others. That is the fear that lies deep down within us whenever we are faced with the prospect of impairment or disability. That fear can paralyze us more than the physical condition from which we suffer.

A Body Image

Everyone builds up a body image of themselves. When we stand in front of a mirror, we may like what we see, or we may not. However, our shape and form is the way we recognize ourselves as persons, and how others see us too. We live in a continual struggle between accepting this body image and trying to improve it. This struggle occurs for most people from adolescence onward. The pressure of modern advertising is centered around this body image and its improvement. The "ideal" is set before us in the hope that the dissatisfaction that ensues when we compare our body image with the media ideal will drive us to spend large sums of money on "improvements." Some people even resort to surgery in the hope of creating a better body image. This can be appropriate for those with visible disabilities, but is it necessary for those without? Of course, it *is* important that we try to keep in good shape for health reasons, but it is also important that we come to fully accept the body images that belong to us. This is who we are in outward form, and we need to give thanks to our Creator God for the bodies we are given. In one way each body is "perfect," because it is the body that has been gifted

[2]For details see Nancy L. Eiesland, *The Disabled God* (Nashville: Abingdon Press, 1994).

to each of us to use as a vehicle to express our inner selves. In another sense, no body is perfect (just look at the shape of your nose!), but every body is good in the eyes of the Creator. If that is so, we too should accept it as good for what it has to offer us.

When the body image is damaged or disabled, our self-image can be deeply wounded. If we are born with a disabled body, this shock to our self-image occurs when we make a comparison (or someone else does) with what appears to be the norm. The bodies of other people become the mirror of comparison, and in that comparison the sense of loss is deeply felt.

If we suffer damage to our body image through an accident or a medical condition, it is then that our self-image suffers severe shock. From that point on we engage in the struggle between hoping for the recovery of our body image and learning to accept the new restricted image as the one we have to enjoy. Some people find that as they go through this struggle, they withdraw into themselves and are tempted to isolate themselves from others. They fear that others will be shocked by what they see and that such reactions will exacerbate the grief over loss of the former body image.

We all need to realize that body image is a key component of self-image. It is also true in my experience that self-image will always shine through body image as long as we allow this to happen and others who meet us learn how to relate to this self-image despite any disability. This is a key point that I hope every reader will grasp. Then, whether disabled or not, we can all be enriched by relationships with others, whatever our body condition.

What Does God See?

We must ask ourselves how, in faith, we respond to the question, What does God see? The answer will help us discover what our attitudes are about ourselves and others. In light of the teaching and actions of Jesus, we can say that God sees the person behind the body. This is the person we shape through our attitudes; through God's grace and our faith; and through the love and care we receive from others. This person will shine through to the outside world if we release it to do so. Normally this self-image is expressed with confidence through our body image. Sometimes disabilities and impairments make it more difficult for this to happen. However, it is still true that we can find ways to reveal our inner selves. For example, a woman we know found that the treatment she was receiving for her cancer distorted her face and body. A dear friend from another city came to visit her.

As our acquaintance opened the door, she saw the look of shock on her friend's face. With a smile the lady with cancer said to her friend, "Don't worry. It is the same me behind the face. Do come in; I am so glad to see you." These words showed her sense of self-value and the sense of humor that so often goes with it. When our body images are damaged, such an attitude can save us from isolation and self-pity.

In my own experience of ministry with people with impairments or disabilities, I valued the occasions of our meetings and our relationships. After a few times of meeting, I was easily able to look past the exterior and find the interior person. In fact, I became so interested in the person that I had to make a conscious point of remembering to take into account the disability whenever this was necessary. Otherwise, I saw not the disability, but the delightful person. I did not see the crumpled ear, the hand with fingers missing, the hearing aid, the burned face, or the spastic body. I saw the person. In the same way, I do not focus on the way that the body of Jesus was damaged by the crucifixion to the extent that we would say that he was disabled. Instead, I concentrate on Jesus' character of love and life, of courage and sincerity. So how do you see other people? How do you see yourself?

On the other hand, to develop relationships with others, we need to respect, accept, and take note of their needs, and they of ours. To be open to another person is vital for fellowship and communication. So I need to be aware of another person's impairment or disability, not because I am frightened by it or feel superior because of it, but because I need to allow for it so that our communication is improved. For example, if the person has impaired hearing, I make sure that I face that person when I speak. This allows the person to lip-read, which assists hearing. I will also use the best register of my voice, and by tone and clarity, but not by shouting, I make communication as easy as possible. If the person is blind, I allow touch to be part of our meeting. I remember to be "eyes" for the other person as well as myself in observing what is happening around us. If the person is disabled from a stroke and speech is difficult, I use a way of conversing that allows for affirmation of phrases but does not require answers to questions.

Sadly, many people need instruction in the means of developing a relationship with those with disabilities, few bother to learn the art, and even fewer are teachers. If you have the privilege of fellowship with people with disabilities, make the effort to discover and learn how best to relate to and communicate with them. I also ask, in all humility, those who have come to terms with bodily impairment or disability to be teachers for those who fellowship with you. This is not only for your own benefit but for the sake of others with disabilities who may be helped by better communication practices from those they meet.

Reaction to Disability

Now it is time for me to offer the fruit of my experience and research to those whose bodies are impaired or disabled, so that with God's help they can build or strengthen self-image.

The following things seem to happen to us when we recognize that we have an impairment or a disability, whatever the cause of the body's current condition.

- There is first a sense of loss. We are aware that we have lost something important to us. It may be the ability to speak or see. It may be a limb so that we have lost the ability to do or go. It may be the loss of looks, such as a twisted face in a post-stroke situation, the loss of hair in cancer treatment, or the scars left on the body by burns. It may be the loss of future possibilities that can no longer be hoped for or enjoyed.
- Loss is usually followed by shock (I can't believe it); by emotional distress (Why these tears and body shaking?); by blame (What did I, or others, do to cause that?); by despair (There is no future for me); by anger (Someone has to be held responsible); by determination (I'll fix it just to show them); by acceptance (There are ways in which I can cope with this); by quiet faith, patience, and determination (I value myself and with God's help will make the best of each situation).

This is a hard road to follow. The order of the above may vary in each case, and we can become stuck at any point along the way. We need lots of encouragement from others, we need faith in God, and we need patience with ourselves. What we are doing on this journey is reconstructing self-image, body image, and our inner personality. To achieve this, be patient with yourself. Remember how God sees you. Be ready to receive and accept the loving support of family and friends, and to learn how to accept God's gift of grace for your future.

A Paradox

For the Christian there is always a paradox about impairment and disability. On the one hand, we want to return to "normal" or, as some people put it, "to be healed." The New Testament seems to show Jesus as the healer who restores all impairments and disabilities. He heals the withered hand; he restores the leper's flesh; he makes the long-term bleeding cease; he makes the lame walk and the blind see.

On the other hand, the cross shows God in Christ accepting disablement. God does not take away the hurt, and Jesus shows love and his truest inner self while restricted on the cross. There Jesus shows his courage and determination, his care of others, and his empathy with others even while his body is tied and disfigured. The witness of the saints, such as Saint Francis, is that their ministries flourished when their bodies were marked with disability. These saints lived fully and gloriously *with* their impairments.

So when faced with the loss of body function, our struggle is whether we should pray for healing or whether we should pray for faith to accept the restrictions in bodily terms. Saint Paul wrestles with this difficult paradox in the second epistle to the Corinthians.[3] There he tells his listeners that "a thorn was given me in the flesh."[4] The word he uses for thorn is the one used for a sharp stake, not a natural thorn from a shrub or a tree. Maybe he means it is like a splinter of wood that sticks into you when working with wood. Clearly, Paul is using a metaphor for something that disabled him permanently. He does not explain what it is, but he does tell us that his first reaction was to ask the Lord to get rid of it. He says that he did this three times, which is an expression in Hebrew for something done completely and firmly.

The answer that Paul received from God was, "My grace is sufficient for you, for power is made perfect in weakness."[5] That expresses the paradox of the Christian faith. Vulnerability is at the heart of love. Unless we are vulnerable, we cannot receive. Unless we are open to God, we cannot find the grace that is necessary for a wholesome life. This grace is the free gift of God's power, and it is most obvious in our lives when we are weak. So Paul's impairment was accepted by him as a means of demonstrating the wonderful power that Paul received to let his life be transformed by God's love and to shine out as an example to all.

In our impairments or disabilities we will always struggle with this paradox. We are to work as hard as we can to restore our bodies to full functioning. Yet if we do not become "perfect," we should fully

---

[3]2 Corinthians 12:5–10.
[4]Verse 7.
[5]Verse 9.

accept the fact so that we can live well with a positive attitude toward life. We do not need to be restored in body image as an assurance that God loves us. God loves us whatever the outcome and will have a place for us as persons of value ready to demonstrate that love by our transformed inner selves.

The Health of Society

Taking Paul's witness seriously, we come to understand that for the health of society, we need the full participation of those who have accepted the vulnerability of being disabled. The truth is that we are all "disabled" from time to time. We are all vulnerable and have a thorn of some sort in our bodies. We all have to live in the frailty of the flesh. Those with more obvious disabilities can minister to us all by modeling how to find strength through weakness. They can help us understand how to receive God's grace. The way we and they live with disability points out the lies in advertisements about the "body beautiful." The body does not make a person beautiful. The beauty in a person shines through, whatever the body's condition.

A healthy society struggles as a community with the paradox of seeking either restoration or acceptance and giving equal support to both. Feeling guilty that the attempts of modern medicine fail to restore everybody, society is tempted to isolate its disabled to hide this fact. What should happen is that those with disabilities are embraced as essential to a healthy society. We can say that the measure of a society's health lies in the success of its care for the disabled. Through disabled persons' acceptance of weakness we can all learn to accept our weaknesses. Only in the mutuality of love can strength and power be shown.

In my own society I rejoice to see every corner footpath sloped for easier crossing, for it means that those in wheelchairs and pushchairs are seen as an essential part of our community. These are the simple symbols of inclusiveness.

Looking after Oneself with Disability

Knowing that any loss of function will hit hard and that with a disability a difficult journey lies ahead, what are ways that we can best look after ourselves? Here are some responses to that question:

1. Know that God is prepared to share fully in your weakness. You are as precious to God as Christ was on the cross. Your disability can never devalue you in the eyes of God. Place yourself in the hands of God and take God's

power to cope with your sense of weakness. Exercise your trust in God so that you can work out the paradox, moving toward restoration and/or acceptance. The greatest healing of all will be the healing of your hurt inner self. Allow Jesus to heal that real you.

2. Know that there are always some means by which you can continue to communicate and fellowship with others. The biggest disability is isolation. Isolation has two contributing factors. First, you may find that you want to shut yourself away from others so that you can hide your impairment or disability. In your isolation it is easy to blame them for neglecting you. Second, other people may lack the sensitivity or willpower to keep up the relationship with you. They will make excuses. Your disability may remind them of their human frailty. Blame and excuses will not solve the problem for either party. Such things only make matters worse. Even with your disability, try hard to create the bonds of fellowship and to communicate as fully as you can. Show that you understand the feelings of others and tell them of the feelings that you have.
3. Know that relationships are built on mutuality. Disablement and impairment often lead to dependency. When you can only move with difficulty, it is obvious that you need help. Receiving such help only highlights the disability, so it may add to your frustration until you find a way of creating inter-dependence. It is useful to ask what you can do for each other that will build up the relationship. Older people have often complained bitterly to me that after being disabled, they were no longer able to be doers and givers. Their Christian faith and witness had been built on the maxim "Be a doer of the word." They would tell me, "I have always done so much for others, and now I feel useless." As I listened and tried to absorb the hurt, I would respond, "If you will receive graciously, others will have a chance to give. In time you will find new ways to give of yourself, which is a different type of doing." Those who learned the art of mutuality were always the subjects of great affirmation and admiration. Others would tell me that they came away from visiting such people feeling much brighter and better. This is true mutuality. With modern communication and

technology, there are many opportunities to create a mutual relationship. If prayer is the highest form of human activity, the opportunity to pray for others and letting them know of such prayers can be a priority task for those in society who are less mobile than others. In the hectic rush of modern society few people have time to listen to others. With the cordless telephone, those still retaining their hearing can be ears to the cries of others. If you are disabled or impaired, see if you can share in this ministry.

4. Know that the body can relearn alternative ways of doing many basic functions if the brain itself is capable and operating accordingly. Many people learn to walk again with the guidance of trained physiotherapists. Many people can learn to write with the "other" hand, and even those without hand movement can "type" using their voice with the aid of modern computers. One of the world's greatest physicists does all his work from a wheelchair with a minimum of movement because of a disability. The deaf have learned to lip-read, and advances in aids to hearing are remarkable. Guide dogs for the blind are a common sight in all communities. One of my enduring memories is witnessing the care a guide dog took in escorting a student into the chapel of an ancient university college. Even the dog seemed to enter into the worship with reverence and thanksgiving. Partly paralyzed people have been greatly helped to "move" in the buoyancy of specially built swimming pools. There seems to be no reason why a person with a disability cannot expect some equipment to enhance their quality of body movement and often their mobility. The common symbol of disablement seems to be a wheelchair, but this is only one of a wide range of mechanical instruments that can make life easier and more independent for people with disabilities. To learn to use these aids takes great patience and courage. I marvel at the human endeavors and divine grace that make such use possible. Know that in disablement there is no reason to feel that "there is nothing that can be done to help."
5. Know that the spirit is the key to the person you are. Use all the energy that you can spare from coping with physical tasks to enhance yourself spiritually. The spirit will be rekindled by a positive attitude toward life and the future.

This will come from prayer, patience, and readiness to take in the hope and encouragement that others give. Our wounded spirits are healed by God if we pour out our deep feelings to Jesus. He knows how to absorb hurts—even anger—by love. Let your spirit be open to receive God's grace in your weakness. We have seen how this weakness can be turned into God's power for good. Let your spirit's communion with God be a two-way fellowship. As you tell God of the realities of your situation, be ready to hear God's words of comfort, reassurance, and renewal. Practice making your spirit "smile" in the warmth of God's affection. Try to uncover a sense of humor about the predicaments in which disability places you. Above all, identify with the disabled and renewed Christ of the cross and resurrection. As your spirit grows stronger, your body will discover a new body image by which you can communicate this inner spirit to others. It will help them to face their frailty and focus on the development of their spirits rather than their bodies.

6. Know that people who care for you or visit you need help in coming to terms with your situation. Do not be put off by people's first reactions. You probably have had more experience of impairment or disability in a short time that they have had so far in their lifetime. Treat them gently. Lead them to understand how things are for you. Use such phrases as: "When you have lost your…, you feel…" Or "When you are disabled, you…" In this way you are helping them to understand you better and, at the same time, helping them to face human weakness and frailty. Your experience forms part of the essential information that society needs to share. It prepares people for their own times when they have less than full body function and makes them more open to see those who are disabled as "part of us," not "part of them." The visibility of the disabled within the community has been a real gift to the whole community. We all know that we no longer have to hide away should we be disabled in one way or another. The quality of society's care is enhanced if the experience of those with disabilities is more widely known. The common relationship within a society is built on the foundation of its individual relationships. The relationships

among those with disabilities and those without obvious disabilities can be as rich as, if not richer than, among the able-bodied alone. The emphasis on the inner spirit creates the possibility of deep, rich relationships.

7. Know that it is right to ask for help without feeling useless and that you have much to give through your vulnerability. The Lord's Prayer shows us how to ask for what we need. It teaches us that it is right to ask for what we need for daily support. There is a note of trust, not of demand, in the prayer. The request is preceded by the acknowledgment of the value of the relationship. If the service we need is done to God's glory, we are offering someone the opportunity to serve Christ by serving us. The humility of Christ keeps us humble, knowing that we are all dependent on God and interdependent with one another. The Lord's Prayer also helps us to exercise the mutuality of forgiveness. In the stress of disability or impairment we all transgress–both those asking for help and those providing it. We must be ready to repent and forgive, to say we are sorry, and to offer pardon.

   One difficulty that our increased dependence on others in our times of disability creates is that our hurt self-images may try to manipulate others emotionally. You have a right in a time of disability to ask, but not to demand or manipulate. The actions of service should be motivated by mutual love, respect, and care, not by compulsion, guilt, or blackmail. I have tried to help those who told me that because they had a disability, I was "duty bound" to do what they demanded. I wanted them to see that this left me no chance to do it out of love for them. In the end I may hate such a person for locking me into "duty." We can only serve one another out of love. Not even love of money can be a true motive for such service. Those providing service as part of their employment have a right to a financial reward. Yet the service they offer may still be motivated by love, and aim at building up mutual relationship.

8. Know that there are those in the community who are skilled and dedicated as helpers for the various types of impairment/disabilities. Be strong enough in spirit to search them out. Be aware that not many people are going

to be skilled at meeting your particular need, so it is important to identify the skilled helpers. Try not to blame those who cannot offer help. They will probably prove unhelpful in the circumstances even if you persuade them to try. My research shows that there are many specialty groups and associations in the community skilled at helping people with particular disabilities. Such associations provide mutual support while at the same time holding the tradition of experience as to who can give help and what assistance is available. Those with multiple disabilities may find that they have to turn to a number of associations or agencies to get help, and this uses valuable energy. If possible, share the load with a small team of those family and friends ready to help you make contact with these groups. When the task falls to one person, the load is too heavy, and emotional tensions mount to the detriment of all. Some friends would rather do something practical to help rather than sit with the person with a disability. Ask such people to help in practical ways.

9. Know that coping with the emotional and physical challenges of living with disability or impairment is tiring, and progress is often painfully slow. In the first instance, it is better to set small goals than aim for the major goal that you would, of course, like to reach quickly. For those learning to walk again, one foot in front of the other with the assistance of parallel bars is the first important goal. The ultimate goal of walking with or without a permanent aid is too far distant for its achievement to be a source of encouragement. Patience, as well as determination, is the quality we seek on such occasions. Tiredness can lead to frustration and irritation so that we often project this onto those who seek to serve us most. They will usually understand this and allow for it, but with a strongly developed spirit we ourselves will learn to deal with it in the presence of God. Often music will soothe our disturbed spirits and give us renewed energy for the next small step along the road.

It certainly lightens the load to build up a routine of ways to help ourselves or be helped. It is less tiring to work with a pattern than to think out each step afresh. Routines may sound boring, but they save energy for the more important parts of life. Establishing a routine is a major step forward, and the routine can be reviewed as new possibilities arise or improvement occurs. The priority goal is the creation and maintenance of the inner self and the means to convey this through a renewed body image.

10. Know that you have many companions on this road. It is said that one in every six Americans is disabled in some way. In most developed countries the average would be about the same. Whether you are disabled or not, think of all those you know who have some level of disability, from the loss of some level of hearing to the total loss of bodily movement. Awareness of the number of such people will prevent too much of the "Why me?" self-pity syndrome. To be aware of these people gives us the benefit of their examples and the accumulated experiences of those who are skilled in caring. It is always useful to relate to others with similar disabilities and to give mutual help to one another with the maintenance of a strong spirit. If golfers, for example, are always sharing their frustrations at being less than perfect at the game and passing hints to one another about improvements that can be made, it seems right that those struggling to play the game of life with a "handicap" should be equally supportive of one another.

People with disabilities often face two handicaps: stigmatization–highlighting the differences; and marginalization–being pushed to the sidelines. By these means the disabled can be kept silent and invisible, the objects of pity and paternalism. The only way of opening up society to see the stupidity of this approach is to strengthen the bonds between those with disabilities and the other members of society so that we all become more inclusive.

A Strong Healthy Spirit

In this chapter I have put a lot of emphasis on a strong, healthy spirit. How can we measure whether we have attained it or not? This applies whether or not we live with impairment or disability. I am indebted to Jessie van Dongen-Garrad for the following list.[6]

With a strong, healthy spirit, people:

[6]For details see Van Dongen-Garrad, 56.

- can acknowledge their feelings and have a strong sense of personal identity, of being "me." To achieve this, we have to have an integrated self-image, body image, and soul image.

- have a sense of direction, provide their own driving power, can take an independent line of action. This goal holds greater difficulty for people with disabilities, but the principle can in most cases be achieved through the use of mechanical aids or the assistance of others as an extension of self. For example, I have acted as an amanuensis for a student unable to write, but the driving force, the thinking force, and the creative force all belonged to the student. I was the pen for the student's thoughts.

- are resilient to emotional stress and are not overwhelmed by their own emotions or by feelings of guilt. This is a difficult goal for us all and is a special challenge for those with disabilities. I have tried to outline some ways that this might be achieved.

- are realistic, seeing things as they are rather than as they might like them to be. This goal can only be achieved by true acceptance and God's grace.

- can appreciate the feelings of others. The goal is important both for those with disabilities and for those who minister to them. Sometimes those with disabilities find it hard to explain to those without what is difficult for them. I had the experience of ministering with a person who did not want to admit that he had a major loss of hearing. As a result he was accused of ignoring requests from others and distorting what had been said. In fact, he did not hear sufficiently and falsely filled in the gaps in what he had heard. Out of his embarrassment about being deaf he failed to appreciate the feelings of others, whom he misled.

I have found this to be a good checklist to measure my ability to maintain my spirit in a healthy condition. My relationship with God strengthens this spirit because in my prayers I have the confidence to see myself as God sees me and to approach others as people valuable to God and to me. I am able to forgive myself and others. I discover my place in God's purpose and know the enabling power of the Hol[illegible] Spirit in the fulfillment of my goals. I endure suffering in the spiri[illegible] Christ and free myself from bitterness and resentment. I am [illegible] from self-pity and am able to reach out to others with se[illegible] Christ's name. With God's help I care for myself so that I [illegible] and sustain my inner spirit as a whole person, whatever the condition of my body.

Where Is God in All This?

The answer to where God is in all of this is: right there with us, even (or indeed most of all) in our times of disability. The wrong answer is to blame God for causing the disability or to expect God to remove the disability without any effort on our part. Because we say that God is almighty and all-powerful, we lead ourselves into the position of attributing all events to God. We thus infer that God either causes events or should have prevented events. The teaching of Jesus is that the power of God lies in the love of God, and love can never be mechanical. So when we are realistic, we know that the created order is open to choice, or, as we might say, open to possibilities. There is always the element of risk in open possibilities. Human beings live in a world of open possibilities. We now know that this is true of our genetic makeup as well as the choice of human behavior. "Accidents" are the results of open possibilities. When choices turn out badly, we say that we prefer a closed system, which we think should safeguard us from harmful effects. When they turn out positively, we fully support the open possibility system. When we are "lucky," we like open possibilities. When we are "unlucky," we like fixed systems.

In Christ, God has fully identified with the open possibility world and showed us how to live in it, accepting the situation by making the most of the possibilities. In the spirit of love, Christ redeems (turns into the positive) every situation, even disablement and death. Hanging on the cross, unable to move, Jesus heard the demands that he come down from the cross and save the world. Instead love demanded that he stay where he was to save us by entering into the struggle with pain and death and showing that love cannot be overcome by it. The presentation of the gospel has often tried to reject this revelation of God and turn God into a magician who would take us out of our situations of pain. God provides us with the open possibility of a new beginning. That is the action of an all-loving God. We are never stuck with the past, for our spirits are freed from simply being extensions of our bodies. Our spirits are created for recovery, and our total bodies, within the limits of human mortal condition, are able to find pathways to recovery. These are the miracles of open possibilities. This is the pathway God walks with us. Sometimes God even carries us in those moments of grace that we experience but cannot explain.

If I look for security in this world, I will only find it in a love that will not let me go. I will not find it in a closed future, in certain health, or in predictable reactions. Many people, even certain Christians, do not like this life of trust. They seek assurance and certainty. They are quick to make others responsible for every evil and cast blame accordingly. Life is not like that, even for God, not even with God. Vulnerability is the state in which we all live. Those with disabilities help us understand that this is so, and in their realism help us to find the God who shares the journey, offering open possibilities for the future, binding us to God and one another in hope and love. For me, that is the only faith worth having, and many of those with disabilities have helped me to discover it. Through them I have found where God is.

Whatever our situations we should be able to share in this prayer:

Christ Jesus, bound on the cross and in pain,
you showed us the depth of love for others,
and the totality of trust in the care of God.
In my times of vulnerability
give me your strength for my weakness,
help me seek the assistance of others without loss of my self-confidence,
still teach me how to give and receive love.
Then will I rediscover my true inner spirit
and follow your example in patience and hope,
for in you love does not come to an end,
but expands and shines through the clouds of loss.
Dear Lord, I am yours and you are mine.
Your grace is sufficient for my need. Amen.

7

Looking after Yourself through Leisure Activities

No Time to Stop

The pace of modern life has become so hectic that some people have forgotten how to stop and be at leisure. I just read that research has shown that a maximum of forty-eight hours' work per week is the best for good productivity and for a sense of personal value. That will be a surprise to some employers and workers, though if we think about it, the research makes good sense. The body was not built for continuous activity. It demands rest periods and needs a change of activity to keep it fully alive.

Christians are aware of the reference to the Sabbath in the Ten Commandments. Obviously, most do not keep the law as laid down in the Old Testament. Christians keep Sunday as the day of worship in remembrance of the day of resurrection. Yet we also know that the concept of rest and recreation is essential to the life that God designed. How do we provide for it in a world that keeps a seven-days-a-week, twenty-four-hours-a-day routine? How do we stop when the world clock goes on ticking, driven by the rotating financial markets open always somewhere around the world? The Internet never sleeps. Neither, it seems, do some of its users. If you have ever been in a casino, you may have noticed the absence of any public clock and the fact that there are no external windows to show whether it is day or night outside. It falsely says to you that your lucky time is now, so keep on playing. Whether the activity is so-called playing or working, we all know that continuous activity is damaging to the health of body, mind, and spirit. Ask yourself: What is the place of leisure in my life? How do I keep the sabbath rule today?

The Purpose of Leisure

The reason for leisure is to help us rest and recharge our inner strength. Our bodies demand that we have sufficient rest to be able to function properly over a sustained period. Lack of rest is cumulative, and if we use up our inner resources for recovery until there is nothing left, the body automatically shuts down, sometimes fatally. We not only need to stop regularly but also to rewind. Our leisure should be regular, relaxing, and recharging. Like the seventh day, it should be part of the routine of our lives. Then it will help us to stay in touch with nature–the essence of all being. We can be more aware of our bodies, minds, and souls and be less "driven" as people. We will notice all that is going on around us.

- Leisure should provide us with the opportunity to stop and look at the beauty of nature and the inspiration of art. If we do this, we will gain a new appreciation of who we are and what God and the world are like. We will watch a sunset; sail on the ocean; or just sit in a chair. We will stop and listen to the songs the birds sing in thanksgiving to their Creator.
- Leisure should provide us with exercise for the body to maintain its fitness. Those with physically strenuous jobs still need exercise for other parts of the body. This leisure exercise does not grind the gears, but oils the wheels of our delicate bodies. Be cautious not to drive the body to its limits as a sign of "better" exercise. For leisure, the human frame needs to be relaxed as well as invigorated. Not all sport is leisure. Some have made it as exhausting as work, even though they are not employed as athletes.
- Leisure should provide the opportunity to stimulate the mind. I hope the concept that education is only for the young is fading away rapidly. People of every age need to stretch the mind to keep it nimble. As we grow older, formal education is often replaced by the stimulation of films, plays, debates, crosswords, reading, research, and wise use of the Internet. As we stretch our minds we prevent hardening of the attitudes and the closing off of viewpoints. Through aging, some minds become more brittle and ossified than the bones of the body.

- Leisure should provide the opportunity to keep the spirit alive. Meditation and silence, reading and praying, all make their contributions to a healthy soul. It is true that Christians have spiritual work to do–intercession for others, proclamation of the gospel, witness through practical caring, and affirming hope for the future. The Christian also knows that the spirit needs leisure to revitalize it. Listening to sacred music, reading about the lives of the saints, breathing in the prayer of grace, and focusing on the love of God all contribute to the refreshment of the soul.

Fanaticism about Play

Some people find their lives "driven" by leisure activities. They become fanatical about their favorite sport or leisure time activity. Leisure, like work, can reveal some basic personality problems. The new gym culture can provide excellent opportunities for keeping fit, but it can also drive us into a competitive spirit, even if the competitor is the goals we have set for ourselves. The game of golf, for example, can lead to fanaticism as skills are pushed to the limits to try to equal those of the professionals. Do you sink into despondency when you fail to sink the putt?

When we suspect that we are becoming fanatical about our leisure activities, we can check it out by asking ourselves:

- What am I trying to achieve through this activity?
- Am I looking for success, personal achievement, or recreative energy?
- Do I feel exhausted or enlivened by my leisure?

Perfectionism can become apparent in leisure activity. It can make us continually strive to achieve the unattainable. Is this a condition we need to face for ourselves? Perfectionism is also becoming a problem in children's games. Parents drive the children to win. The eight-year-old is expected to play like a professional adult. Young gymnasts must put their health at risk by training to the limit despite the fact that their bodies are growing and changing.

The critical part of our judgment can get out of hand. Many a game is ruined by those who condemn every "mistake" and loudly trumpet the failure. Some people will not play the card game bridge because of such attitudes. We need to ask: When is a game only a game? and, Where is the fun in all this?

The other trap we need to guard against in leisure activities is the attitude of dominance. Games can become a place where we seek to overpower others or even outshine others. Such leisure will not fulfill the purpose of providing an opportunity for recreation. We may feel uncomfortable about our domination of others and uncertain about our value as we struggle for power. If we are dominant in our leisure games, we are likely to end up isolated and lonely.

Positive Goals for Our Leisure Activities

Here are some of the positive goals that we should be able to achieve in our leisure time:

- Renewal of feeling good about ourselves
- Re-creation of body, mind, and spirit
- New or complementary skills put into practice
- Outlets for various personality traits; for example, reflection for the extrovert and socialization for the introvert
- Use of senses that are not employed in our "work": woodcarving and pottery for those who only use their minds at work, or crosswords and card games for those whose work involves more brawn than brain
- Training in relationships. Leisure provides us with opportunities to meet people, to be part of a team, to be valued for our participation, and to develop our interpersonal skills.
- Opportunities to use special gifts or skills in the areas of music, gardening, painting, sculpture, dancing, or animal care.
- Widening of our knowledge and experience. In our leisure we see new people, encounter fresh ideas, travel to new places, and engage with different cultures.
- New challenges. For many people, life is very routine, and leisure provides adventure and daring.

Pause now and look at your own leisure activities. How do they line up with these goals? Ask yourself whether you have special gifts that you fulfill through your leisure activities.

Choosing a Hobby

Hobbies are a vital part of our leisure activities because they allow us to express key parts of our personalities. Hobbies can provide opportunities for our more creative talents. They can allow us to keep our bodies and minds fully fit. They can ensure that we have a wide circle of acquaintances and maybe friends. It is interesting to note that hobbies or recreation are listed in most editions of *Who's Who*. People obviously think that hobbies are important in the description of a person.

How do you decide about taking up a hobby as a leisure time activity that re-creates your whole person? The process that I have outlined in chapter 2 can be a useful guide. Some choices come easily. We discover a natural ability when we are young and give it continuing expression through a hobby rather than through work. We may be musical and learn to play an instrument, and the enjoyment of it means that we allocate considerable free time to playing. Those with artistic gifts may do the same. Many find that they have to make a conscious decision as they grow older about how much time and energy they will give to a hobby when the pressures of work and family responsibilities restrict their choices.

Many adults find that they need to make new decisions about hobbies as life changes. Gardening is a hobby for some and a chore for others, depending on attitudes and responsibilities. Those beginning retirement suddenly realize that hobbies will be a major component in the use of time and the meeting of friends.

Choosing a hobby can consume as much energy as any other long-term decision. We have to find out as much as we can about the "facts." How much will it cost? How much time must I spend on it? What natural talents must I have? How much training do I need? How can I try it out? Are there any health considerations? What sort of people will I meet through this hobby?

Because hobbies are considered subject to freedom of choice—we do not *have* to take them up—our feelings about a particular hobby will strongly influence our choices. We want to feel good about our hobby, and it should reward us with delight. There may be some pain before this gain, but the positive outcome must be obvious to us fairly quickly.

Most hobbies involve us in the company of others. It will be helpful to seek advice from those already engaged in the hobby to see why they enjoy it. They can advise us of its benefits and often answer our practical questions. Hobbies are the subject of individual choice, but it is wise to seek advice before taking them up. There is usually a setup cost. Unless we have an unlimited budget, we need to be fairly certain before we start that we will enjoy this activity. So accompany your friends around the golf course before you pay a fee to join the club.

For many people, their hobbies are the best opportunities to express "the way of love." In the mutuality of shared delight are frequent occasions for care, affirmation, and support. Through hobbies we develop friendships that help us share our inner delights and our times of crisis. A hobby often allows us to share in the wider community firsthand in a practical way.

We need to take note of the consequences for ourselves and others when taking up a particular hobby. If you commence playing the trumpet or the bagpipes, others will be affected. A married couple often want to have some shared hobbies and some that they carry out on their own. Such decisions should be made with mutual consent and encouragement so that a spouse does not feel abandoned in favor of a hobby.

Our principles and boundaries come into play in making decisions about hobbies. They may rule out certain activities. Some people will not follow the recreation of travel to certain countries where they consider the local people to be corrupted by tourism. Others will not attend a casino because of their moral objection to all forms of gambling. A boundary may apply to a sports club that overindulges in alcohol in its program.

Our dreams of success are a spur to undertaking a hobby. For many, life is or has been a hard grind. They look to their hobbies to relieve the feeling of nonfulfillment. They dream of success in something that they freely choose. This is an important part of their care for themselves and provides an essential balance to their lives. Through hobbies we can often fulfill our dreams and develop a rounded personality.

In weighing the factors behind the decision to take up a hobby, we may not think that prayer and reflection are appropriate. Yet if we see God as involved in the whole of life, we should recognize that our hobbies are important for us–and therefore for God. In our hobbies we can grow; we can walk the way of love; we can experience the revelation of God; and we can express our faith. We can also have a lot of fun!

Fun and Games

When we are young we are encouraged to play. Such activity brings delight, allows us to act out our ideas, gives us the chance to make mistakes without having to take them too seriously, helps us prepare for the real situations that face us in life, and above all makes us smile and laugh. As we grow older it is important that we still have opportunities to play. We need fun and games. In our over-serious contemporary world we certainly need laughter. We need to see the funny side of so much of life before the weight of seriousness pulls us down. We also need to continue with the art of play and to enter into games as an arena where we can act out some of our plans for life.

Much of family life can be enlivened by games, be they indoor or outdoor, depending on the weather and people's abilities. Such games allow us to learn how to win and lose without being dependent on winning for a sense of value. Games also provide a focus for interpersonal relationships within the family as different ages and different abilities are brought together in a common purpose–to have fun together. Without the experience of games, we may never learn how to accept and support others who are "not very good at it." Through games we learn to encourage other people and to help them face challenges. We also learn to receive praise and encouragement without giving way to pride. Games give us the chance to develop our abilities to plan and execute, to work as a team, and to gain the patience to strive for longer-term goals.

Sport

What I have said about games applies to sport as a whole. Yet sport has some special qualities to offer us. Sport stimulates the mind and the body in the same activity. We have to learn special coordination to achieve our goals in sport. Sadly, sport often begins as leisure and then governs our lives to such an extent that it is no longer relaxing and reviving. Instead we come back from sport exhausted and worn out. Many people cease to play a sport as soon as their body protests at the pain inflicted. Yet we should continue and find a type of sport that suits our body's condition. Sport is an important means of socialization and gives us good opportunities for working on a cooperative team. There is a sport for most stages of life and seasons of the year. What would you list as your sporting activity? To fulfill its goals, it should exercise mind and body together–and of course be lots of fun.

What Does the Sabbath Mean for us Today?

The First Testament and later rabbinical injunctions hold a clear view that the seventh of a cycle was for nonwork activity. This was true for both the seventh day of the week (being Saturday) and the seventh year as a necessary year to allow the land to lie fallow and uncultivated. The seventh or rest day was for the worship of God,[1] as well as for the rest and recreation of human beings, those they "employed," and the animals that served humanity.[2] To achieve this rest, strict rules were composed as to what constituted "work" on the Sabbath–the gathering of food and its cooking,[3] or even the lighting of a fire.[4] The attempt to legislate a Sabbath continues in some parts of the world to this day, though legislation has been dismantled in other countries through the so-called pressures of tourism and convenience.

The principle of the Sabbath's being a day of total rest as well as a day for worship was only brought into prominence among Christians in England and Scotland following the Reformation. Subsequently, it was "exported" to other countries in North America, Africa, and the Southern Pacific as the culture of the "old country" was spread abroad through empire and trade. The principle of Sabbath was easier to impose on an industrialized society, where the machinery could (and probably had to) be rested, or on a community with a system of tilling and harvesting land that was subject to the laws of fallow restoration, than in an agricultural society with animals to be cared for. Now we must consider how it is best to apply the principle of the Sabbath to our particular society.

In societies both past and present, there are different views about the place of recreation on the Sabbath. One view was that as long as worship and relaxation were encouraged, people should be free to follow their own choices. The other view was that the cessation of all work was so important to society as a whole that any activity other than worship should be forbidden. With the general liberalization of society and the support for individual choice, freedom to do as one likes on the Sabbath has been encouraged. This has raised a number of vital issues for both society and individuals:

1. When modern life as a whole never pauses, where are the opportunities for corporate rest and recreation? Where can we find the essential sabbath rhythm in society?
2. Family life is suffering because, with scheduled work on any day of the week, there is no common time off for parents and children or between the different generations.

---

[1]Exodus 31:13–17.
[2]Deuteronomy 5:14.
[3]Exodus 16:22–30.
[4]Exodus 35:3.

3. Shopping has become a major leisure activity. In what way does shopping fulfill the purposes of leisure, and does leisure for some mean work for others?
4. Professional sport is a major activity on the Sabbath. Does this leave enough time for participatory sporting leisure? Have we become a nation of spectators rather than players when it comes to leisure?
5. Young people involved in a team sport find it difficult to exercise their freedom of choice about worship and leisure when the team competition requires them to play on the Sabbath.
6. The feeling that the Sabbath was a "different" day of the week has been lost for most people. One reason for the Sabbath was to define the week and give it proper shape within the created order. Now every day is becoming the same. How does this affect the corporate psyche?
7. Does the normalization of the Sabbath give Christians a better opportunity to witness to the difference that their faith makes to them?

What Does the Sabbath Mean for You Personally?

When society set the rules, you probably found that you were drawn into the common system. Now you will probably have to make your own set of rules. You may be helped to formulate these by asking yourself these questions:

- How do you establish your time for rest and recreation?
- What are your arrangements for regular participation in worship?
- How do your needs on the Sabbath affect the opportunities that others have to exercise the best choices for their sabbath times?
- What do you think that Jesus was indicating when he said that "the sabbath was made for humankind, and not humankind for the sabbath"?[5] Does this mean that you can do what you like or that it is your responsibility to determine how you can best keep the sabbath principle?

---

[5]Mark 2:27.

Clearly, there are no easy solutions to how a modern, complex society can find a common day of rest and recreation and give people of different faiths opportunities to gather in corporate worship. Individuals are forced to make decisions for themselves in providing the necessary opportunities for worship and recreation. In this we have to be sensitive to the needs of others and to foster the attitude in society that shared practices of rest are vital for its long-term welfare. Try to come to a decision, share it with others, and keep witnessing within society to the benefits of keeping the Sabbath.

Vacations

A major part of our annual program is our provision for holidays, or vacations. We need these longer breaks for fuller recreation and to achieve some of the goals that we have set for ourselves, which take a longer consecutive period of time to accomplish. Vacations are the human equivalent of the "fallow" period for the land. After a while the soil will not respond to regular tilling but needs a fuller rest for its goodness to be revitalized. So it is with human lives. Vacations, with their greater depth of relaxation and recreation, are necessary.

Originally holidays were just that–a series of holy days when people had a longer break from work with time to celebrate and rejuvenate. These holidays were connected to the cycle of the church's holy days: Christmas in winter, Easter in spring, the Patron Saint's festival in high summer, and the All Saints celebration in autumn. Some of these holidays are still celebrated by society, but the school calendar has set a more dominant pattern of holidays for most families. In the workplace the pattern of holiday breaks follows more closely the choice of the individual, with a preference for breaks when the climate is most extreme–be it winter cold or summer heat. The emphasis here is on holidays that care for the body rather than those that re-create the mind and spirit.

We need to plan our vacations with a clear aim in mind. Do we need rest and relaxation or revival and stimulation? Do we need new experiences or the affirmation that comes from familiar places and faces? Do we need to develop and maintain existing interpersonal relationships or make new friends? Do we need to "get away from it all" and claim our own space or counter our loneliness with involvement in group activities? Do we need opportunities to use our creative talents or to "chill out" or "vegetate"?

Pause now and think about your next vacation. When should you take it? What sort of vacation do you need most? What did you do on your last vacation? Did you meet your needs on that occasion? What has God got to do with your vacation plans? When did you last plan a vacation in response to your body's needs, your mind's needs, and your spirit's needs?

Some of you will protest at this point that your home, work, or financial situation is too pressing to allow for a vacation at all. Without knowing your individual situation, I cannot put this response into perspective. However, I do know that it will be detrimental to you to allow this situation to continue for long. You need a vacation, and you have a right to plan for it. If it is a financial situation that is too pressing, you can take a vacation from (rather than at) home. Home can be used as a base for a fresh routine. If a vacation is to be taken at home, try to get out and about, or at least do different things than your normal routine at home. Every home takes work to maintain it, but we need a Sabbath from that work as far as is possible. Many activities from home can be free or achieved at minimum cost. May I suggest a walk through some local gardens, a visit to an art gallery or an art shop (where I am sure you would be welcome even if you were not intending to purchase), attendance at a local youth sports match on a public field, a swim in the lake or sea if distance and weather permit, a visit to the local library to look at recent book purchases, a prayer time in a local church, or a call on friends or relatives. The list is long if you will sit down and think about it carefully without the feeling of panic that nothing can be done from home that does not cost a fortune. I have stated the obvious because in the midst of financial difficulties we tell ourselves all the things we cannot do instead of working out all the things that we can do in our vacation periods.

Those with work pressures that are constant and those who work with animals on the land often feel that they cannot take a vacation. However, if we live by cooperation rather than competition, we may well be able to cooperate with colleagues, neighbors, or family to allow for *some* vacation time each year. Cooperating with these folks may also allow them to take a much-needed vacation in their turn. If the restraint on taking a vacation is our involvement in our own business, we have to consider the cost of not taking a vacation. There are certainly economic as well as personal gains from taking a vacation. If we are concentrating only on work, we may be severely limiting the opportunities we have for affirmation and success from leisure, thus becoming slaves to our work. This is not good for us or for those we meet through our work.

I am glad that a number of organizations have been set up to provide relief for those who have responsibilities for others day by day. Vacations are not only important for the carer but also for those for whom they care. A fresh face and a new routine are good for both. Part of our responsibility as a society is to see that such relief is available. You may be able to offer such a service to others in your neighborhood.

If this paragraph has been important for you in your care of yourself, I suggest you talk it over in person with a trusted friend. The answers you discover together will tell you a lot about yourself. Listen carefully to his or her advice and remember to listen to the affirmation and guidance of God through the Holy Spirit. Recall that even Jesus knew the importance of taking time out.

Vacations and Pilgrimages

For members of Christian congregations, many of their vacations in the past were associated with local church activities. There were church outings, vacation camps for various groups, retreats, and even pilgrimages as the most popular form of national and international travel and sightseeing. Such activities provided for fellowship, companionship, new experiences and perspectives, cross-cultural education, and space to pray and listen to God. In the last few decades the pilgrim industry has flourished again with the emphasis on travel in groups for safety's sake and on being in touch with "holy places" as a way to find God. These pilgrimages may take us to centers where people have experienced God afresh in our generation, such as the Toronto Blessing, or to places of continued experience of God over many generations, such as the Holy Land or the shrines of saints in Italy, Britain, or other parts of Europe. In addition, places such as Taizé in France and Santiago de Compostela in Northern Spain attract pilgrims from around the world in the thousands to centers of corporate worship and care.

These pilgrimages are often led by guides who provide for the spiritual appetites of those who find that it is the soul rather than the body that needs to be fed on such occasions. In former times the body was renewed by the walking exercise that was part of every pilgrimage, and even today most pilgrim sites are accessible only on foot from a distant parking lot.

The tourist authorities in Israel and the areas under the control of the Palestinian people are keen to encourage pilgrims to visit the sites that are connected with the life of Christ. All of us who have had the privilege of "walking in the footsteps of the Lord" have found that it is hard work physically and emotionally. The fact that we have seen the geography of the gospels is especially important, and we are far more aware of the cultural issues involved for all the peoples of the land. For those who want a time of leisure, it is important to build into your visit space to rest and reflect and times to be away from the tensions that are part of this land and of the gospel itself.

Christian pilgrims throughout the world must always be sensitive to the local people who carry on their ordinary lives in the places that are labeled holy by the pilgrim/tourist. We know that we find God both in the routine of life and in those special times and places through which God can reveal the Spirit to those with eyes to see and ears to interpret the Divine. Within the church community, holidays and pilgrimage have been closely intertwined, serving the twin goals of bodily and spiritual refreshment. A place for pilgrimage can be found in every country, and its identification is an important task for every group of Christians. We need to find where in our areas are traditions of discovering God in relation to a person or a place. This then becomes a true shrine for those who wish to touch the holiness of God through the sanctity of a person or place. Once or twice in a lifetime we should plan to take one of our vacations in the form of a pilgrimage. Many young people want to discover the "roots" of their faith as well as of their family. Later, when we have a wider perspective and a greater knowledge, it is often good to refresh our faith and gain a renewed feeling of holiness through a pilgrimage. This is best achieved in the company of a guide who can stimulate our sight and feed us with background information.

Refreshment for the Soul

The pressures of modern living are so oppressive that from time to time we should plan to go apart in a form of retreat. This does not mean that we are running away from life's issues, but that we are taking time out to put them in perspective and arrange a new list of priorities. On retreat some Christians follow a fixed form of activity that can be quite strenuous. Accommodations often offer no more than the essentials, and long hours are spent in meditation, prayer, and silence. It is almost as if we are returning to a monastic way of life and trying to discipline the soul into goodness. All this has its place, but it may be classified more as work for a Christian than leisure.

A retreat for leisure contains much more rest and relaxation. It gives time for us to stop and listen in wonder rather than eagerness.

Such a retreat is possible in some religious communities, and it is also possible for us to create our own surroundings for such leisure activities. What we seek is a place for periods of rest and quietness where we can restore the easy rhythm of the body, mind, and spirit. We will breathe the fresh air as well as the air of the Spirit. We will stimulate the mind rather than educate it. We will take time to work out our priorities and find a fresh center for our being.

Obviously, such activity for a Christian will include prayer, but these prayers will fill us with grace rather than empty us of spiritual strength. We will also take time to read for leisure and let our minds run in new lines of thought. It is often with such contemplation that we regain mental energy to face some of the hard issues that are before us in the complexity of modern life. When we can go aside to think and plan, there are long-term advantages to such retreats. No doubt this is why some business firms have introduced the practice of taking their staffs away to undertake team building and new planning. If it is right for those conscious of the profit at the "bottom line," it is probably a sure sign of its value for us all.

Take time now to consider your own needs for a retreat experience and how this might be achieved. You may have a vacation house available to you from family or friends. You may know of a place in the countryside that offers opportunities for you to spend some time on your own with space for your own activities. Some religious organizations may provide just the type of vacation I have described. If you are unaware of any of these choices, ask your friends and church community. There always seems to be someone who knows of such places. Part of the reason why such places are not so well known is that they are hidden from the popular round, thus providing space for those who need it most.

Planning for Leisure

In planning any type of vacation, we need to set aside both time and resources. For this reason we must plan ahead. I hope that what I have written will encourage you to put time and resources aside so that you can take regular vacations. In some ways I admire the Japanese custom of paying workers in thirteen installments per year–one for each month and one for a vacation. We should be able to do such planning ourselves with the incomes that we have. Set aside a sum for vacations each month, or use a special, extra source of income. Even planning for a vacation is a foretaste of leisure as our minds focus in anticipation on the pleasure. The principle of the Sabbath strengthens our resolve to take regular vacations and provide for them. To take a good vacation, we need sufficient finances to cover the expenditure so that the vacation is not ruined by anxiety and strain.

We should also plan for a rotating type of vacation. One year we may want to use our vacation period for recreation of the body. This may take the form of relaxation or exercise through walking, swimming, or sporting activities. Another year we may want to pursue mental activities–reading, visiting art galleries, or undertaking research on some new topic. Then there will be times when we want to refresh the spirit, either on our own or in a group, with such activities as I have outlined above. These vacations will mostly be spent not too far from home base, but every now and again we will want to travel farther afield to see new sights and new cultures. Such trips will require practical and detailed financial planning.

Summary

As we look after ourselves, we realize that leisure is an essential part of a balanced life. It complements our work activities, whether this is paid employment or our day-to-day tasks for others and ourselves. The objectives for this leisure are rest, relaxation, and recreation. Such leisure allows an outlet for many aspects of our personality that are not engaged fully through our work.

Following the law of the Sabbath, leisure is taken in regular patterns of short and extended times. We need to plan ahead for both types of sabbath rest. In looking after ourselves through leisure activities, we need to be on guard against fanaticism and perfectionism. These, if present, should be corrected so that leisure is part of our renewal by God. Enjoy your leisure and give thanks to God for the way it contributes to your fullness of life.

God of the Sabbath, we thank you for the rhythm of your world,
its creativity and rest, its changing seasons and stimulating scenes.
Guide us as we plan for our vacations.
Help us to set aside regular times for rest and recreation,
and give us companions for our play and pleasure.
Renew, through your Spirit, our bodies, minds, and souls,
and refresh them with activities that bring them the fullness of life.
May the gift of joy brighten our days, and peace rest our nights,
as we find in our work and leisure the blessing of Christ,
in whose name we make this prayer. Amen.

8

Looking after Yourself in the Search for Truth

What Is Truth?

To make the best possible decisions for ourselves, we need to be fully informed. We need to find what is called "the truth." The truth is that point of reference that clearly establishes the principle of fact, taking into account emotional considerations and the way that the facts relate to the situation. Truth in this sense is a working principle rather than a philosophical absolute. Herbert Waddams once wrote, "The Christian religion holds that truth is paramount in all moral decisions."[1] Without establishing the truth, human beings cannot exercise their reasoning faculties in making judgments of what action is right and appropriate for the situation.

Yet it is difficult for us in many cases to say, "This is the truth." In our younger years we suppose that things are either true or false. We are not able to distinguish shades of gray. We are aware from conscience and training that when we tell a lie, this raises feelings of guilt and unease, which are essential ingredients in moral capacity. We dislike telling lies and prefer to search for the truth. As young people we are encouraged to tell the truth, even when that means we have to admit that we have acted wrongly. This is part of our moral upbringing and part of the development of internal conscience. This is our guide to choosing behavior that is positive for us and the

[1]Herbert Waddams, *A New Introduction to Moral Theology* (London: SCM Press, 1964), 184.

community around us. It is essential that we develop this capacity so that we can make moral judgments. To do this we have to search for the truth and recognize it for what it is. The focus of truth at this stage is the establishment of facts about what is or what has happened.

As we grow up we realize that truth consists of more than facts. We start to consider experience and emotional factors. We know that what is true for us is not always true for other people. We realize that the truth in one situation is not the truth in a different situation. The way that we express the truth must also take more than fact into account. We ask ourselves whether the starkly told truth will be hurtful to the person to whom it is revealed. The mature person realizes the dilemma in telling someone that he or she is ugly or stupid. It may be the truth as far as we discern it, but it would be hurtful to express the truth in this way. We take into consideration emotional factors and learn to rephrase the truth. For example, we might say, "Your features are not your best attribute, but your bubbly personality is what I like most about you." (Of course, *how* one says this can be even more important than *what* one says.) To take another example, we can be put on the spot when asked point blank for our opinion about a painting. The truth may be that you think it is dreadful, but you are aware of the emotion behind the question. To reply, "I think it is dreadful," may damage the relationship with the questioner. On the other hand, to say that you think the painting is nice just to please the questioner would be to lose the principle of truth in regard to both fact and experience. Taking all aspects into account in this case, we learn to give a "qualified" opinion of the truth. We may say, "I do not find the painting good according to my criteria, but how do you see it?" The truth is established but is stated as a subjective opinion, not an objective truth. We imply that we are aware that people hold different criteria by which they establish the truth for themselves.

These examples help us to see how we color the truth by the way it relates to our situations. In the case of the picture, the truth about its quality may not be as important for us as the issue of the relationship with the other person. This may be our priority consideration. On the other hand, if the issue were whether we would purchase the painting as a source of inspiration, delight, and investment, we would see the truth about the picture from a different perspective. We would want to determine whether we "liked" the picture (a subjective opinion of truth) and whether it was a "good" picture in the eyes of the experts (a more objective opinion more widely based). We would pay serious attention to establishing the criteria for deciding whether it was true to say it was a good painting. We would ask, Does the painting fulfill its purpose? Does it conform to the conventions of design? Do the colors harmonize, or do they counterbalance one another? Are the perspectives correctly portrayed? Experts would give a true opinion in accordance with their own predetermined principles.

I have used this art example because it illustrates a number of issues about truth from a more neutral position than if I had used a moral situation. Yet in moral situations similar factors apply. We see the truth first from a subjective point of view, but we soon come to realize that truth is more than personal opinion when the judgments made affect more than just ourselves. The circle of people around us and the wider community are usually affected by the decisions that arise from what we establish as the truth. We therefore have to take into account an external point of reference. If we also believe that there is a further point of reference which is God, we will want to consider the principles of truth within this wider framework.

Relativism

In the complexity of modern living, with its multiplicity of choices for many people, considerations of truth can be centered on "relativism." In this way of thinking, all truth is relative to the person making the judgment and to the particular situation in which the judgment is made. There is therefore no "external" truth. By the method of relativism, truth must be established on and for each occasion. At first this idea looks attractive, but it places a heavy burden of responsibility and energy on the individual. It would seem to free us to make an assessment for ourselves without having to take into account any external references. Soon we come to realize that as our decisions about truth affect our neighbors, this solo assessment can be a source of conflict and uncertainty for us. It would be like a jury at a trial making up their minds about the truth without the help and guidance of the judge. Each member of the jury would interpret the law as she or he wished. There would be no common point of reference and no agreed criteria by which to make judgments. This would be anarchy and would destroy the foundation of justice, which is truth, commonly held. All the people in the justice system would be subject to extreme anxiety about whether their version of the truth was only their opinion. Experience has shown that the better way is to seek both an exterior criterion (the law) and communal support for the truth.

From this example we can see why many people reject the proposition of relativism because it is too difficult, too uncertain, and too subjective to operate well. In the way that relativism thinks, the truth is only my opinion, and each person is left to make her or his own decision. Tolerance at that point undermines truth, for it implies that truth does not matter in itself. The facts are unimportant; feelings alone predominate.

Establishing a Set of Working Principles

A better way to establish truth would be to work out a set of principles on which we can make a judgment whenever one is required. In so doing we take into account the wider perceptions of truth that we might call common wisdom. Some hard work is necessary to establish principles for ourselves, but once they are in place, each subsequent decision about truth is a little easier to reach. I want to state my principles as a series of questions through which I search for the truth. I ask myself the following:

- What are the "facts" of the situation?
- Who are the people involved, and how will they react?
- What moral outcomes will flow from the decision?
- What similar decisions have been made previously, and is this situation similar to or different from the previous situations?
- What factors are special to this situation, and how do they affect the decision?
- If this decision about truth is made, how will it affect subsequent decisions?
- What wisdom do the past and the community have to offer me in this search for truth?
- Is it possible to make a "qualified" decision about truth that will more effectively take all the factors into account for the time being?

The Bigger Picture of the Truth

The set of questions above helps us establish truth on an individual basis for particular situations. However, we have to face the fact that the establishment of truth cannot be limited to our own personal spheres. There is a bigger picture of truth that has to respond to these questions:

- What is true about the nature of the world in which we live?
- What is true about the nature of the community to which we relate?
- What is true about God?
- What is true about human nature?

These so-called philosophical questions may seem remote or too difficult for some individuals. These people claim that they only want to establish the truth for themselves on a day-to-day working level and do not need to worry about the bigger picture. However, our small picture is always set in a larger frame. We make our small decisions about truth on the foundation of some very important assumptions. Our decisions about truth are always affected by the assumptions we hold. If we hold the assumption that the world is the result of a series of random responses without an overall design and purpose, we will not take into account any long-term consequences as we come to our decisions about truth. Each decision will be "ad hoc" and for a specific working occasion only. We will delete from the set of working principles those about moral outcomes and subsequent decisions.

Here are some further examples. If we assume that it is true that we live in an interdependent community in which neighbors have rights and responsibilities as well as we do, we take that into account as we establish the truth. If we assume that there is a God who has helped and guided human beings to discover the truth, we aim to search out that truth as one of the objective principles to heed. If we assume that a proposition cannot be true because it is not based on scientific fact, our minds will be restricted in the way we establish truth.

So the truths we hold in the bigger picture are a major influence in the establishment of truth in our personal and limited situations. As usual, unconsidered assumptions have greater influence on us than considered ones. This is because they set the framework, and we do not even think about their influence on our judgments. However, when we consciously check out these assumptions, we are aware of how they may alter our final decisions about the truth of the current situation, and therefore take them into account.

When I make a radical change in my basic assumptions, my day-to-day decisions about truth will be transformed. When I change from seeing my neighbors as a personal threat to seeing them as those wanting to cooperate with me, I will make different decisions about the truth concerning their actions.

Consider now, before you read on, what you hold as the truth in answer to the four questions above. How do these affect your day-to-day decisions about truth?

Changing Conceptions of Truth

The assumptions behind my attitudes may be taught to me, or accepted as "normal" by me, or worked out as truth by me. These assumptions usually build up over time and develop into a set of principles that govern my attitudes and behavior. However, my assumptions about what is true are never static. They are open to challenge, change, consolidation, or entrenchment. The challenge can come from a radical experience. Take for example the onset of a serious illness. My assumption about human nature was probably that I had a life expectancy of some eighty years. I was told it was true that this was the average life span. Now I have to admit that it is true that people can die at any age. The radical experience of illness may make me change my assumptions about the truth. After a severe illness I may live each new day as a bonus–to be treasured, enjoyed, and employed to the fullest.

Another example of a cause of change in our conception of truth is a major shift in public opinion. The "norm" is changed. This has happened in the truth about gender. At one time it was believed to be true that "women are the weaker sex." Alongside that statement was another: "Women are the fairer sex." Now public opinion challenges both statements. The assumption has changed. Attitudes and behaviors are now "normally" very different. The perception of truth has changed, to the delight of many and the anger of a few.

Another example of a change in the public perception of truth is in the area of religion. One of the current assumptions in society is that all religions are equally "true." It does not matter which one you follow. Yet each religion has a unique statement about the nature of God that is held to be true. These statements conflict on a number of points. Unless these statements are reduced to the lowest common denominator, they cannot all be "true." An adherent of a particular religion will be challenged by its teaching and have to reach conclusions about truth that will then influence the set of principles by which he or she decides about truth in all situations.

When the assumptions about truth are radically changed, it is important that a person look after her- or himself with care. The mind can become very confused, and the principles on which that person operates will need to be reconstructed. There will be a good deal of uncertainty and anxiety. Inner stress can manifest in outbursts of emotion. Relationships with others will be affected for good or ill. In the period between the breakdown of the old perceptions of truth and the establishment of a new acceptance of it, we need to be patient, communicate why we are finding life difficult (or exciting), and work to uphold a structured routine in those things that have not been subject to change. It often helps to sit down and affirm those things that are still held as true. This provides a sort of anchor in the midst of general anxiety about truth.

If the change is in the "big picture" of truth, we must be ready to review most of our assumptions. This will take a great deal of energy. A new view about the nature of the world, the nature of God, the nature of human beings, the nature of myself, will cause a major upheaval–positive in the long term, very disturbing in the short term. Recognize that such a change will consume much energy. Try to establish a firm routine for daily living. Ask for the understanding and support of those around you. Have patience with yourself and be patient with others, especially those who are fixed in their perceptions of truth. Wait until you have a new set of principles for establishing truth in place before you begin to challenge others.

Truth and Trust

Something in each one of us makes a close link between truth and trust. When a person shares the truth with us as she or he sees it, and we accept that truth, a bond of trust builds between us. We begin to put confidence into our relationship. Children naturally expect parents to tell the truth. They believe this must be so because most parents regularly stress the value of truth. Parents say frequently: "Now tell the truth." Children see this attitude about truth reinforced by the attitudes of other significant adults. Schoolteachers emphasize the importance of truth and declare that the system of justice and fair play rests on the truth. Most children, therefore, grow up expecting high standards of truth from adults. As adults consistently tell the truth, children learn to trust them. Any adult found to be untruthful is no longer trusted. Parents and other adults therefore have a responsibility to the next generation to build up trust in the truth. As an adult do you think that you are worthy of this trust, and what responsibilities does it place on you?

In the middle years of youth, young people want to prove their independence by establishing their own principles of truth. This is one of those disturbed periods that I described. It is a time of high emotion and consumption of energy. The patience that I encourage is often hard to hold on to for both adults and young people. The questioning of truth can sometimes appear to be the condemnation of truth. The young person may want everything to be "proven" as true, often lacking the wider experience of truth that is able to cope with its complexity. If you are the parent of teenage young people, you might like to share with them the series of questions I use to establish truth (p. 132). This may broaden their perception of truth and allow you to give them the benefit of some known examples. As young people explore the meaning of truth for themselves, remember that truth must always be open to question, and that a firm basis of trust will keep you interdependent at this crucial time. Young people may be able to help you see things in a new way, so all are open to change.

Sadly, the bond of trust between parents and children, and significant adults and young people, can be easily broken by a breakdown of truth. In hurtful situations adults and children or young people can choose half-truths or even lies as a way of covering up pain. I suspect that we tell lies or half-truths to others when we cannot face the truth ourselves. We talk of "shielding children from the truth," as if the truth as we have defined it could be bad for them. If we have created ways of communicating the truth, it should be possible to keep the rule, Always tell the truth. As we tell the truth to others, we are also helping ourselves to hear and accept it. The truth builds up trust, and that is an essential ingredient in hearing the truth well. I am certain that a lie, or any version of the truth that is seen as a lie, so damages the bond of trust that it is never the best option. This is true even if we know that hearing the truth will be painful.

What are some examples? First, parents sometimes tell children that a grandparent or a loved one is "sure to get better," when in fact there is a chance that he or she will die. If that person does die, the child has not been prepared for the shock. The child may be devastated by not only the death but also the broken trust resulting from the perceived lie. In such circumstances the child will often burst out in anger with the words: "You told me she would get better!" The parent may reply with the excuse: "I did not want you to worry." When we examine the situation, we can see how the bond of trust, so essential to coping with loss, collapses. The child has to face the death even more on her or his own because of the loss of trust in the parents' ability to tell the truth. The child may be reluctant to ask questions for clarification or information, which often leads to wrong conclusions about the truth.

A second example in the same category is when a child has to have an operation or it is time to explain the "facts of life." Parents who fail to tell the truth about such situations are in danger of breaking the bonds of trust and withholding from their children the information they need to face major changes in their lives. At this point I want to stress again that in communicating the truth, consideration should be given to the reactions of the people involved. Sometimes there is a need for a "qualified" decision about truth. Parents may need to explain the truth in a series of statements rather than "dumping" it on their children all at once.

This is especially appropriate in my third example, the painful breakdown of a family. Adults may be aware of the deterioration of the relationship and express the truth between themselves in a series of statements. Many parents shield (if that is possible, which I doubt) the children from the truth until everything is decided. It is not surprising that the children are shattered by the shock. This is likely to cause withdrawal, the deep silence of resentment, and possibly guilt. The children are profoundly disappointed that the adults are not able to love each other enough to make reconciliation possible, and they are angry that their whole world has been disturbed through no fault of their own. Additional disappointment and anger is felt about the adults' not trusting the children enough to share the truth with them earlier. They know that such decisions are usually reached in a series of stages. Because they were shut out of the truth earlier, children are reluctant to search for the truth now. They are hesitant to ask questions for clarification. Many therefore imagine that they are the causes of the breakdown. To overcome this, parents will have to tell the children the real causes for the breakdown and painfully own their responsibilities for it. Maybe parents hide the truth from their children because they cannot face it themselves.

These examples highlight the important connection between truth and trust. Those we can trust tell us the truth. When we hear the truth, however hard it is to accept, we need to be reassured that the mutual trust between us will continue to support us and help us make the best possible decisions.

Facing the Truth

The most often cited example of the difficulty with telling the truth seems to be when doctors or family members have to tell a patient about a terminal disease. Because it is hard to face up to the truth on such occasions, the patients are often told only as much as those telling the news consider them able to accept. Some in the medical profession believe that it is not possible to establish the truth about the patient's condition with sufficient certainty to "tell the truth." Some family members are told rather than the patient on the grounds that they are more trusted by the patient and therefore can reveal the condition more sensitively. My experience is that it is difficult to tell a patient about a terminal illness but that the revelation of a "qualified" truth may be the preferred choice, if there is indeed some uncertainty about the outcome of the illness.

It is possible to ask the medical authority to clearly set out the current condition using this method. For example, the authority may explain that the illness is severe, there is failure in the operation of certain functions in the body, or disease exists in certain organs. This establishes the truth about the current condition. It is then possible to set out the truth about any treatment that is advised and how this will be carried out. Finally, there is "qualified" truth about the forecast for the future. It is possible to say: "In most cases with your condition, the body..." It is important that the relatives also express the fundamental truth that they will love, support, and care for the patient now and in the days ahead. The medical authorities should also express assurance that they can give treatment for the condition to give the best chance of recovery and for any pain and distress that might arise. As we will see in the final chapter of this book, our approach to the possibility of death goes through a number of stages, including the struggle to face the truth, and in most cases the final acceptance, in peace, of death. However, we will not be able to go along this pathway if we do not have the facts before us. We need the truth so that we can deal with it in our own way and in our own time. Hearing the truth from those whom we trust helps us to accept it and make the required subsequent decisions.

Truth and Freedom

The promise of Christ in the scriptures is that "the truth will make you free."[2] How are truth and freedom connected? The answer lies in the reality that when we know and face the truth, we are free to make the best decisions in response. We are free from the darkness of ignorance, from the doubt of anxiety, and from the entangling web

[2]John 8:32.

of lies. The truth may be tough to face, but it is the only foundation that leaves us free to decide our next course of action.

When the concept is used in Holy Scripture, it points to the need for us to make up our minds about the truth of the claim of Jesus Christ to be our guide and reference point in the search for truth. The gospel makes it clear that we are free to make this choice and that once we do so, we will find a new freedom.

Earlier we considered the implications of establishing truth on a wider basis than just personal judgment. The teachings Jesus gave established a new set of truths about the nature of God and the nature of humanity. Jesus taught that in God we would find mercy and justice linked by love. Because of this truth, we could seek and find forgiveness from God and from those who shared this truth with us. For those who accept this teaching as true, it is possible to be free to tell the truth about ourselves to God. We are not tempted to lie in the hope that we might escape retribution. The truth about God sets us free to be honest before God and before God's community.

The teachings of Jesus also exposed the truth about sickness. Sickness was not due to the curse of God. God's purpose was that the sick should receive the gift of life—that is the gift of recovery within the limits of human mortality or the gift of resurrection of life. It is true to Christ's teachings that some sickness is a consequence of the misuse of the body. Any of us might have to admit this truth to ourselves. But the truth as Jesus taught it was that if we did admit this, we could be free and sin no more,[3] thus starting on the road to recovery. The cause of other sickness was seen as neutral ("Neither this man nor his parents sinned").[4] In light of this truth, the community and the individual can work positively for a cure for the sickness, trusting in God's guidance and comfort.

We can also see the connection between truth and freedom when we consider the opposite of truth. The lies of propaganda are spread so that the powerful can retain power. Their aim is to create a set of assumptions that everything the powerful do is good for you, that you have no need or right to think for yourself, that any opposition is against the good of all and therefore deserves and receives severe punishment, and that they alone have all the facts to determine the truth. In the midst of such corporate lies, it is hard to establish the truth. You are not free to exercise judgment and decide behavior.

[3]John 5:14.
[4]John 9:3.

One of your main principles, "What are the facts?" is distorted by closed information. You are chained to lies. You have been robbed of the power to think clearly. Your experience of reality may be contrary to the propaganda, but the wider picture you are given dislocates your critical faculty. You have lost your freedom along with your responsibility. Those who have suffered from propaganda will tell you how hard it is to remain free. You become a slave unwillingly, without a simple alternative. Corporate refocusing on the truth is required to combat propaganda. Only when we are free can we see how much we were enslaved. That is why those who hold power over us (rather than on our behalf) can continue to distort the truth and keep us in slavery. We can be denied the facts and fed the lies as if they were the truth, but only the actual truth can set us free.

Truth in Suspense

In the complexity of modern life, when we are aware of more facts that can easily be processed, it can be helpful to suspend judgment while we go through a fairly lengthy process of establishing the truth. If we do suspend judgment about the truth, we must not do so because of laziness or ignorance. We must simply set up a process in which we actively pursue the search for truth until we find it.

Take, for example, the search for truth in the record about Jesus in the gospels of the New Testament. The gospel record about the life and deeds of Jesus seems confusing and sometimes conflicting if a modern historical approach is used. If that is the only criterion of truth, some would quickly dismiss the gospel record as untrue. However, people would be better advised to suspend judgment until they have considered a wider range of "facts." This will entail study and research. It will mean seeking people with knowledge of alternative definitions of truth. It will mean considering the purpose of the record and the reasons why it has made such an impact on generations of Christians. During such an investigation the questions asked will be different from those normally asked of a modern biographer. Such investigations may well cause revision of the bigger picture in the way we see the historical record of many events. There will be a comparative study of the other literature of the period and an overview of oral and written traditions at the time of writing. After this process we will be able to reach a fuller conclusion about the truth of the gospel record.

Even if we suspend judgment about the truth for a while, in the end we must still reach a decision. The process we follow during the time of suspended judgment may help us widen our horizons, find deeper meanings in many matters, and fine-tune steps by which we reach conclusions about the truth in general. This attitude of suspended judgment is often used by the scientist, on the one hand, and the music critic, on the other. The scientist may consider it premature to come to a conclusion about a theory. More evidence is needed. There must be more experiments performed to test the theory in different circumstances. A new overview of the working of creation might be necessary to take all the recent evidence into account. The only course of honest action to take is to suspend judgment about the truth until the full process of gathering and interpreting facts can be carried out.

The music critic may also want to suspend judgment about the truth. When faced with a new composer or a new work, the critic may have to establish new criteria by which to judge the composition. It will be proper to consider the opinions of others. Time will be required to gauge the impact of the music. The critic may wish to seek from the composer an explanation of the purpose behind the radical changes of style. The objective behind suspending judgment about what is true concerning this composition is to gain a deeper appreciation of the music. In the end, the critic must come to a conclusion, but in this case it would be advisable to take time making that decision.

Think now of some situations in which you find yourself, and see if it would be best to follow such a process before reaching conclusions about "truth." Identify how you would handle the situation and the practical steps you would take in your search for truth.

The Spirit of Truth

Jesus promised to send the Spirit of truth into the hearts and minds of his disciples to guide them in establishing the truth.[5] The teaching of Jesus was not propaganda, because he always gave the hearer responsibility for deciding on the validity of what he said. Jesus was clear that people had to reach the truth for themselves. Some in the Christian church have not always followed his example and instead have tried to force the truth on people. We have already seen why this is both futile and dangerous.

However, I am sure that you are fully aware of how hard it is to carry out your responsibility to decide the truth. Jesus knew this. In his lifetime he was able to give guidance to his disciples. When he

[5]John 16:13.

faced his death, he promised them that after his ascension he would send the Spirit as their guide. The Spirit would help the disciples recall his teachings and apply them to new situations. It would be an inner voice of wisdom. The Spirit would help them see reality clearly; it would give them hope and patience to work through issues; it would be a Spirit that would work with and through the fellowship and community of the church. The Spirit would help them reach common decisions and establish guidelines for what was true. The Spirit working in community would allow individuals to suspend judgment until they had gained more information and experience. This common Spirit would provide a framework of truth within which each one could make personal judgments. The responsibility could be shared between the individual and the corporate wisdom. The principle of interdependence can work well in this search for truth. One person can help the other find a greater picture of the truth. Generations of Christians have testified to the positive work of the Spirit in guiding them to conclusions about the truth and in helping them live their lives based on those judgments. For them the Spirit *is* the Spirit of truth.

The Model of Truth

Jesus claimed to "embody" the truth. The gospels record his saying, "I am the way, and the truth, and the life."[6] This mature claim about Jesus shows him as replacing the reference point of the Torah, the previously accepted teaching of the truth through scripture and applied word of the rabbis. Jesus lived his life based on a series of convictions that he held to be true. In this way he was the model of truth, showing us how to do the same. I am sure that teachers of wisdom convey their messages best by providing models of such teachings. People accept the truth more readily when they feel that they can trust the one who reveals it. Jesus lived according to convictions of truth about the nature of God, about the nature of creation, and about the nature of humanity. For Jesus, God was known through an intimate relationship of love, goodness, purpose, and caring. God worked in partnership with those who entered into such a close relationship. Jesus was convinced that humanity was capable of entering into this relationship through being bound to himself. The symbolic way for people to do this was through the rites of baptism and communion.

[6]John 14:6.

Jesus was convinced that the natural world was created for the purpose of giving delight to God and providing a home in which humanity could reach full potential. The natural world and humanity are subject to the system of recovery within finite limits, and people have been given the gift of life beyond decay if they are willing to share in God's eternal existence. Jesus claimed that he could reveal these convictions to be true because he was one with the heart and mind of God. He spoke with God's authority, and God alone knew what was true because God was the ultimate reference point of truth. Jesus called upon his followers to consider these convictions and respond to him as the one who was worthy of their trust.

Jesus also models for us how to face up to the truth. He was able to accept the truth about the opposition that confronted him. He knew that they held opposing views about the truth. Jesus also knew that this opposition would result in violent conflict. Some people would try to eliminate his convictions about the truth. At this point Jesus was able to accept as true the promise of God that he would be vindicated through death and resurrection. He was able to live the truth that God would forgive the sinner, even those who betrayed, deserted, and destroyed Jesus in death. He models for us the courage necessary to reveal the truth to those who are threatened by changes to their perceptions of truth. He also models for us the patience that is required before reaching final conclusions about the truth.

Jesus calls on us all to establish the truth and to live by it. In the search for truth, we can gain strength by reading the record of Jesus in the gospels and noting the convictions, the methods of establishing truth, the freedom we must give others in reaching their conclusions, and the courage that is required in helping people change their conclusions about the truth.

We can also turn to the Spirit in prayer and seek guidance. You may like to use the following prayer as a model for your own prayer as you search for truth.

Spirit of truth, I ask for your guidance as I search for the truth.
Give me clarity of thought and breadth of vision.
Help me to see all the issues involved and the ways that people will react.
Hold in my mind Jesus as the model of truth,
so that I can recall his teaching of the way to follow.
Give me patience with myself and others as I fulfill my search,
and then give me courage and strength to face the truth for myself and others.

If I need to make big changes in my conception of the truth,
help me to take the time required and ask for the support of others.
Support me in the routine of life until a new set of principles is established.
Above all, help me to see the truth about God and about myself
that, in the relationship of the Spirit,
I may be free to be fully myself,
and so fulfill my responsibility for the truth.

Let this prayer come true and be my true desire. Amen.

9

Looking after Yourself in Action for Justice

"I have a dream."

One of the high points in the struggle for justice in the twentieth century was a speech by Martin Luther King, Jr., with the memorable line "I have a dream." That speech called for justice for all people, especially the future generations of King's own people. Such justice would bring with it freedom, unity, respect for all, and open opportunities for every member of society. "I have a dream," he shared with the crowd gathered to listen. The crowds and the media shared the dream with the world. Many felt that a new spirit of courage and hope pervaded the world. Many wanted to stand for justice and walk tall for equality. The prophets of the Old Testament had found a new voice. The call had gone out, and many people were determined that the dream should not fail before justice prevailed.

Working for Justice

As we look back on this struggle for justice and examine the parallels in South Africa, we are well aware of the cost of struggle and of the long period it takes to bring forth the fruit of the dream. In this chapter I want to look at the ways that we might be asked to work for justice in our communities, to stand up for justice for ourselves as well as others, and to survive the stress of the justice system. My own experience is that many of those involved in pursuing the cause of justice do so with mixed motives. I know that when the issue of justice affects us personally, it takes inner courage to persevere. However just our position, we need support from other people to prevent our collapsing under the load of stress. In today's world the increasing use of litigation or legal negotiation means that most of us will be involved with the justice system in one way or another.

What Is Justice?

Let's begin by clarifying what we think justice is. Here is an attempt at a full definition. Justice includes:

- The maintenance of respect for each person as a human being, worthy of full consideration and care
- The acknowledgment of the rights of each person as a full member within society
- The establishment of rules and laws that uphold these common rights
- The determination of the responsibilities and contributions to be accepted by each member of a society in order to provide for the welfare of the corporate community
- The exercise of authority to maintain these rights and enforce these obligations
- The protection of members of society from harm from other members of society
- The reflection in our relationships with others of the attributes of God's character that we experience in God's relationship with us

Each individual has a responsibility to honor the rights and obligations of others so that justice is achieved. Society has a duty to uphold the fabric of justice in such a way that individuals can exercise their responsibilities, that the rights of individuals are protected, and that injustice is remedied when necessary.

The Breakdown of Justice

Justice fails when *individuals* cease to care or when they harm others. Such harm can take the form of lack of respect for others, denial of open opportunities for others, actions of violence, and pursuit of dominant power.

Justice fails when *society* ceases its care and protection of its members; when society excludes some members from contributing to its decisions; when society deprives its members of their rights to share fully in the benefits of that society; and when society fails to uphold the rights of individuals in accordance with the principles of justice.

The Mosaic Commandments

Moses formed a society of Hebrew people out of a group of those who fled from slavery in Egypt, where the laws of justice were imposed by others. Moses is said to have received from God a set of principles by which this society should operate and establish justice. These principles were recorded as ten "words" or commands from God. The first four in the ten laid out the responsibilities of each member in his or her relationship with the God who bound the group together. The remaining six were expressions of duty or restraint that had to be imposed on members so that a just society could be maintained. It was clear to Moses that the breaking of any of these commandments would cause the breakup of the society as a whole. Therefore, those who harmed others were harming God, and such people would have to be restrained by penalties or, in severe cases, eliminated from participation in the society by banishment or death. Many subsidiary laws and regulations were codified and set down for later generations in the biblical books of Exodus, Leviticus, Numbers, and Deuteronomy in particular.

When we consider the list of six clauses concerning the community, we realize how important these principles are for the maintenance of justice in any society:

- Honor and respect shall be given to parents and the generation before you.
- No one shall be free to murder another person.
- No one shall be free to break up a marriage by adultery.
- No one shall be free to steal from others.
- No one shall be free to give false evidence against another.
- No one shall desire or envy that which belongs to another person.[1]

Some of these clauses seem to refer more to the behavior of individuals than to society as a whole. However, the behavior of

[1]Deuteronomy 5:1–21 and Exodus 20:2–17.

individuals and the working of society as a whole are too intertwined to say that one does not affect the other. We know that when the fabric of justice in society breaks down, everyone is affected to some degree. The same is true in reverse. The behavior of individuals affects the corporate behavior of everyone. Where children do not respect their parents, divisions between the generations in society at large quickly appear. Adultery by individuals will soon undermine the stability of families within the whole of society.

Pause now and consider how your society is trying to uphold the principles on which the Mosaic commandments rest. Once you have done this you might like to include a prayer before you move on to the next part of the chapter.

God, you act justly toward us and all people,
respecting our humanity and calling us into mutual community.
Give us your spirit of justice
so that we gladly fulfill our responsibilities and uphold the rights of others.
Guide our lawmakers; uphold our judges; restrain the lawless; and restore the rights of the deprived.
Let our society reflect your justice with each person enjoying a place in our community.
Help us to love others as ourselves as we have been taught by Jesus our Savior. Amen.

The Call to Justice

Now that we are clear about what justice is and how it affects us as individuals and in our society, it is time to consider the call to act justly. The best summary of this call in the Bible is in the book of the prophet Micah. On God's behalf the prophet declares, "He has told you, O mortal, what is good; and what does the LORD require of you but to do justice, and to love kindness, and to walk humbly with your God?"[2]

This verse brings together the twin aspects of justice: restraint and respect. We are to restrain ourselves from doing what would harm others. We are also to respect others by doing what shows them love and kindness.

The generality of this call is grounded in the concrete examples given in the book of the prophet Amos, who calls on the people to

[2]Micah 6:8.

"hate evil and love good, and establish justice in the gate."[3] In other parts of the book, Amos gives these examples of injustice in his time:

- Moving landmarks to enlarge the fields of the powerful
- Falsifying the weights used in commodity trading
- Exploiting labor by not giving workers a fair share of the produce
- Enslaving the poor by tying them to crippling interest rates on loans for the essentials of life
- Ignoring the needs of those stuck in poverty while idling in rich circumstances

Amos helps us to see that the call to act justly is not simply a call to fulfill an ideal, but a call to action in a particular set of real circumstances. The principles of justice are embedded in a series of "laws" that are enacted by the representatives of society. These laws have a restrictive aspect–setting out actions that are *not* permitted. The laws also have a supportive aspect–setting out those actions by which resources are collected to care for those without the means to live and participate in society.

In the New Testament, Jesus in his teaching interprets the law through its positive side–love, respect, and care for others. He declares that we are called to extend this care to those we might consider our enemies. Love involves forgiveness of those who have harmed us. Such love transforms justice into peace through reconciliation.

The epistle to the Philippians has a summary of how Christians should behave if they are to follow the call of Christ:

> Finally, beloved, whatever is true, whatever is honorable, whatever is just, whatever is pure, whatever is pleasing, whatever is commendable, if there is any excellence and if there is anything worthy of praise, think about these things. Keep on doing the things that you have learned and received and heard and seen in me, and the God of peace will be with you.[4]

So there is no doubt that we are called to justice. We cannot stand aside and disengage from the obligation to see that justice is

---

[3]Amos 5:15. The gate was the place where the appointed elders sat in the communal area ready to declare justice for those people who brought to them complaints about injustice or requests for the protection of their rights.

[4]Philippians 4:8–9.

upheld in society, and that any examples of injustice are corrected both in law and in attitude. The persecution of Amos, the cross of Christ, and the violent deaths of so many prophets of justice over the centuries all remind us that actions for justice are costly to us personally. However, to let injustice prevail is even more costly. Then we all become less than human, and the corrupting influence spreads its evil into the lives of all in society. The call to act for justice is to both the individual and the corporate whole. It is a matter of the law and the spirit. In heeding the call, we must look after ourselves with care. We need courage and energy to make progress toward full justice. As we respond to the call for justice, we need spiritual balm to prevent or overcome stress and burnout.

God, you have called your people to act justly and love with kindness.
Give us your spirit to respond to this call.
When the way is hard and the cross is heavy,
give us your courage and strength.
When we are tempted to give up the struggle for justice,
keep the example of Christ and the prophets before us
and inspire us with their determination and their teachings.
Keep us always loving and hopeful,
and gather around us a community to support us.
We make this prayer in the name of our Savior Jesus Christ. Amen.

Justice in Action

To respond to the call to act justly is always a struggle for the individual as well as for society. It means putting the care of others high up on the list of priorities. This brings satisfaction but not comfort. It means considering the welfare of the whole as vital to the welfare of each individual.

Here are some examples of justice in action that illustrate these principles:

1. *Paying taxes* is one form of justice. Our taxes provide
    - support for those in need
    - machinery to establish and maintain laws
    - resources to restrain injustice through a police force
    - compensation and care for victims of injustice
    - means to enforce the law through penalties and imprisonment

Most of us are willing to pay these taxes but usually feel the burden of tax should fall more heavily on others in society than on us. We need to consider the positive side of paying taxes and its role in upholding justice. Ask yourself how you approach paying taxes and whether you see the connection with justice.

2. *Achieving a fair and just commercial environment.* In commerce many people consider that they should get the best deal possible on every occasion. In action for justice we need to ask ourselves the question, What is a fair margin for the supplier of goods at every level to obtain? Should it be 50 percent, 20 percent, or 10 percent? After expenses, what is a fair profit? The supplier usually argues that it should be the maximum that the market can stand. The buyer or user, on the whole, argues that it should be less than that demanded. The constant round of "sales" in the retail sector has confused the consumer. If the retailer can still make a profit at a sale price, why was that not the price in the first place? Suspicion is aroused that there is injustice involved in pricing. Has the original price been inflated just to give the impression that the sale price is a bargain? Should the buyer attempt to lower the price even further to see what the market will stand? Should every price be the result of a direct negotiation between the buyer and the seller? Would this be fair to all? If, as a buyer, I obtain the goods too cheaply, who am I cheating? Is it the retailer or the workers who made or who sell the goods? If the price is too low, are they receiving a fair wage? From this example in the struggle for fairness you can see how difficult it is, both for the individual and society, to achieve true justice.
3. *Acting justly in the court system.* Over the generations, society has set up courts of law to maintain justice for all. The courts have prevented the perversion of justice that would result from the passionate judgment of mob rule, on the one hand, and the freedom of wrongdoers to harm others with impunity, on the other. In the end, the general standard of justice in a society rests on the common behavior of the individuals within it. The lawmakers and the courts can only try to enforce the common mind of the people, reaching for the top end of consensus. Because this

common mind is complex and uncertain, the judicial system has become ponderous, time consuming, and expensive. In some cases the cost of justice to society is using up more resources than the care of the needy. Restraint is receiving more resources than respect. Many societies spend more money on convicting the wrongdoer than on supporting the victim. How can the balance of justice be restored, in your opinion? How can you contribute to the common mind of your society in this regard? This is all part of the struggle for justice.

4. *Being personally involved in the legal system.* If you are or have been involved in some way in the legal system, you know all too well its stresses. If you are a judge or court official, my advice in your care for yourself is to see that you develop a deep, reflective prayer life through which you can refocus on yourself as a person precious to God. You also need to shed the images of violence and injustice that are a part of your job. Maybe you would like to use the passage from the epistle to the Philippians to refill your mind with all that is wholesome. As a person who has held authority, I know how difficult the task of being a judge is. On you rests our hope that justice will be done in a particular situation. You have to exercise your judgment about the actions and intentions of the accused or guide the jury in the struggle to determine justice. Ideally, all judges and court officials have a "chaplain" to act as a confidant, spiritual adviser, and counselor to whom they can unburden themselves before God. The standards of judges and officials in most societies in the world are very high. They have achieved this through common support and self-imposed high standards. This is a cause of great thanksgiving in society, and part of that thanksgiving can be shown in providing support for all court officials through our prayers, the respect we extend to them, and the practical care that they are given in society.

Care for Yourself as a Victim of Injustice

If you have been or are a victim of injustice, you probably need to build up your self-confidence, your perseverance, your faith in God, and your faith in humanity and its normal behavior. You may need to overcome deep disappointment in some aspects of the system and in the behavior of some of humanity. You need strong inner resources and financial support.

Society and the churches are recognizing more fully the need to provide support for the victims of injustice and harm. Every victim needs a "friend at court" to see him or her through the ordeal, which can often give victims the impression that they are "guilty." To take a simple example, the person who is robbed of possessions can be blamed for not having sufficient security for them or even for possessing such precious objects in the first place. If the victim is required to give evidence against those accused of injustice, such evidence can be "tested" (and this is essential to ensure accuracy), but this testing can turn into a trial in its own right. During the process of cross-examination, the victim often feels like an accused person, and, if violence has been involved, the victim as witness can often feel violated for a second time. In such confusion the victim needs a friend at court to comfort and reassure her or him of sanity and the truth of the situation. This friend at court should be more than the appointed lawyer, for it is not the facts of the incident that are in danger of being contested, but the inner person and integrity of the victim.

When the injustice is between two persons in a "civil" situation (that is, one involving the two parties without the intervention of police or other agencies of the state), the establishment of justice is particularly difficult. The court on behalf of society often tries to get the parties to bargain their way toward settlement. This may well settle the dispute but ignore the rules of true justice. Both sides often come away dissatisfied, with the feeling that justice was not achieved. If you find yourself with these feelings, identify someone who can support you and help you reestablish your worth as a person.

Restorative Justice

When we are the victim of injustice, it is quite possible that our basic drive is for revenge as well as justice. Whenever we are hurt, the temptation is to strike out at others to inflict on them the hurt that we feel we have suffered. It is healthy not to hide this fact but to recognize that such an attitude lies deep within us. We can only add love to this feeling of revenge when we know what we are really like inside.

Society also has similar feelings of being hurt by injustice. Individuals will share the agony of the victim because all know that they could have been hurt in similar circumstances. Society also adds fear to the feelings of being hurt, so collectively its members want to hurt the person who caused the harm or injustice as much as they can. As they do this, they isolate the accused in such a way that they do not consider the person any longer "one of us." The accused becomes an object of hatred, a thing rather than a person with rights and needs. With a guilty verdict, the penalty, especially if it involves imprisonment, isolates the convicted even further. Society expresses satisfaction about the level of hurt put on the guilty when they are locked away in their pain. Society makes it even easier for individuals to hold this attitude because it lays all the blame for the hurt on the guilty person. They say that the guilty have brought the pain upon themselves. Society deludes itself into thinking that it has no responsibility for the crime, and then goes on to consider that it has little responsibility for the conditions of prison facilities.

Christians over many generations have tried to combat this denial of responsibility and in its place to express the love and care of God for prisoners. Part of the reason for this is that many Christians have found themselves in prison for their faith or their opposition to injustice. There they have understood that the guilt of one member of society has, to some extent, to be shared by the whole of society. These feelings of compassion for prisoners were not made at the expense of proper feelings of compassion for the victims. Both victim and prisoner are children of God needing different types of support and care. Christians are also aware that most of those in prison will rejoin society at some time in the future, and they hope that those same persons will not resume their harm of others. Rehabilitation and reform are the goals for all.

Restorative justice is the name given to attempts to restore dignity, rights, and attitudes of restraint to all those who suffer or cause injustice. Both the victim and the perpetrator need to have their humanity fully restored to them. Love requires reconciliation and the restoration of relationships. Repentance, restitution as far as is possible, forgiveness, and mutual care are all needed, even though they are difficult to achieve. In my experience, restorative justice can only be accomplished by the full support of the whole community. The individuals on their own find it hard to regain their respect for themselves and others without affirmation from those close to them. They also need acceptance and forgiveness from God.

Christ's command to love one's enemies can be put into practice by restorative justice. The accused has to admit the wrong, accept the need to show in practical ways that they have repented, and give themselves the space and care needed to change their behaviors.

The victim has to find the grace to forgive, to heal the hurts in him- or herself, to reestablish a sense of worth, and to share something of the risk that God takes when it comes to the behavior of humanity.

Where restorative justice has been attempted with clear goals and positive support for the concept, much has been achieved to reconcile and reincorporate both victim and perpetrator into the care of society. Where restorative justice is seen as a "soft option" for those who have hurt others, the concept fails. Restitution and reconciliation are never soft options. Both sides have to fully feel the pain of the other, not in the sense that they have to carry the pain of the other, but they have to acknowledge what such pain means for the other. The community is then responsible for supporting the healing of pain and the beginning of the new growth in restored lives.

The other option, that of continuing revenge, leaves lives permanently damaged. Hatred, fear, and hardness of heart can never produce a positive future. For this reason it is important for individuals, society, and indeed for the world community, to work harder to achieve a sense of restoration and reconciliation. The peoples of South Africa have modeled for the world community a new way of restorative justice through their recent Truth and Reconciliation Commission. Desmond Tutu provides us with important insights into the issues in his book *No Future without Forgiveness*.[5] In chapter 4, titled "What about justice?" he compares the old system of retribution with the new system of restorative justice. The reasons he gives in asserting that the new system is the only one that will work in the long term are compelling. Many indigenous peoples have experience of such a system because of their keen sense of communal responsibility. The cost of restitution to the victim is often borne by the extended family of the wrongdoer. This not only acknowledges the family's basic responsibility for the actions of one of their own but also adds weight to the call for the reformation of the guilty.

Ask yourself what you would have done as a victim of injustice, maybe even torture, in South Africa. Would you be ready to forgive your oppressors if they had confessed their crimes to the tribunal? What would you expect the oppressor to do for you? What ways can you see yourself and the oppressor living together in the new society that is responsible for you both?

[5]Desmond Tutu, *No Future without Forgiveness* (London: Rider, 1999).

Campaigning for Justice

The twentieth century saw many campaigns for social justice in those societies that looked for ways to make equality of opportunity and relief of hardship two of their main goals. In the complexity and diversity of modern society, deep divisions continue to exist in most countries. The rights of individuals have often been suppressed on the grounds of gender, race, age, or social status. The struggle for justice goes on in this generation, and most people are caught up with it in one form or another. This struggle may be on behalf of "causes" for justice or on behalf of a particular person who has been treated unjustly by the "system."

When we become involved in campaigning for justice, we need to know how to take care of ourselves. The struggle is likely to cause divisions and sometimes injustice in other directions, and we may well become confused as to the justice of the original cause. We may see innocent people blamed unfairly. The innocent might be those who work in agencies of the state, such as the police, immigration, or social welfare. These people can become the "meat in the sandwich." They are between those who struggle for justice and those who make the rules to maintain justice. As we see such people hurt, we may have feelings of confusion and guilt. We have to keep a clear perspective on the whole situation. To do this, we will need to share the issues with the wider community so that all can support one another.

In caring for yourself, first identify the issues. Justice is about law and respect for rights. It is not immediately about compassion. The struggle for justice involves changing attitudes and principles, which in turn results in a new sense of the dignity of each person. It is noteworthy that Jesus did not try to overturn social systems in themselves. Instead, his teaching focused on the need to see others in a new way–not as threats and enemies, but as fellow children of the one God. Forgiveness for all was more important than a system of privilege or penalty. So if you are campaigning for justice, measure the principles behind your struggle against the teachings of the gospel.

It is also important in the struggle for justice to allow others to help you judge whether your main reason for taking up the cause is some unresolved hurt or anger of your own. It is all too easy to project your own frustrations, anger, and hurt onto a righteous cause without realizing that you are doing so. It is therefore important to sort out with a good friend whether, in addition to your positive motive to see justice done, there lie hidden motives that distort your judgments. If there are, make certain that you deal with these separately and, if possible, concurrently.

Our struggle for justice for others demands stamina and spiritual strength. The saints for justice have all been spiritual giants who were able to sustain their struggles by deep spiritual awareness and dependence on God. Particularly in the struggle for justice, you will feel at times that you are being treated as less than a full human being. You will be called a nuisance, a busybody, a do-gooder, as well as more impolite names to describe the outsiders in society. Unless you are secure in the knowledge of your own person in the eyes of God, these "curses" will undermine your self-esteem. This, in fact, is the objective of the person issuing the verbal barrage. The temptation is to return fire with similar language, but this destroys the very respect for people that is at the root of the tree of justice.

In your struggle for justice, try to identify what laws are in place that support injustice. Then the struggle can focus on changing the laws and the attitudes that support them. The struggle is with the law, not with the agents charged with implementing that law. There are times when the injustice results from the decision of a particular agent in society, rather than from the law itself. In that instance it is usually possible to obtain a review from the lawmakers. Determine which sort of injustice you are fighting before planning a course of action.

In your struggle for justice, try to reaffirm the respect and dignity of all involved—even when the other person seems to be the "enemy." Some struggles for justice are, in reality, simply struggles for power. The cause is made a substitute in the battle for supremacy. If you happen to be the object of the cause because you have been treated unjustly, be careful that you are not trampled in the rush for power and self-righteousness. Many individuals who take an issue to others become bitter as they soon become unimportant in the battle and are used and abused in the political arena. Everyone in such a case is a loser because dignity and respect are lost in the overall struggle.

The call for involvement in the struggle for justice must be heeded, but the wise person is careful to establish the motives of all who share in the cause. The sensitive person operates in a supportive network. The Christian spends much time in prayer and always seeks the good of everyone involved. The root principle is one of love, not of winning a battle by destroying the opposition, even if the foes are unjust. Look back on the causes you have supported and see how love was, or was not, operative in all that was done.

Seeking Justice for Oneself

Nearly everyone suffers injustice at one time or another. Here are some routine examples.

You may have placed an order for goods to be delivered and, after sending the money, discover that the article is out of stock. Then there is the struggle to obtain a refund, or locate an alternative supply, or wait your turn without hearing any report while another line of the article is manufactured. In most cases this small instance is a good "trial run" for seeking justice in more serious hurts.

Injustice in employment situations may come your way. You may be passed over for an employment opportunity on the grounds of age, race, gender, lack of formal qualifications, or simply out of jealousy by those responsible for making the appointment. It will probably be the case that most people recognized that you were the best person for the job and that you should have been appointed. The hurt is intensified if you are given a less than honest reason for why you did not get the job. Everyone struggles with the best way to react in such situations. There are two options. You can take up the cause of justice for yourself and hope you can muster the support of others; or you can turn your back on the situation and put your energies into seeking alternative opportunities. It is wise in such circumstances to seek the advice of others, particularly those with some detachment from the situation, to help you sort out the best way to move forward and to recover from the hurt. If you choose the course of justice and appeal the decision, you must be ready for further hurts to occur–both to yourself and others. Even if you win the appeal (as I know can happen), you will still need to win over, by respect and warmth, those who resent the success of the appeal. However, this level of pain may be an important contribution to the cause of justice as a whole. If the appointment is to an institutional position, your appeal may result in a full review of the appointment process, and important procedural changes may follow. In this way you will have contributed to the cause of justice for future applicants as well as for yourself. Justice is served because people will be treated with dignity, and their rights will be protected. In an appeal such as this, you should be able to summon major support from the wider community. One of the positive aspects of the trade union movement has been the corporate support given to combat acts of injustice in the workplace. If your case is supported by a community group, you need to watch for mixed motives in the struggle. The focus of the case must be on justice, not on power, dominance, or money.

Another example of injustice often faces us when we are concerned about the rights of residence. Whether we rent or own our home (with or without a loan), there will be occasions when we come up against "laws of residence." If renting, we may believe our rights as tenants are not being honored because the maintenance of the property is not being carried out satisfactorily. Maybe it is not done on time, the materials used are second rate, or our requests are ignored. If we own our homes we may find that we are in conflict with the local authority about boundaries, rates, or services. In these cases the individual seems powerless against the institution. In other cases, we may find ourselves "harmed" by neighbors in that they do not respect rights to privacy, quiet, or access. The fight may even be about trees and fences. Neighbors can turn out to be enemies instead of friends. The real cause of the argument may be a conflict of personalities, but often there is an injustice as well. Deep hurt can result from these struggles, and the law may not prevent further hurts. The principles of restorative justice will have to be applied to resolve such conflicts. If you are caught up in such situations, try to engage a mediator who can help you find a just solution and facilitate reconciliation. Sit down with a wise friend and try to establish what the real reasons for the struggle are. This may make it possible for you to face up to the reasons and prevent you from focusing on what you think is simply an injustice done to you.

In all cases of personal hurts caused by injustice, make sure that you have the support of family and friends in the wider community. Such support is best if it is not recruited from "soldiers on your side," but from those who will affirm your dignity as a person and be able to clarify your thinking so that it docs not bccomc swampcd in cmotion. Try always to keep the goal of justice clear so that it is not confused with other motives. Remember that God requires us to respect everyone involved as full human beings. Draw deeply on God's affirmation of yourself. Be ready to be corrected by God when you descend, either in thought or action, to less than proper conduct. Learn to forgive, as well as to fight for justice. Try to keep the struggle focused on the issue and not on the person who seems to be opposing you. Above all, look to the cross and see that Christ's struggle for justice and love for all has been won. You do not need to win your individual struggle at all costs. Your worth as a person does not depend on that. It is already given to you from the victory of the cross. Aim to let love abound as the final result of all your efforts to see that justice prevails, both for yourself and for your community.

This prayer may help you in those times when you are engaged in the struggle for justice.

Lord Jesus, from your cross draw near to me as I struggle with this issue.
Let your Spirit give me affirmation that I am fully a person of dignity in your sight.
Clarify the causes of injustice so that I can identify them clearly.
Make me aware of those things in myself that may get in the way of achieving justice with love.
Help me name those friends who will give me the best support.
Make me realize that there are others who have been hurt by injustice,
and guard me from passing on the hurts that I have suffered.
Like your servant Amos, help me to love the good and hate the evil and to respect and support all those appointed in society to uphold justice.
May your love transform all our lives so that we become reconciled to one another and so build a community where truth and justice prevail.
Then will your name be praised, your kingdom come, and your will be done now and forever. Amen.

In your actions for justice, take good care of yourself and remember to support others in their struggles to see that justice is done.

10

Looking after Yourself in the Face of Death

Mortality

Nobody really likes facing up to the fact that we are mortal creatures. We find it hard to say bluntly—"I am going to die." It sounds so final and harsh when there is so much yet to do, and we enjoy being alive to all our opportunities. Yet our birth and our death are the two certain facts of our existence. I see both as gifts from God. We speak that way about birth, but it might be a new concept for you to speak about death as a gift from God. If we acknowledge God as creator, designer, and the one who sustains our universe, it is God's gift to us that we are born and that we die. The saints, like Francis of Assisi, are able to accept this truth with joy. I haven't quite gotten to that point yet, but I am working on it.

Your mortality is necessary if you are to be open to receive God's further gift, the gift of eternal life. This is not a continuation of human existence, but a new experience of living in relationship with God. We cannot describe it, but we can trust Christ's words that God gives it to us if we accept it in faith.

So our mortality, our death, is to be accepted as the opening of the gate to this new existence. The means of that death, like all the other circumstances of life, are not known to us beforehand. If we live to an older age, we are given some opportunities to let go of what we previously thought was important and to focus on the precious and the eternal—love in our relationship with God and with those human beings to whom we are closely linked. If we die suddenly, the quality of our day-to-day living, especially our loving, will allow others to let go of us with sorrow, but also with love and hope.

It is probably true that the "advances" of modern medicine make us more aware of the process of dying and can allow us more time to prepare for death. Some people find knowing of their impending death a burden, while others rejoice that they have time to affirm relationships and, if necessary, take practical steps to ease the transfer of their possessions in a way that satisfies the requirements of the law. My experience is that most people fear the collapse of the body rather than death. We will look at ways of caring for yourself in these circumstances in the main part of this chapter.

For the moment, the important issue for us is to accept that we *will* die and to work out what this means for us so that we can accept it fully. If we do, we can get on with the task and joy of living well so that we can die well.

God's Love Never Ceases

For a Christian the message of Christ is that love does not end, especially God's love for us. Therefore, dying cannot stop God's loving us or our loving God. The same is true about the deep love between mortal human beings. Death cannot put an end to the relationship of love. Death forces us all to learn to love in a new way. In faith we can say that we will still love in the resurrected life. In the reality of earthly experience we can say that about those who mourn the death of a loved one. We know that there has to be a new way of loving, but love is still there in its new form, and there are new possibilities for the growth of this love.

Death provides a further opportunity for love in action, and, of course, it is also a time when love that is not genuine will be tested with the possibility of rejection. Love has to leave that two-sided option open to remain love. But having said that, I believe that most of us can be helped to see that love does not cease in the face of death.

Emotional Reactions to Dying

The various emotional reactions that people experience when they hear they are in the final process of dying are now well recorded.[1]

---

[1]For example, see the series of books by Dr. Elisabeth Kübler-Ross: *On Death and Dying* (London: Tavistock, 1970) in its various editions; and *Living with Death and Dying* (New York: Macmillan, 1981).

These books, and many others that may use different terminology to describe the same reactions, all show that, in earlier times, most people faced death in the context of their own families. Many modern people are isolated from these emotional reactions to death because, in our era, death has become a subject of silence. The naturalness of death has been denied by the attempts at all costs by medicine to overcome it. Death in this sense becomes a defeat, and we do not talk about defeats, only victories. Fortunately, some cultures have kept alive a healthy attitude toward death and have shared with others their corporate experiences of dying and mourning. In an extended family, deaths occur more often than in the nuclear family. The experiences of close extended families are therefore more current and the wisdom more widely shared. It is fortunate that the hospice movement has created a reservoir of knowledge about death and the care of the dying, which is available to individual members of the community in many places. As a priest I have also had the privilege of sharing with hundreds of others the journey to death and resurrection and, in turn, have made this knowledge available to those who need it. I hope that the summary below will make all this more widely available.

The following is a brief description of the typical emotional reactions of those facing the likelihood of death in a fairly fixed period of time. I set this out in the hope that it will give to those now experiencing such reactions a sense of their commonality with others on a similar journey, and to those who watch a loved one's reactions with concern, an understanding of what might be going on. I pray that it will help all take better care of themselves and one another at this difficult time.

Shock, Denial, and Withdrawal into Self

Our bodies seem to have a built-in system to cushion the effects of an awareness of a major change in our circumstances. We may see shock as a problem, but in fact it is essential if we are to carry on functioning at all. The numbness we feel is like an anesthetic that gradually wears off, giving us time to come to terms with the crisis situation. When we are first told, or when we ourselves become aware, that we are dying, we may feel that the news is about someone else. We deny that this is happening to us and instead consider that it is happening to a person called by the same name–but not to us. We might even say that the information cannot be true because we do not feel that sick, or have enough pain, or are too young to die. Such things only happen to other people. The numbness of shock allows us time to "play the news over" in our brains until we can take it into our inner consciousness. Of course, our great desire for life means that we resist accepting death at this point. If the desire for life has waned because of long illness or the extreme weakness of old age, we might accept our dying more readily. This is because we have already accepted our "little deaths"—the gradual withdrawal of our powers of life—and are now more ready to take on board the news of the concluding chapter.

Some protest at this point that if we had more faith in resurrection, we would be able to incorporate the news of impending death more quickly. Such faith may help, but I doubt that this is the right response of faith. God has gifted us with the desire for life. Our faith keeps this desire strong in us despite the knocks, hardships, and disappointments that we suffer in life. Faith keeps this desire alive during our living, and we then need a different side of faith to change directions in our dying. We have to let go of one type of living to accept death as the gateway to another type of living—eternal life. This change of direction takes time to accomplish, which is how it should be.

Note the picture of this struggle in these words of Saint Paul:

> For to me, living is Christ and dying is gain.
> If I am to live in the flesh, that means fruitful labor for me;
> and I do not know which I prefer.
> I am hard pressed between the two:
> my desire is to depart and be with Christ, for that is far better;
> but to remain in the flesh is more necessary for you.[2]

The numbness and denial of the fact that this is happening to us may last for some time. We may even appear to be brave and accept the fact quickly, but still have to process what it means for us. A proper part of the denial process is the struggle to recover and stay alive. In this we may well rush around trying to find a cure. Usually we at least look for a second opinion. We want to have the diagnosis checked and then repeated to us time and time again, while we search for any fact that does not fit and will allow the hope of an escape route.

This stage of denial is often difficult for the circle of loved ones—spouse, partner, children, other family members, and close friends. They know the "secret" but are not certain that it can yet be said to be a fact. All in their own shock can join in the circle of denial. This

---

[2]Philippians 1:21–24.

can be confusing for all concerned. No one can be quite sure that the opinions of the doctors will turn out to be true. Even they are cautious about making firm predictions. No two people are alike, and all illnesses are particular to the patient.

Some people never progress beyond the denial reaction until a day or even a few hours before death. Plateaus in declining health are seen by some as periods of possible recovery. No one wants to take away the hope of recovery. In such circumstances we need to ask the question, Is it important that we move beyond denial now? My advice is that when the time is appropriate, we need to move beyond denial into acceptance of the *strong possibility* of death, even if we do not shut the door on the chance of recovery. If we fail to do this, we will not attend to the vital art of seeing each moment remaining as an opportunity for new depth in loving relationships. Our inner selves will be so busy debating the "maybe-maybe not" possibilities that we will not have the energy to turn outward in our relationships with others–God, family and friends, and yes, even those who care for us in our sickness.

The withdrawal into self is natural as we come to terms with this new turning point in our living, facing our dying. "He turned his face to the wall" is a good descriptive phrase for this condition of withdrawal. One looks at the blank wall and sees no opening there. There appears to be no way out. Death walls us in, and its finality overwhelms us. Only as we turn and look out the windows to see the new possibilities will we be able to return to our loving selves. Looking at the wall, we cannot even see the others in the room who are ready to surround us with courage and love. I recognize that in this condition it takes a real effort to "turn around." In my visiting the very ill and dying, some have quite literally turned their faces to the wall. They refuse to relate, to talk, to share their feelings of shock, fear, or possibly hope. Yet I know that the one release that such people find from a "frozen position" is to share feelings, questions, and concerns with a person ready to listen and affirm, but not to judge or argue. It requires patience and persuasion to be there for others at such times. The inner struggle is very real, but we should not (maybe even cannot) resolve it on our own. If you are in this position now, or at some time in the future, have faith in yourself and trust in others to share in your confusion and uncertainty. Sometimes people hesitate to share with other members of the family, particularly those that close to them, because they sense that these persons have their own confusion and turmoil. Openness is better than silence. Tears may unlock the door just as readily as words. Remember that what matters is the new opportunity to show love, not the correctness of the factual information. The dying, above all, need to hear that they are valued and loved, and always will be, even when they die.

Anger

Some people come out of the withdrawal phase expressing deep anger and resentment. This also is how we are made to respond. The struggle to accept the truth about oneself generates a lot of energy, which can be directed positively or negatively. With help we can channel this energy to good use. Our love of life will make us angry that we are in danger of losing it. The older we are, the less energy we are likely to have to let this anger spill over into destructiveness, but this is not always true. Whatever age we are, we will probably feel that it is too soon to die. We may wish further opportunities for loving, and we want to enjoy our time. We may feel we deserve a better deal. We might ask angrily: "What have I done to deserve the death sentence?" We may suddenly become angry with God, whether or not we have believed in God up to this point. We may be angry with the messenger of the news that we are dying and hold her or him responsible. We may be angry that we did not get better, or earlier, treatments for our condition. We may be angry that others seem to be healthy even though they have not taken good care of themselves. We may even be angry with ourselves for not doing something to prevent the current situation.

Anger is a strong emotion, and though it is part of the process of breaking out of withdrawal, it can be destructive unless channeled properly. It can be like a torrent of water that can be harnessed for good or left to tumble destructively on its path. Anger can be particularly damaging to relationships at a critical time. It is better to share anger with those capable of receiving it without being hurt by it, than with those who probably share the reaction of anger because they are too close to the same situation. It is at this point that the hospice movement has been so effective. It has made sure that trained personnel are at hand whose task is to support and counsel the patient. This staff is separate from those responsible for physical and medical care.

Anger must be expressed, or it will burn up energy inside us that we need to relate to those outside us. Expression of anger also helps us to accept that mortals are not in control of all they survey. When we hear ourselves declaring in anger that not everything is in our control, we begin to realize that it is silly to think that we control life to that extent in the first place. Once we begin to see that we cannot control life, we start to let go and see life more as a gift than a right. This is a key turning point in our emotional reaction to death itself.

Telling others of our anger at being "cheated" out of life should help us accept the challenge of what we will make of each opportunity remaining in our lives. At this point, we can be helped to let the anger over the past abate and allow the energy to be rechanneled into making the most of the future. The expression of anger may lead to the search for forgiveness and reconciliation. We can be helped to forgive the mistakes of others, as well as those that we have made.

If anger is retained in its negative aspect, it can seriously disrupt our dying well. It can even prevent the attainment of the peace of dying. So the anger must be expressed, accepted, released, and examined. The question we need to ask ourselves is: What can I do creatively about the causes of my anger? The answer in some instances will be obvious: Nothing, because that is past. The answer may also be: I can help the person with whom I am angry stop hurting others as much in the future. To help them will require forgiveness of the hurt caused and encouragement to do better next time. Another answer may be: This anger only shows that I was wrong to think that everything in life is perfect or can be controlled. Life can be accepted more fully as being worth living despite its limitations and imperfections. To come to such a conclusion will assist us in making much better use of the life that is still available for us to live.

So our anger, if rightly used, will help us to reassess the future as well as the past. It can motivate us toward seeing the opportunities for loving and caring that are the precious qualities of living (and dying) well.

Striking a Bargain

When the attempts through anger to get our own way and escape our destiny subside, we often try another tack. We can use the same technique as the child who, having tried shouting and stamping feet, uses pleas for kindness and ingratiating behavior in an attempt to get his or her own way. In the face of death, people may try bargaining. They think that the way out is to cut a deal with God, the doctor, the priest, or the minister, delaying or eliminating the threat of death. All of us try this method when faced with extreme danger. I am sure you can recall taking such actions. Some people take up praying to a God they have ignored for years. Others try to correct their diets, quit smoking, or take exercise. Some make firm resolutions to amend their behavior. The thought is that if we are good enough, nothing bad should happen to us.

This stage of facing death can be confusing. Doing better things looks like a positive outcome from the resolution of our fits of anger. We are determined to lead a better life, and we are more pleasant to live with. Our health may indeed improve from the correction of bad habits or laziness. If we were difficult to approach before, it makes life more pleasant and peaceful in our relationships with others if we take this new approach. Some people even look so happy and positive that we think they have accepted in full the fact of their death and are finding new ways of living. They say their prayers; they say they believe in God; and their behavior has taken a turn for the better. Even their general health may have improved. All around, things are brighter.

However, if all these "improvements" are simply part of an attempt to bargain with God, there will be a rude awakening when it becomes obvious that death cannot be avoided. We will be furious to find that all our efforts have been in vain. It is especially difficult when a plateau in our deterioration occurs. Then hope rebounds, and the idea of bargaining gains weight. We think that if we can make a difference by a new attitude, then by greater efforts we can take control and postpone death altogether. On a plateau, we cannot be certain whether we have halted the decline and can hope to climb back up or if the plateau is just a temporary stopping place on the way to the depths. This is a hard stage for everyone. We want to rejoice in the improvement of feelings and behavior, and at the same time we either fear it will not last or know that it is only a diversion from the final reality.

In our bargaining with God we need outside help to see that God's love for us is not greater if we should get better than if we die. God does not show more favor to us by giving us a miracle of healing. God's love for us and the value in which God holds us is constant. Resurrection and healing are equally miracles of love. Each gives us new opportunities to respond to God's love and to show our love to others. Both are unknown futures in the sense that the choice is not predictable. Only the constancy of God's love is predictable. If we can grasp that, sooner or later, we will begin living fully again.

It is especially difficult in this reaction to facing death when folks around us promise that if we do this or that, we will become better. Alternative therapists and spiritual healers can be brokers in the bargaining stage. They encourage us to drink this, take that, have more faith, pray to a special saint, as *the* way to get better. A change of lifestyle or of medicine or a renewal of faith may be beneficial to general well-being, but not if it is the result of a bargain. Life is a gift. Remember that we did not cause our creation. We cannot earn love. All is given to us. So we may want to undergo treatment or change our habits, but we do so for the value of the actions themselves, not as part of a bargain.

Depression and Pain

If our condition is now serious and it is obvious that no long-term reversal can postpone death, we may find that with the collapse of our bargaining efforts we become very depressed. This stage usually occurs at the same time that the resources of the physical body are failing. The two happen simultaneously because the signs of weakness in our bodies make clear to us that none of our attempts to bargain have been successful in the long term. We are forced to face up to our mortality. Our souls have to feel what our bodies are telling us. The information of the head must flow into the heart, and the issue cannot be postponed or avoided any longer. Our search now is for an answer to the question, "What will my death *mean* for me?" As we are asking that question, those near and dear to us are pondering the parallel question, "What will the death of my loved one mean for me?"

If we are able to be honest, we know that the answer will at first bring us pain. Death will mean the end of earthly life. It will be painful to let go—all that we hoped yet to do; all the relationships we hoped to develop further; all the honor we hoped to achieve; all the generations yet to come that we hoped to see; all that we hoped to bring to full completion—all that will not happen. The child in every one of us always thinks that one day we will grow up and make everything perfect. Some people do get more of a chance to round out their lives, and these folk may find it less painful to let go. Facing death, a friend of mine once remarked that his pain lay not in knowing that this was the end of his hopes of a great career, but in the ending of his relationships with those he loved. For whatever reason, most people find that there is pain in placing a full stop at the end of the sentence.

In our depression and physical pain we look for love and care. We know that this cannot take away the feelings that we have, but it can support us so much that the feelings do not become the focus of our attention. We learn to live with and through the pain. In recognizing that the end of life is near, we can also turn to thanksgiving. The past becomes important for us. We want to share with others how much we enjoyed the good times and are grateful for them. We want to thank the people involved. We want to see the future and hear the plans and hopes of the next generation. It may be difficult for young children to be taken to visit a relative at this stage, but it is positive both for them and for the dying. The handing over to the next generation is an important part of letting go for both children and adults. Both need to share love and express thanks for life–past, present, and future.

Acceptance and Hope

There is also another part in the answer to the question, What will my death mean for me? The first answer affirms that my death will mean the end of my struggle for life. If we have pain, it will also mean the end of pain and weakness. We might be able to give ourselves the answer, My death will mean release and peace, not only for me but for those anxiously supporting me with love.

We may also be able to answer, My death does *not* mean the end of loving. My faith and hope is that God will love me to the end and to my new beginning. My trust in those around me whom I love makes me hope that our love will not be broken by my death. Death may refine that love, change its shape and its expression, but it will not destroy that love.

As we accept the reality of both our impending death and of the continuity of love, we can be filled with hope. It is a hope born of deep experience, tested by life's fortunes and misfortunes, and strengthened by quiet words of reassurance. It is a hope created out of sharing and built on mutual trust. If this hope is to remain with us at the end, we will need the love and support of others who can share this hope. We may need to borrow something of their faith when the struggle to let go bites deeply into our last energies. We may be able to enhance the faith of those who watch and wait beside us when their faith runs low with the thoughts of how they will possibly cope in the future without our physical presence. The prayers and words of the faithful community, which has grown from the seeds of the martyrs and the saints, is often of supreme value to the dying and the grieving. At death we are never individuals. We are companions of humanity, linked to the past by those who gave us life and to the future by our gifts to others of life and meaning.

Acceptance and hope affirm our yes to God's gifts and open us up to the future of love in resurrection. If, with the support of all those whom I have mentioned, we can reach this point of living, we will have no fear of dying. We will be content to leave the future of our loved ones on earth in God's care and our own future with God's love. Our good-byes will be said in faith: "God bless us on our journeys, I in mine, and you in yours, safe in God's keeping." What more fitting ending could there be?

Pause now, as I have done as I write this, and let your emotions rest. If you are in the midst of a journey toward death for yourself or for another, take the opportunity to share your feelings with a person you trust. If you find such a person hard to identify because you think all this is too painful for any of your friends or family, call on the resources and people of a faith community of your choice. Give them this chapter or one of its sections to read and then share your feelings and reactions with them. Help them to listen so well to you that you, in turn, can listen to your soul and to God. Ask for the care that you think is appropriate. Do not be shy in asking them to help you communicate with those you love. As we have seen, love is the goal of living and dying–for in love, there is God.

Take time to reflect on that.

Some Practical Considerations

Our emotional needs as we face death are paramount, but our minds often want to deal with practical considerations as well. In dealing with our emotions, it helps to have something to do as well as feelings to share. Here are four practical steps you might want to consider.

Instructions about Medical Care

In our efforts to take some responsibility for ourselves and not just opt out of everything, we may want to leave instructions about our medical care. Some people are very definite about their wishes to be allowed to die in due time. They do not want the use of endless medical procedures in an attempt to prolong their life "unnaturally." Obviously, the medical profession is dedicated to the cause of helping people live as long and as well as possible. Yet it is right and proper to leave some guidelines as to when such attempts should cease. These should be in the form of our permission, rather than of our control. I suggest that you consult your medical and perhaps legal advisers to see what options are available in your own country.

The Making or Revising of a Will

If it is at all possible, everyone should leave legal instructions concerning the transfer of their property and possessions in the event of death. These instructions are usually contained in a will. If you are reading this and do not have a will, my advice is to have one drawn up as soon as possible by a lawyer or other official. Please do not wait until your death is in sight before you do this task. We do not know when and how we will die, and it is most helpful to those who are left to have the legal arrangements in place for the transfer of our possessions.

Some people facing death with time to consider the provisions in their will may want to revise some or all of it because of changed circumstances. If you want to do this, my advice is to seek the counsel of your lawyer and a trusted family member or friend. It would be best to follow these guidelines:

- Only change something for the better.
- Do not act out of anger, resentment, or bargaining for love.
- Only make changes that will make it easier for those left to accept your loss.

Remember that the hurt left by your death should not be aggravated by any hurts caused by your will. One way of lessening the pain is to be open with those most affected about the contents of the will once you have completed the document. You are not under any rules of secrecy about its contents. Remember, love cannot be obtained by bargaining.

Donating Parts of Your Body for Medical Use

In your will you may make the provision for some parts of your body to be used by doctors to help other people or for research. You may feel that your body has been a blessing to you, and you want to share that blessing with others who need a vital part of your body to help them live more fully. Some people facing death are greatly helped by knowing that their bodies will not be "wasted," but will be useful to others. Other people consider the body to be personal and private to them and do not feel it right to take such action. It is very much a matter of choice. Again, if you wish to leave instructions, discuss it with the family and your legal and medical advisers.

Arrangements for Your Funeral

Some wills contain requests in regard to burial or cremation and the sort of ceremony appropriate for the funeral. Other people advise their closest relatives of their wishes, as those are the ones responsible for such decisions.

In recent years, when I have been asked to participate in a funeral service, I have become aware of clear instructions that have been laid down by the deceased. Some of these have been helpful; others have been inappropriate and unhelpful for those for whom the service has been designed. They often created difficulty both practically and emotionally and added to the confusion and stress. The more I consider the issue, the more I would advise that as we face death, we trust those responsible with the task of deciding on the details of a funeral. The service is the gift of the family and the community to you. It is for their strengthening and comfort. It is the acknowledgment of the gift of your life and what it has meant for all. Above all, it is there to affirm the belief in God's care for you and for those who mourn your death. It will include thanksgiving for your life and for your resurrection. If it is a secular occasion, it will be the opportunity to dispose of your body with respect and to share feelings of grief and thanksgiving within the community whose lives you touched.

Obviously, it may help you to accept the reality of your death if you are able to talk about your funeral. However, this can be part of the denial of your dying if your mind plans the funeral as if you were present. You will not be there in that sense. You will have said your good-byes. The funeral may be an opportunity for others to say their final good-byes to your body, but resurrection means that by then we have begun a new experience of life. Love and God's care will remain, and the future will enfold both. There is a new form of living, and the care that we have received and given in our dying shapes that future.

In the beginning was God. In the ending is God, embracing us and our dear ones with equal love. That is the assurance we need to live well, and to die well. Share this faith with me as you pray:

God our Creator, you gave us life and gift us death.
We entrust ourselves into your care
in life, in death, in life beyond death.
Keep us aware of your love for us.
Give us grace to love one another

and to trust that love by sharing
all our hopes and fears,
our feelings and failures,
our faith and doubts.
Christ Jesus, in our dying, walk with us to the cross and grave,
and share with us your resurrection,
and the life of fellowship with you.
Enfold us and those we love in the arms of your mercy,
bring our lives to completion
through forgiveness and renewal,
and teach us to live well,
that we may die well,
and enjoy you, our God,
forever and ever. Amen.

The Process of Mourning

Those who are left behind after our death will enter a period of mourning. Much has been written about this process, and the knowledge of its stages is becoming more fully known within our communities. There are a number of similarities to the various stages we pass through as we face death. Because I think this information is readily available to you,[3] I will not repeat it in detail here but simply give this summary:

Those who mourn have

- A feeling of numbness, shock, and disbelief that the death has occurred. This seems to occur whether or not the death was "expected."
- A feeling of extreme sadness over all the memories of the past and the gaps of the future. This is the time of many tears. It is accompanied by a search for a cause of the loss and some anger at the circumstances. There may be times when the mourner sees hallucinations of the loved one returning or sitting in a favorite chair.

---

[3]Standard authors are C. M. Parkes, *Bereavement: Studies of Grief in Adult Life* (New York: International Universities Press, 1972); Granger E. Westberg, *Good Grief* (Philadelphia: Fortress Press, 1971); Delores Kuenning, *Helping People through Grief* (Minneapolis: Bethany, 1987). I have written a fuller description in my contribution "No Justice in Grief," in Philip Culbertson, ed., *Counselling Issues and South Pacific Communities* (Auckland: Accent, 1997).

- A feeling of disorganization and despair. The awareness of loneliness is very much present, and the body finds it hard to do the regular tasks required for living. Panic may set in as the person realizes that the deceased is no longer available to perform her or his usual functions. This is particularly relevant in the case of the death of a parent of young children or a spouse. New skills have to be learned, but there is not enough energy to do this. The condition has parallels with depression.
- A feeling of anger about the loss of the person and the causes of that loss. There may be feelings of guilt involved, but these can be projected onto others and external causes. This anger is the beginning of the recovery of energy, but it must be channeled into a positive force for it to be helpful.
- A feeling that life must go on despite the loss, that things must be reorganized for the new shape of living. There comes an acceptance that the loss has happened and that there is nothing we can do to reverse it. In the end, we begin to see some good points about the circumstances of the death. We readjust to a new reality, especially if we feel that love does prevail, and that we continue to be loved by God and others.

The best way to walk this journey is in the company of those with experience of how grief feels. Many support groups have been formed for those in the first year of grief. The encouraging thing is that most people do reach a readjustment to life in its new shape after a due period of time. This seems to occur best when no one tries to push the process along, and when love holds the person secure during the shaking of the foundations of life. Children as well as adults go through the process, but the speed is usually different. The child goes through the stages more quickly but then may have to repeat the process later. The adult takes at least a year, so that all the "first anniversaries" are experienced and coped with. Children are often neglected in the care given by family and friends, and I would urge those able to help such children to make special efforts to attend to their needs.

Do not try to walk this journey alone. Share it with those close to you and particularly those who have had a similar experience but are now able to move on to a new space. Do not suppress your feelings or think that you must be peculiar to feel or act as you do. The process is part of the essential preparation for a new pattern of life. This is your "resurrection," somewhat like that of the one you mourn.

They and you are held securely in God's love, and you and they have been built in such a way as to be able to make this transition. Let your tears flow and become the water that gives life to the seeds of hope.

Let this prayer help you accept God's love even in your time of grief:

God of resurrection, hold me safe in your love as I put my life together again.
I loved_______, and love him/her still,
and in that love I am free to move forward.
Help me to grieve for the past with thanksgiving,
to look to the future with hope,
and to work through my feelings with patience.
Give me confidence that I can reshape my life and live it to the fullest.
Let my heart be open to the ministry of others
so that they can be a balm for my sorrow and the spur for my hopes,
and then assure me that I in my turn have a place in your design
and a future of care for others as well as myself.
God, your love continues for me and for my beloved,
in time and in eternity. Amen.

Conclusion

Ways to Care for Oneself

Having looked with some detail at the major individual situations that we face in life, we now need to see whether we can discover some principles of self-care that we can apply in general.

I began the first chapter with the image of the triangle of love: love of God, love of others, and love of self. We saw that each aspect of love was interdependent with the other two. Only as we receive love and affirmation from God can we establish them in ourselves. Only out of a heart of love are we able to respect and care for others. These are the most important facts that we need to absorb if we are to look after ourselves well for the journey through life to death and beyond.

In this conclusion I want to expand on how we might achieve the goal of giving and receiving mature love.

Love of Self

For many this phrase is still a shocking imperative. It smacks of arrogance, self-centeredness, insularity, and intolerance. My experience is that all these occur more often when people do not truly love themselves than when they do. It is out of lack of love of self that a person projects negativity toward others and tries to pretend to be more important than anyone else. Love of self in its true expression releases a person to reach out to others with respect, love, and care.

My love of self includes a proper estimation of my gifts and abilities. It saves me from feeling that I need to dominate others by trying to force them to love me to fill the void in my feelings. I realize that I have no need to succeed in all areas of life, because my love of self has affirmed what my best gifts are to offer to my community.

Out of love of self I am able to recognize and respect my body as the gift I have been given to communicate my personality to those around me. I love my body and keep it functioning to its fullest ability. My affirmation of my body saves me from being jealous of the "ideal" body presented to me by the media. I am aware that my body is not and cannot be perfect, but that does not stop me from valuing it for what it is and does and keeping it fit to the fullest extent. I learn to accept my disabilities, cope with them, and find ways to see that my inner spirit is still visible to others.

My love of self expands my love for those around me as I recognize our interdependence. As I love myself, I try not to grasp at the love shown to me by others, so that they feel drained of love. Instead I am able to circulate love freely so that there is more than enough for all in my community. In such circumstances, love expands and grows as all feel respected, affirmed, and warmed in the atmosphere of love.

Faith in God

My experience of the triangle of love builds up not only my love of self, but also my faith and trust in the power of God's love for me. In our love of self we are strong enough to know that we need loving, especially in those moments when we are challenged to seize our opportunities, and in those moments when we are shocked by life's losses and pain. We are more ready to accept the love of God without losing our sense of self-esteem. We show our trust that God's power of love, though greater than ours, does not diminish our love, but adds to it. We know when we ought to release ourselves into the arms of God's love and are aware of those times when we need to rest in God's love to regain our strength and courage. Our faith in God allows us to see God as a partner in love, not as one who seeks to dominate us with love.

Our faith in God also helps us to see the true causes of events, so that we do not seek affirmation from our "lucky breaks." Our faith does not demand of God what is contrary to the way of love chosen by God. That way must leave the possibility of rejection open for its love to be genuine. We in turn accept our responsibilities for mistakes and messes without becoming despondent and feeling that we are failures, because we know that love allows for forgiveness and recovery.

Confidence in Self

Our love of self and our faith in God build up a continuing confidence in ourselves that allows us to know that we can face all of life's situations. Such a confidence does not mean that we pretend we can cope immediately with life's shocks. Rather, it helps us to know that with assistance from God and from others we can gain the courage and strength to move forward on the journey of love. Our confidence allows us to relax and savor some of life's pleasures. It prevents any sense of "being driven," of thinking that we can acquire external honor to cover our own lack of confidence in what we are doing.

Such a confidence helps us to see our proper place in all of life's activity. We know that we cannot do everything, but are dependent on and interdependent with others. Our confidence means that we can ask for help and receive it gratefully. Such an attitude about self makes us a full participant in community.

Humility, Realism, and Discernment of Value

Our love of self, our faith in God, and our confidence will make us a person with three distinctive characteristics: humility, realism, and discernment.

First, we have humility. The word comes from the root "humus," meaning the earth. A person of humility is aware of his or her place in the created order. If we have humility, we know that we are nurtured by the Creator and by the environment in which we live. In turn, we nurture the earth and all that grows from it. Those who sit on the ground are in touch with their roots and whatever shares this created order with them. The mighty raise their sky towers to try to dominate the earth from above. The humble share their place on earth with everything that lives at that level. "Out of the (ground) you were taken; you are dust, and to dust you shall return."[1] This verse is not a threat, but an affirmation of your gift of life in its given status. Such humility removes all false attempts to dominate, exploit, and escape our mortality. In humility lies the knowledge of our place, our purpose, and our potential as part of the natural order.

Second, we have a realism about life. We are saved from false expectations and, therefore, the wrong kind of disappointment. We realize that life is not easy for anyone; that it takes time and help to reach maturity; that it takes time and help to recover from life's knocks and hurts; and that we have to work hard to achieve our goals. Our realism stops us from expecting everything in life to be presented to us on a plate. It also prevents feelings of jealousy that destroy the energy for good. Our realism extends to what we can do and offer others from our limited abilities and resources. Our faith in ourselves helps us to know those things we have to share, and our realism helps us to know that what we most have to share is an inner self and a unique personality.

---

[1]Genesis 3:19.

Third, we have a clear discernment of the value of all things. We are able to reach a true estimation of the value of material things and of invisible attributes. We are not misled by the power that money and position are thought to gain. We are able to give proper weight to the things of the Spirit–both the Holy Spirit and our own. We prize love above all gifts, and honesty above all virtues. Such an attitude of discernment enriches our lives. In poverty we do not look for pity. In wealth we do not pursue power. We see the value in the person, not the product. Our possessions are the treasured memories of the giver or the occasion of the purchase. We give and receive presents as symbols of the giver's love. We know the value of every person, not the cost of every article. We know the worth of what brings us joy and are able to share that joy with those around us.

Scripture and Prayer

What can teach us to live like this in confidence, faith, and truth? You have seen how scripture and prayer have formed part of the inspiration for our journey to maturity. Neither is a magic source of instruction, but they are the springboards for God's teaching and our response. The Spirit moves in both, enlivening the words and helping us apply them to our situations. The Spirit helps us express our deep feelings and hopes in prayer to a listening God. In the dialogue deep inside your being, the creative Spirit is molding and shaping your maturity for living. Receive this help gladly, even if you are a little mystified at its source and power. Trust God to work in you, even if you cannot know why and how. The Creator knows the creature and how to give the best care.

The Care of the Community

In this book I have frequently drawn your attention to the help you need to find from others in the community. You cannot look after yourself on your own, not even with the help of God. God has placed you in community. There you will be supported for living and find the opportunity for loving others.

The care of the community is expressed through family and close friends. It is vital that we use the experience and wisdom of the generations ahead of us. Sometimes a lack of maturity in the older generation leaves them feeling isolated and impotent. By our attitudes we can help such people to see that we need their wisdom, but not their attempts at control. Sometimes we are the ones who empower that control by our protestations that we do not want it. Confident love assumes that only wisdom will be offered, and in most cases such love disarms the weapons of control.

Families can be places of cooperation or competition. Our own self-confidence and our secure love of self mean that we can aim to emphasize the mutual support that we can give one another and take away the need to compete for places and love.

To achieve this miracle, we may need to seek the help of the wider community. There we should find wise pastors and counselors who can listen and help us establish a sure inner self. In our hurts they may be best able to facilitate our healing with God's power of love. Be realistic about those who offer such a ministry. It is hard work, and they do not always succeed. However, they do hold up the way of love as the true road to follow and give support as we take steps along the way. You will need to do your part in the gathering of knowledge, energy, and determination for such a journey, but these representatives of the community's support are there to assist you.

My hope is that this book will give you the knowledge to face many of life's situations and will inspire your love of self and your faith in God. Then you can live confidently, humbly, realistically, and with discernment of the true value of life. Live in the love of God and to God's glory!

Bibliography

In this list of reference books, I have placed the number of the chapter covering the special topic in brackets in the hope of providing readers access to supportive literature for more in-depth study.

Anderson, Herbert. *The Family and Pastoral Care.* Philadelphia: Fortress Press, 1984. [Ch. 1]

Armstrong, D. M. *Belief, Truth and Knowledge.* Cambridge: Cambridge University Press, 1973. [Ch. 8]

Atkins, Peter G. "No Justice in Grief." In *Counselling Issues and South Pacific Communities.* Auckland: Accent Publications, 1997. [Ch. 10]

——. *Soul Time.* St. Louis: Chalice Press, 2000. [Intro., Ch. 3]

Badham, Paul, and Paul Ballard. *Facing Death.* Cardiff: University of Wales Press, 1996. [Ch. 10]

Brizee, Robert. *The Gift of Listening.* St. Louis: Chalice Press, 1993. [Concl.]

Browning, Don S. *Religious Ethics and Pastoral Care.* Philadelphia: Fortress Press, 1983. [Ch. 8]

——. *A Fundamental Practical Theology.* Minneapolis: Fortress Press, 1992. [Intro.]

Carmody, John. *Conversations with a Dying Friend.* New York/Mahwah: Paulist Press, 1992. [Ch. 10]

Clements, William. *Ministry with the Aging.* New York: Haworth Press, 1989. [Ch. 1]

Cotter, Jim. *Brainsquall.* Sheffield: Cairns Publications, 1997. [Ch. 3]

Couture, Pamela, and Rodney Hunter. *Pastoral Care and Social Conflict.* Nashville: Abingdon Press, 1995. [Ch. 9]

Covey, Stephen, and Roger and Rebecca Merrill. *First Things First.* New York: Simon and Schuster, 1994. [Ch. 2]

Culbertson, Philip. *Caring for God's People.* Minneapolis: Fortress Press, 2000. [Intro.]

Eade, John, and Michael J. Sallnow. *Contesting the Sacred.* London: Routledge, 1991. [Ch. 7]

Eiesland, Nancy L. *The Disabled God.* Nashville: Abingdon Press, 1994. [Ch. 6]

Eiesland, Nancy L., and D. E. Saliers, eds. *Human Disability and the Service of God.* Nashville: Abingdon Press, 1998. [Ch. 6]

Erikson, Erik. *Identity: Youth and Crisis.* New York: W. W. Norton, 1968. [Ch. 1]

——. *The Life Cycle Completed.* New York: W. W. Norton, 1982. [Ch. 1]

Forrester, Duncan B. *Christian Justice and Public Policy.* Cambridge: Cambridge University Press, 1997. [Ch. 9]

Gaede, S. D. *When Tolerance Is No Virtue.* Downers Grove, Ill.: Intervarsity Press, 1993. [Ch. 8]

Gallant, Donald M. *Alcoholism.* New York: W. W. Norton, 1987. [Ch. 4]

Gerkin, Charles V. *An Introduction to Pastoral Care.* Nashville: Abingdon Press, 1997. [Intro.]

Gilligan, Carol. *In a Different Voice.* Cambridge, Mass.: Harvard University Press, 1982. [Ch. 5]

Higginson, Richard. *Transforming Leadership.* London: SPCK, 1996. [Ch. 5]

Klein, Donald F., and Paul H. Wender. *Understanding Depression.* New York: Oxford University Press, 1993. [Ch. 3]

Kübler-Ross, Elisabeth. *Living with Death and Dying.* New York: Macmillan, 1981. [Ch. 10]

——. *On Death and Dying.* London: Tavistock, 1969. [Ch. 10]

Kuenning, Delores. *Helping People through Grief.* Minneapolis: Bethany, 1987. [Ch. 10]

Linn, Matthew, Dennis Linn, and Sheila Fabricant. *Healing the Eight Stages of Life.* New York/Mahwah: Paulist Press, 1988. [Ch. 1]

A New Zealand Prayer Book/He Karakia Mihinare o Aotearoa. London: Collins, 1989. [Ch. 4]

Parkes, C. M. *Bereavement: Studies of Grief in Adult Life.* New York: International Universities Press, 1972. [Ch. 10]

Scarf, Maggie. *Intimate Partners: Patterns in Love and Marriage.* New York: Ballantine, 1987. [Ch. 2]

Spickard, Anderson, and Barbara Thompson. *Dying for a Drink.* Waco, Tex.: Word Books, 1985. [Ch. 4]

Tutu, Desmond. *No Future without Forgiveness.* London: Rider, 1999. [Ch. 9]

Van Dongen-Garrad, Jessie. *Invisible Barriers.* London: SPCK, 1983. [Ch. 6]

Waddams, Herbert. *A New Introduction to Moral Theology.* London: SCM, 1964. [Ch. 8]

Warren, Neil Clark. *Finding the Love of Your Life.* New York: Pocket Books, 1992. [Ch. 2]

Weatherhead, Leslie D. *Psychology and Life.* New York: Abingdon Press, 1935. Reprint, London: Hudder and Stoughton, 1957. [Ch. 3]

Welch, Don D. *Conflicting Agendas.* Cleveland: Pilgrim Press, 1994. [Ch. 2]

Westberg, Granger E. *Good Grief.* Philadelphia: Fortress Press, 1971. [Ch. 10]

Winnicott, D. W. *Playing and Reality.* London: Routledge, 1991. [Ch. 7]

Worden, Mark. *Adolescents and Their Families.* New York: Haworth, 1991. [Ch. 1]

Index

LADY OF HOPE

A Journey of Faith with Breast Cancer

Ellen Washburn Gragg

Foreword by Carmen Falls Redding

CROSSBOOKS
PUBLISHING

CrossBooks™
A Division of LifeWay
1663 Liberty Drive
Bloomington, IN 47403
www.crossbooks.com
Phone: 1-866-879-0502

First published by CrossBooks 7/6/2011

ISBN: 978-1-6150-7874-5 (sc)
ISBN: 978-1-6150-7875-2 (hc)

Library of Congress Control Number: 2011932908

Printed in the United States of America

This book is printed on acid-free paper.

QUILT PHOTOGRAPHS BY: VICTORIAN ROSE victorianroseweb.com

Few families have gone untouched by the plague of the "C" word, cancer. One's pattern to that point in life changes; the knowledge of mortality enters; relationships are challenged; financial security is questioned; and eternal concerns are raised all because of the diagnosis represented by the "C." Resources of various kinds are available for these issues, but the one crisis that may not be as well documented is the very personal one which Ellen Gragg's book seeks to deal with here, i.e. the day to day struggle as one attempts to battle this monstrous disease.

She shares out of her personal walk the important lessons learned, the steps which anyone in similar circumstances needs to take, and the pitfalls and roadblocks which are all too often a part of the struggle. One major difference in Ellen's writing though is the revelation of the power her unwavering faith gives her in the midst of this fight. Family, friends and faith are the sources of her strength. Ups and downs are a given, she tells us, but not in regard to those three certainties of her life.

Included in this book is the voice of another whose journal entries reflect a different perspective on Ellen's battle with cancer. As Carmen Redding informs friends of Ellen's faithful fight she writes eternal truths which would be applicable to any challenge a Christian might face. One can sense her love and admiration growing for her friend as she reports on the ups and downs of Ellen's walk through treatment after treatment. In our hectic lives we are reminded through this journal of the precious gift of time, perhaps the crowning gift of friendship which Carmen gave so generously.

Read, even if you have yet to face the "C" word personally. Read for inspiration, read for information, read for encouragement of what the human spirit can accomplish when redeemed and filled with His Holy Spirit, thanks to His Eternal Son, Jesus the Christ.

Rev. Bill Fryar
Pastor, Double Springs Baptist Church

CONTENTS

LIST OF ILLUSTRATIONS/PICTURES

Embracing Ellen With The Fabric Of Friendship

At the 2006 San Diego Delta Kappa Gamma Society International Convention, a circle of North Carolina friends presented Ellen Gragg with a beautiful prayer shawl, fashioned by Betty Marshall. Prior to the presentation, each of the friends had tenderly held the shawl and each had offered a blessing over the sacred garment. Our friend, surprised and deeply touched by this gesture, was consoled by this loving act. While Ellen anxiously awaited the second surgery following her lumpectomy performed one week prior to the West Coast event, this circle of friends quietly enveloped her with the fabric of friendship; thus, began our vigil of Ellen.

Ellen's fight to live began in the remaining hot, humid days of summer as the relentless sun bore down on leafy, green treetops. Like the turn of a kaleidoscope, the summer treescape shifted to the riotous, sassy trees of autumn, shimmering in golds, oranges, reds, and shades of umber. Then, the blaze of autumn faded and changed to the somber, contemplative days of winter with barren, black trees etched against leaden skies. In time this monochromatic season passed. At last, the prelude to spring arrived with the first tree buds, bursting with the promise of new life and hope. This kaleidoscopic change of seasons echoed Ellen's battle to overcome cancer cells lurking in her body.

As a longtime friend of Ellen, I offered to inform the circle of friends of Ellen's weekly progress via email. After the Sunday supper hour, I looked forward to leisurely, gentle, and free flowing conversations with Ellen. With a reverent, respectful heart I felt privileged to enter my friend's world, a most remarkable world. I learned of her cancer treatments and mundane but powerful events of her everyday life that strengthened and supported her. In this world the superfluous and trivial were stripped away. What clearly emerged were those elements of life that were vital and nourishing to one looking death in the eye.

With this eight month watch over our friend, the sweetness and preciousness of life loomed large in our hearts. This circle of friends marveled at Ellen's strong Christian faith, her courage to confront cancer, and her indomitable spirit to live. Each of us was deeply touched by the tender love and care given to Ellen by her steadfast family, loyal members of her church, and concerned Cleveland County friends. We, too, were impressed by her skilled medical team who advised, cared for, and supported Ellen on every step of her journey.

Indeed, as Ellen's friends, we were honored to witness her overcome cancer. This event imprinted upon our hearts the sacredness of life. May each of us treasure our lives and live them fully, reflecting integrity, purpose, compassion, and a humble spirit. Each of us is only "a moment of sunlight" in the dark eons of time.

Carmen Falls Redding
Greensboro, North Carolina
November 27, 2010

Preface

Me? Write a book? Never! I knew it was out of the question for me to write a book on my own. But the idea kept popping up in my head! My experience with breast cancer had certainly been a journey of faith and I felt that with God's help and the encouragement of my family and friends that I could do it.

This book has been written in an effort to share my experiences with breast cancer with those who either have or will have this disease. It records my notes of the journey as well as a journal written weekly by my dear friend Carmen. I hope that by relating my experiences others can know what to expect if faced with the disease or if one becomes the caregiver.

Names and places are included as well as quotes from the National Cancer Institute, Carmen and others. Experiences learned throughout my life that have influenced the person I have become are also included.

My vision for this book is that those who read it will have a better understanding of breast cancer and its treatments but especially a deeper understanding of how one's faith is essential to true healing.

Acknowledgments

Supported by the efforts of Jon Lineback, Echo Fluharty and others of CrossBooks, I was able to navigate the maze of challenges involved in getting my manuscript ready for publication

I have been extraordinarily fortunate to have Dr. Warden Woodard as my oncologist and to have the support of my medical team.

Thanks to Dianne, Linda, Glenda, Patsy and Pastor Bill Fryar for their suggestions and help.

My church family at Double Springs Baptist Church in Shelby proved that "Work is love made visible" as they worked to care for me in every way possible.

I am grateful to my friend, Carmen for her weekly record of my journey to health, and also, my friend, Kathy Mosdal O'Brien, whose encouragement and editing have helped bring this book to completion.

I am thankful for all who assisted me in any way during my cancer journey and especially to my loving husband, Larry, and all of my family.

Introduction

Psalm 23:4 (King James Version) [4]Yea, though I walk through the valley of the shadow of death, I will fear no evil: for thou art with me; thy rod and thy staff they comfort me.

Four years ago I was on the mountaintop of life. My husband and I had both retired, our children were grown and married, and we had eight beautiful grandchildren. Life was good! We had reached the time in life when we could travel and enjoy the wonders of the world without worrying too much about schedules. Every day was as busy as we wanted it to be with the farm, Angus cattle, meetings, helping with grandchildren, and church. But in May 2006 I hit the depths of the valley. While visiting in Japan I found a lump in my right breast. This was my first experience with breast lumps and I was taken aback somewhat at first. I knew that we had two more weeks abroad so I tried not to think about it. I didn't tell anyone but my husband Larry so that everyone in the group would enjoy their visit without thinking of me.

Back home, the doctors' appointments, tests, and treatments began immediately. A friend, Linda, and also my oncologist's nurse, Kim Rippy, encouraged me to keep a journal. The thought of someday sharing my journey to health with others never entered my mind. That journey has taught me many lessons but even in the depths of my own valley I knew that **life was good!**

The idea of writing a book kept popping up in my head. I had shared my experience with several women who had been diagnosed with breast cancer since my treatment. I felt that they were more prepared to make decisions about their treatment after asking me questions about my experience. I had asked my survivor friends about their experiences, and I know it helped me. With the encouragement of several close friends and family, I began to consider the idea of a book. Writing a book was a task that I didn't believe that I could accomplish since I have never had any courses in writing. Through the years when I have had an important decision to make I have put the decision in God's hands. With God's help and the nudging of family and friends, I have now accepted the challenge. The experiences since 2006 have been a walk of faith.

The book begins with a testimony of my life before cancer. To understand my cancer experience, it is important to know of things in my life that influenced me. Threads of strength and love weave through my life: a loving and supportive family, friends, education, and church.

This book is documentation of a journey that begins with the discovery of the lump and tells the story as I experienced it, from discovery until the present. My cancer journal, as well as one kept weekly by my friend Carmen, is included. With each procedure or decision I attempted to *tell it like it is* so that someone facing the same procedure would know what to expect. I have included the names of the medications used for chemotherapy and I explain why each is given, as well as the side effects that I experienced with surgery, chemo and radiation. If you don't remember anything else, remember that breast cancer is a marathon, not a sprint! With each step, I have included how I walked in faith *through the valley of the shadow of death without fear. (Psalm23:4).*

Some would call me crazy to say that I have been blessed by breast cancer. I realize this is a strange statement, but even in the depths of the worst effects of the chemotherapy I was at peace with the situation. Because of the cancer, my life is richer! I learned to live *one day at a time*, to enjoy the beauty of mountains, trees, flowers, birds, and all of nature in more detail, to be more thankful for my heritage and to strive to *make a difference* with my life. I am grateful that my experiences may help others who are either facing breast cancer or those who will be their caregivers.

My Story

A small community in rural Cleveland County, North Carolina, at the foothills of the Blue Ridge Mountains is my home. The nearest small town is Lattimore, where I grew up. I am the oldest of four children born to Dietz and Elizabeth Washburn. Our home was rich in love, family, and friends. We had everything we needed and most of what we wanted. My paternal grandmother's example taught us this. Even in her nineties, she would say she had always had everything she wanted but she always knew what to want. Our parents were living examples of a "Spirit-filled" life. I can recall many times finding them studying their Bibles. Daddy was a substitute Sunday School teacher for his men's class and we have his notes from some of his lesson preparations. Our parents took us to church and encouraged us to study the Bible and participate in various activities at the church. As a result of this, I memorized Bible verses and learned words to hymns that comforted me later as I experienced cancer.

One of the things I have missed most about Daddy is hearing him pray. Prayer and Bible study were both very important in our family and in our community. I can remember hearing Grandfather Washburn and Daddy tell this story:

> Daddy's cousin Yulon had a serious sawmill accident in which his hand was almost cut off; it was barely hanging on. His father rushed him to the hospital where the doctors told the family that the hand could not be saved and that it would have to be removed. Preacher Gordon Washburn,

> Yulon's father, told the doctors for them to do their part by reattaching the hand. He called several friends to come to the hospital and pray with him for Yulon during the surgery. Two of his preacher friends, John Suttle and Zeno Wall, joined him and prayed during the hours of surgery for the hand to be successfully reattached. The hand healed and years later Yulon became a skilled surgeon.

The year before I graduated from college I married Larry; this has proven to be one of the best decisions of my life. He has been a loving help-mate for 47 years and four years ago became my dedicated caregiver. We have enjoyed a blessed life, enriched with three sons and their spouses: Kelly and Wendi, Lee and Kim, Jeff and Lea. Our lives have also been blessed with eight grandchildren: Lucy, Jane, Jacob, Kate, Troy, Ella, Joe and Izora.

The Gragg Family
L to R front row: Troy, Joe (in front), Lucy, Izora, Ellen, Larry, Ella, Jane, Jacob and Kate
L to R second row: Lee, Kim, Lea, Jeff, Wendi and Kelly

My plan for a profession was to become a nurse because medicine was an important part of my Washburn family. Two of my uncles were doctors; my mom and two aunts were nurses. I was accepted into a school of nursing in a nearby county, but in the end felt led to attend Gardner-Webb College, now a university near our home. I convinced myself that after I received a bachelor's degree, I could always go to nursing school. My biology professor, Paul Stacy, was a dynamic teacher who inspired me from the very beginning of the course. He taught almost word for word from the text, giving page number and general location on the page but never looking at the book. His enthusiasm for biology was contagious and finding the only example of an amoeba or a cat's cranial nerve in lab would bring a loud "hallelujah" and a wonderful smile from him that made your day if you were the finder. In addition, he taught us so much about life and what is really important. He loved teaching and he loved his students. It was his example that influenced me to change my plan from nursing to teaching.

I graduated with a degree in biology and a minor in chemistry and began a 34 year teaching career in high school sciences. The last 15 years I taught human anatomy and physiology but the last six I "team taught" with Wanda Scruggs, a nurse who was an instructor in Health Occupations. Most of our students were juniors who would then take a senior level of Health Occupations II as seniors. Both Health Occupations I and Human Anatomy and Physiology courses were a system-by-system study of the human body with different emphases. Health Occupations I included many skills needed for nursing, and Human Anatomy and Physiology had more labs. By teaming, we had twice the teaching time, were able to cover more material and labs, had visiting speakers, taught nursing skills, and enjoyed field trips. Our students earned two credits.

At the end of the first semester as seniors, these students were honored with a "pinning" ceremony to honor them as CNAs (certified nursing assistants). In my memory, every student accomplished this goal. This experience spanned some of the best years of my career. We had the cream of the crop in students who wanted to learn and prepare for health-related careers. Wanda and I had been trained in integrated curriculum, and we both learned from each other as well.

During my experience with cancer, this science training enabled me to look realistically at what was happening to me and to have a better understanding of what doctors were explaining to me. My knowledge of the human body gave me insights that many patients would not have.

My professional career was enhanced when I was invited to join an honorary international organization for women educators. The Delta Kappa Gamma Society International became an important part of my life as an educator. I was selected in 1990 by the Society to attend a Leadership and Management Seminar at the University of Texas in Austin with 29 other members. Since that time I have had responsibilities at the international and the state level. These *sisters* in the Society were encouraging and supportive during this entire cancer experience.

In 1990 Larry and I joined the Friendship Force, an international organization based in Atlanta, Georgia, which arranges home hosting exchanges between countries. We have enjoyed many inbound and outbound exchanges. Our experience in Friendship Force has given us the opportunity to visit Argentina, Austria, Australia, Brazil, Costa Rica, Denmark, England, Finland, France, Germany, Japan, The Netherlands, New Zealand, Norway, Panama, Scotland, Sweden, Switzerland, Taiwan, and Wales. This organization has given us the opportunity to make friends all over the world. I am convinced that if I had not had the Japanese exchange I would not have found the cancer until it was much larger and more dangerous. In chapter three I will explain why.

Throughout these years I have striven to live a good life and live up to my profession of faith that I made as a young teenager. Larry and I have taught our children as we were taught by our parents and grandparents. What an awesome responsibility it is to be a parent and grandparent. We are so pleased with our children, their choice of spouses and the wonderful grandchildren. We hope that our lives will be an example to others of the *golden rule* and of how we deal with life's challenges.

You may be ready to begin my cancer journal now, but I hope you will first read the following chapter which is an overview of breast cancer diagnosis and treatment. I have tried to simplify the information so that a lay person could understand the decisions that have to be made. This overview is important, because if you find yourself or a loved one having to make these decisions, you can be an advocate.

Medical Decisions Simplified

Even for a biology teacher with knowledge of many facts concerning the diagnosis and treatment of breast cancer, having to make those decisions was not easy. As a result, I have written this chapter to help others with those decisions.

"Statistics on the prevalence of breast cancer in the United States are alarming. It is estimated that in 2010 there will be more than 207,000 cases of breast cancer in women and about 2,000 cases in men. Breast cancer among women is the most common cancer with the exception of skin cancer. Breast cancer deaths are second only to lung cancer in the USA. Deaths in 2010 from breast cancer are estimated at 39,840 for women and 390 men. Most doctors quote a one in eight diagnosis in women yearly. The good news is that the USA has more than two million survivors. Success in breast cancer treatment depends on finding the cancer early."[1]

The following screening techniques are used to find cancer before any symptoms are noticed: mammogram, self-breast exam or clinical breast exam. Any change in breast tissue such as a lump, dimpling, discharge, irritation of the nipple or breast should be examined by a doctor. There are some women who are considered at high risk due to diagnosis of breast cancer in several family members.

When tests indicate the possibility of cancer a biopsy is performed. A biopsy can determine if the tumor is cancer or not. There are different kinds of biopsies and doctors will choose the best ones for the patient.

1 www.cancer.org/cancertopics/types/breast

Needle biopsies and surgical biopsies are often used. A needle biopsy can aspirate fluid from a cavity or obtain tissue through the long, hollow needle. A surgical biopsy removes tissue and can remove part or the entire tumor.

In order for physicians to evaluate tumors they use a method known as staging which helps them determine the size and possible spread of the tumor. This staging method known as "TNM" provides for a common language among health professionals.

"The TNM staging system is based on the extent of the tumor (T), whether cancer cells have spread to nearby (regional) lymph nodes (N), and whether distant (to other parts of the body) metastasis (M) has occurred. Most tumors are described as stage 0, I, II, III, or stage IV.

"Stage 0 is called *in situ* meaning it is localized and has an excellent cure rate. Stages I-IV are ranked as to the seriousness of the malignancy: the lower the number, the less the cancer has spread; the higher the number the more extensive the disease."[2]

Next, the doctor determines whether the cancer has spread. There are several tests used to determine this. The mammogram and ultrasound may be able to determine if the cancer has spread in the area where the cancer was found. X-rays and bone scans may identify the spread of cancer to chest or bones. "Computed Tomography (CT scan) is used to take pictures inside the body. The CT scan can detect or confirm tumor presence, provide information about the size and location, guide a biopsy, and help plan radiation treatment. The Magnetic Resonance Imaging (MRI) scans use radio waves and a powerful magnet to create detailed pictures of areas inside the body. The Positron Emission tomography (PET scan) uses a small amount of radioactive glucose injected in the vein. Cancer cells often use more glucose than normal cells. These pictures can be used to find these *hot spots* of cancer cells in the body.[3]

Types of treatment depend on the results of many of the previous tests. Treatment may depend on whether the tumor can be treated with surgery or radiation without affecting the rest of the body. If treatment

---

2 www.cancer.gov/cancertopics/factsheet/detection/staging

3 www.cancer.gov/cancer/factsheet/detection/ct

is systemic it is given by mouth or in the bloodstream to travel through the body to find cancer cells.

"Breast cancer is commonly treated by various combinations of surgery, radiation therapy, chemotherapy, and hormone therapy. Prognosis and selection of therapy may be influenced by the following clinical and pathology."[4]

Surgical procedures vary depending on how large the tumor is and where it is located. These factors can determine how much tissue is removed. The mastectomy removes all of the breast tissue and in some cases even surrounding tissues and muscles.

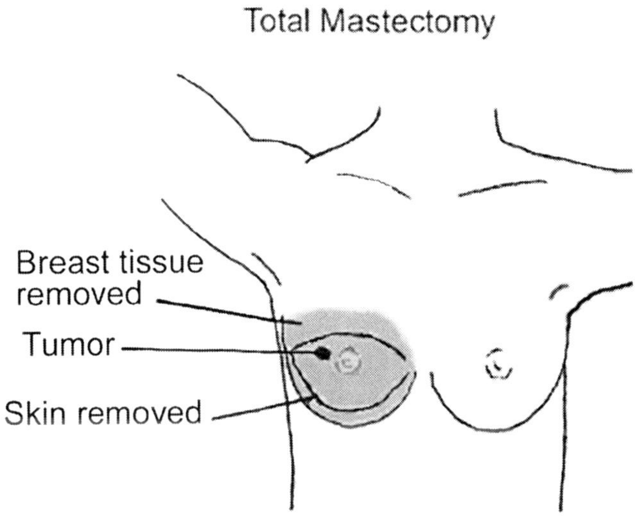

"Adapted and reprinted by the permission of the American Cancer Society, Inc. from www.cancer.org. All rights reserved."

Two methods of breast conservation remove only part of the breast tissue. A lumpectomy removes only the tumor and some normal breast tissue. If there is no clear margin (the clear margin method involves removing tissue until no cancer cells remain) that is free of cancer, then additional tissue would be removed. Radiation or chemotherapy may follow the surgery.

4 www.cancer.gov/cancertopics/pdq/treatment/breast/healthprofessional

Lumpectomy

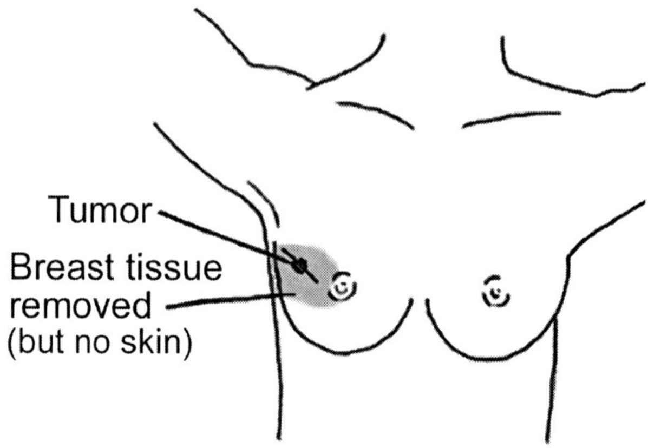

"Adapted and reprinted by the permission of the American Cancer Society, Inc. from www.cancer.org. All rights reserved."

A partial mastectomy removes more of the breast tissue and skin than the lumpectomy. The partial mastectomy may also be called a quadrantectomy. This procedure removes about one fourth of the affected breast. It may be followed by chemotherapy and/or radiation.

Quadrantectomy
or Partial Mastectomy

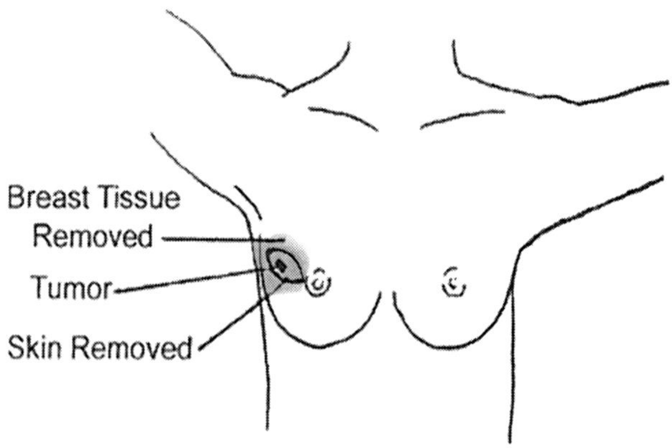

"Adapted and reprinted by the permission of the American Cancer Society, Inc. from www.cancer.org. All rights reserved."

Another surgical option is reconstructive surgery, if the breast is totally removed or if the size difference is noticeable. This reconstruction may be done at the time of the first surgery or sometime afterwards.

"If someone is diagnosed with breast cancer, the next question is usually if it has spread to other parts of the body. The underarm or axillary lymph nodes are removed for examination in the lab. The standard dissection once removed most or all of the axillary nodes. Today, biopsy of the sentinel node and one or two others is examined. A sentinel lymph node is the first lymph node(s) to which cancer cells are likely to spread from the primary tumor. Cancer cells may appear in the sentinel node before spreading to other lymph nodes. Since the sentinel nodes would likely come in contact with cancer cells traveling away from the tumor they are often referred to as guards for the breasts."[5]

The procedure for the biopsy includes being given a blue dye and/or a radioactive substance which will both help to identify the sentinel node. A Geiger counter will identify the radioactive substance and the blue dye can be identified visibly. The nodes are sent to a pathologist for examination to determine if they contain cancer cells.

When several lymph nodes are removed there is a greater chance for the patient to experience lymphedema or swelling in the arm due to fluid retention. Some patients experience numbness or even some pain under the arm. Many patients must wear a sleeve that compresses the arm and helps control the fluid. Exercises to prevent lymphedema may be suggested by the doctor.

---

5 www.cancer.gov/cancertopics/factsheet/therapy/sentinel-node-biopsy

Lymphatic System

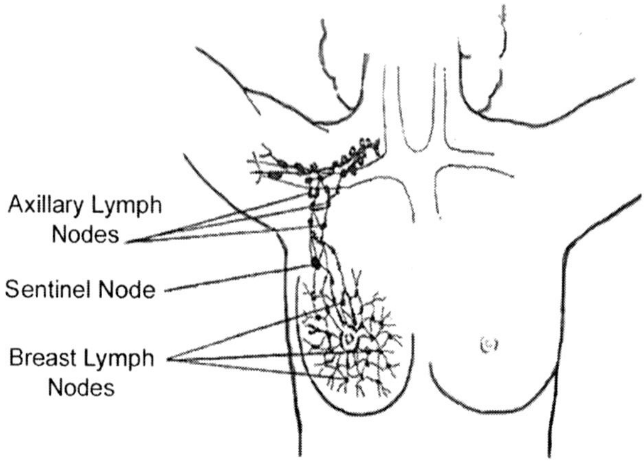

A radiation oncologist will decide which radiation therapy is best for the patient. The external-beam radiation therapy (EBRT) is painless and takes only a short time usually five days weekly for about six weeks.

There may be damage to surrounding tissues with this method. Patients are marked with tattoos to help focus the rays on the exact area determined by the radiation oncologist. I understand that the tattoos can be removed but a friend suggested that they could be *battle honors like medals.*

Tattoos

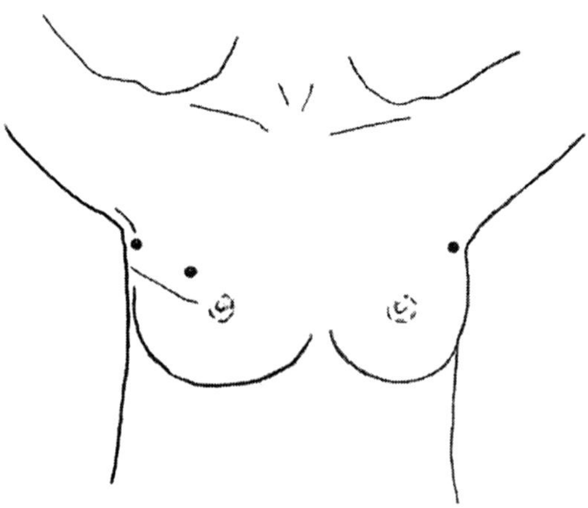

EBRT Radiation Therapy a more common method of radiation is called External Beam. "Dosimetry is the determination of the correct dosage of radiation. A treatment team for the EBRT treatment consists of a:

- radiation oncologist--a doctor who uses radiation to treat cancer
- dosimetrist—a person who determines the proper radiation dose for treatment
- radiation therapist—a health professional who give radiation treatments
- radiation physicist—a person that makes sure that the radiation machine delivers that right amount of radiation to the correct site in the body. The physicist works with the radiation oncologist to choose the treatment schedule and dose that has the best chance of killing the most cancer cells."[6]

A new method of radiation is called Brachytherapy. This new method places a radiation source inside the body near the tumor. An advantage to this method is that one can avoid damaging the surrounding tissues.

The radiation oncologist determines the treatment that is most appropriate and also the area to treat. The physician and the physicist determine the techniques that should be used to deliver the proper dosage. The physicist and dosimetrist make the detailed calculations for the treatment being careful to include quality control before the prescribed treatment is given. The therapist operates the accelerator and administers the treatment.

LINEAR ACCELERATOR

The external beam radiation treatment (EBRT) often uses the linear accelerator for patients with cancer. The accelerator is used to treat the whole body and uses a high-energy x-ray. The linear accelerator "uses electricity to form a stream of fast-moving subatomic particles. This creates high energy radiation that may be used to treat cancer." [7]

---

6 www.cancer.gov/dictionary

7 www.cancer.gov/cancertopics/factsheet/therapy/radiation

A large gantry or arm rotates around the patient as the x-rays are delivered to the patient. To insure safety, thick lead and concrete walls surround the accelerator. The machine is turned on from outside the room.

Safety of this machine is insured by a daily inspection. The accelerator has built in systems for quality control. The physicist makes more detailed checks weekly and monthly.

Today, radiation treatments are very precise and there are no immediate side effects. Most patients tolerate the treatments very well but over time side effects do develop. Most patients develop mild fatigue that builds gradually over the time of therapy. Skin reactions are most common and may have a sunburn-like effect on the skin. Dull aches or sharp shooting pains may occur. In some cases the breast may swell or feel heavy. These side effects may continue for years. Some patients may have a rib break but this is rare. The radiation on the axillary area may cause the extreme swelling of the arm called lymphedema, radiation pneumonia, or heart damage. Years later the patient may develop cancer somewhere else in the body.

CHEMOTHERAPY

The dreaded treatment chemotherapy or simply chemo can be administered in a variety of ways and frequencies depending on the type and stage of the cancer. Some chemotherapy is designed to destroy cancer cells although for some cancers they may only slow the growth. Administration of chemotherapy can be as simple as a cream rubbed on the skin or a drug taken by mouth or by intramuscular or intravenous means.

"Chemotherapy is treatment with drugs that kill cancer. It works by stopping or slowing the growth of cancer cells, which grow and divide quickly. But it can also harm healthy cells that divide quickly, such as those that line your mouth and intestines or cause your hair to grow. Damage to healthy cells may cause side effects. Often, side effects get better or go away after chemotherapy is over." [8]

Chemotherapy for breast cancer is usually given in cycles, and may be given in two or three week cycles for a period of months.

8 www.cancer.gov/cancertopics/coping/chemotherapy-and-you/page2

Chemotherapy has many more side effects than radiation: nausea, vomiting, loss of appetite, low blood counts, hair loss, mouth sores, diarrhea, heart changes, sinus congestion, bleeding, and irritation of the bladder wall, neuropathy, and increased risk of leukemia, fatigue, chemo brain, or feeling tired and unwell.

HORMONE THERAPY

Physicians have a better way to plan treatment for patients when a target therapy is available. Hopefully, the future targeted cancer therapies will become more specific to cancer cells and reduce normal cell damage. "Targeted cancer therapies are drugs or other substances that block the growth and spread of cancer by interfering with specific molecules involved in tumor growth and progression. Because scientists often call these molecules 'molecular targets,' targeted cancer therapies are sometimes called 'molecularly targeted drugs,' 'molecularly targeted therapies,' or other similar names. By focusing on molecular and cellular changes that are specific to cancer, targeted cancer therapies may be more effective than other types of treatment, including chemotherapy and radiotherapy, and less harmful to normal cells."[9]

To reduce the risk of recurring cancer, hormone therapy is used often following surgery. The female hormone, estrogen, promotes the growth of breast cancer so in an estrogen positive cancer patient, attempts are made to reduce the levels of estrogen in the body.

"HER2/neu is a protein involved in normal cell growth. It is found on some types of cancer cells, including breast and ovarian. Cancer cells removed from the body may be tested for the presence of HER2/neu to help decide the best type of treatment."[10] This protein makes cells grow and spread faster.

"A monoclonal antibody that binds to HER2 (human epidermal growth factor receptor 2), and can kill HER2-positive cancer cells. Monoclonal antibodies are made in the laboratory and can locate and bind to substances in the body, including cancer cells. Monoclonal means that it is made for only one substance. Herceptin is used to treat breast cancer that is HER2-positive and has spread after treatment with

9 www.cancer.gov/factsheet/therapy/targeted

10 www.cancer.gov/dictionary

other drugs. It is also used with other anticancer drugs to treat HER2-positive breast cancer after surgery." [11]

Overwhelmed? A quote from Ralph Waldo Emerson says *Knowledge comes by eyes always open and working hands; and there is no knowledge that is not power.* I think knowledge can be powerful! With knowledge you can be a better advocate for your own health or even be better advised to help someone else.

---

11 www.cancer.gov/dictionary

The Land of the Rising Sun, Japan

Our Friendship Force Club had been invited to Japan for two weeks of home hosting. We would have one week in Yamaguchi and one in Oita. I was so excited that our club had been given this opportunity, and I definitely wanted on the list. Larry at first was not interested. As the weeks and months of planning continued, Larry showed more interest in the exchange and the added possibilities of doing some touring prior to the exchanges and the trip to Taiwan following the exchanges. The Floyds, our long-time friends, and Larry and I decided to go a few days early and visit the ancient cities of Nara and Kyoto. Also, following the two weeks of exchanges the four of us would fly to Taiwan. The Floyds had hosted an exchange student from Taiwan some years ago at the school where I taught. Caroline and her parents invited the four of us to visit with them for a week.

We left the United States on May 8, 2006, and arrived after lunch at Kansai Airport, Japan, the next day. The airport rests on a constructed island one and one half miles long. It was reasonably new and very clean. After going through immigration and customs we were met by our driver for a two hour transfer to Kyoto. Surprisingly we had no problem with language since most Japanese speak at least some English.

The next morning our tour began at 8:40 A.M. We visited Ninomaru Palace and the Golden Pavilion. Our lunch break was a buffet with Western selections as well as Japanese. In the afternoon we visited Shinto Shrines and several of the sixteen hundred Buddhist temples.

On May 11, we had the morning free and the afternoon in Nara. During the morning we had to send our two large bags to Yamaguchi with a delivery company that charged us $32 for two bags. Marietta Floyd and I walked to an internet café and sent messages home and then did some shopping. The afternoon in Nara featured viewing the largest Buddha in the world and a shrine that had more than one thousand statues. For dinner we walked to the JR train station where we chose our meal from a visual menu of plastic foods. Back at the hotel after dinner we called our taxi driver to pick us up for our transfer to Osaka, where we would join the other Friendship Force Ambassadors.

The trip from Osaka to Yamaguchi was to be on the famous Bullet-Train. The group of ambassadors met at 8 A.M. to walk to the train station. I wondered if we'd get on the right train. No one knew exactly what to do. We did have our tickets. The 20 of us made our way through a full, moving crowd of Japanese that seemed to know where they were going. As for our group, I wasn't sure we'd get to the correct track because the station was like a maze. Our train was Number 3, Car 13, and seats were in Rows 15-18, and was due to leave at 8:59 A.M. We had been told that the train stopped only a few minutes so we had to get in position quickly. The different trains whizzed by like large puffs of wind. I realized why we had sent our luggage ahead when our train arrived and we rushed on. The train was full of people and we barely had room for our carry-on bags. The train arrived a few minutes before 8:59 but left on time. The speed of this train was 180 miles per hour. The ride was smooth but so fast that you really couldn't enjoy the countryside for specific details.

Our hosts for the first week of exchange were waiting on the platform when we arrived. All the hosts were holding signs with the ambassadors' names on them. Dr. and Mrs. Shinya Kawai were our hosts. Shinya, an orthopedic surgeon, at this time was in charge of the Medical School of Yamaguchi. Ikuko Kawai, a retired pharmacist, ran up to me and gave me a big hug. She said she had seen Larry first. I had told her that he would be the tallest man in the group. We both had shared photographs before the exchange so we knew what each other looked like. The Kawai family had spent three years in Chicago, Illinois, many years ago when Dr. Kawai was studying there. They spoke great English; it was OUR Southern Style English that they had trouble understanding. Our week in their home was wonderful. Larry and I both slept on thick futons in an upstairs bedroom. They were comfortable, and most nights we were so tired from the day's activities that we could have happily slept on concrete.

One of the highlights of this week was a visit to Hiroshima and hearing stories from some of our hosts who had family or friends still suffering from the exposure to radiation or were themselves still suffering these effects. The city now is modern and has only one partial building left from the bombing. The museum was interesting and informative but too real for most of us. We spent time in a public school, which was especially interesting to me as a teacher. Students in Japan all wear uniforms, which was a big change from students who I had taught. One day we learned how to make Japanese characters and fold paper to make Origami animals. As always with exchanges, departing makes for sad good-byes, because by this time you are dear friends.

Dr. and Mrs. Shinya Kawai

On May 19 the group boarded a bus for a day's ride to Oita, Japan, further to the east than Yamaguchi. Oita and the surrounding towns and villages have many hot springs that encourage tourism. Our hosts there were Mr. and Mrs. Joshihiko Goto, a young couple with four daughters all in school. The girls range in ages from 15 to 6 years. Taki was oldest, Azu was 13, Kayo 7, and Saho was the youngest. This family lived in a small village called Naori a 30 minute drive away from Taketa, which had a train station that Taki rode to school each day. Naori had one of the most famous of the hot springs. Mr. Goto was the director of the municipal hot springs facility, and Mrs. Goto was a nurse and taught health in the local middle school.

The father spoke some English, the mother understood some English and the girls were all studying English in school. We used hand signals and Japanese/English dictionaries for much of our communication. The Kawai family had provided us with silverware and chopsticks but not the Gotos. Mrs. Goto "gently" insisted that we use chopsticks. They had bought a set for us to use and then take home with us. The girls got great pleasure out of seeing us struggle with the chopsticks. Rice was growing in paddies all around us, and we actually had a very narrow road into the house. Mr. Goto's father and mother lived close to them and we spent one day with them, watching as they planted rice.

The two Japanese families were similar but different. The Kawai family had married after an arranged marriage. Ikuko spoke with me about the match-maker that suggested that the two of them marry. She said she could have refused but was pleased with the matching. They seemed very happy and compatible. On the other hand, Joshi and Chie were much younger. Chie, with Joshi's help, told me that they made their decision to marry without a matchmaker. They didn't have the usual roles that I had seen in the Kawai family. Both helped with cooking and housework and entered the same door and walked beside each other. Both couples were happy and very gracious to us.

The Goto Family
L to R first row: Kayo, Saho
L to R second row: Ellen, Larry, Azu, Chie and Joshi

This week had been much different from our initial exchange in Japan. Living with a working family with children enabled us to see how young families in Japan share similar scheduling problems with American parents. Taki had to get up at 5 A.M. in order to be driven into another village for a train ride to Oita to her high school. This school provided the opportunity to be in a marching band. Azu rode her bike to the local middle school, and the younger girls walked through the rice fields to their neighborhood school. Mrs. Goto drove to another village to her school and Mr. Goto went to his local hot springs director's position.

Larry and I were given an opportunity to visit the springs. Most of the local patrons went to the segregated public pools, but we chose a western private room with a hot bath. Bathers must follow a procedure. First you shower and bathe with soap, and then you enter the pool. The water is always 108-110 degrees F. Larry braved the water first and then I began my entry into the hot water very slowly. If you moved it seemed hotter. The whole process was to last about 50 minutes. After several minutes I had been able to sink to mid-chest but I was not a happy camper. This water was really hot! My hair began to drip with perspiration and I lasted about 15 minutes before I told Larry I had to get out. For two or three hours I was the color of beets from chest down. I will have to admit, however, that my arthritic hands and knees felt better for a day or so. Our beds here were actually wooden slatted beds with the slats about two inches apart. We had thin futons or cushions to put on top of the beds. My body seemed to slide into every crack along that bed, and I was miserable. During the week I was turning often so as to relieve the parts of me that pushed through the cracks. On the night of May 23, when I turned from my right side to my left, I slung my left arm over my chest and hit a "tender spot." I sat up and discovered a lump in my right breast. To make sure that I was really feeling something, I asked Larry to feel it too. He confirmed my findings. Normal self-breast exams would never have found it as it was almost under my arm. Try sleeping after finding something like this!

Larry and I both prayed that it was not cancer; but, if it were, that I would be okay. Knowing that there was nothing that I could do until I returned home, I tried to just enjoy the days left in Japan and Taiwan. We were not due home until the 31st. so we just kept this new finding to ourselves. With two days left in Oita, I tried to keep my mind off the lump. From the very beginning of the discovery, I was at peace with it, whatever it turned out to be. This peace came from my faith and the promises in the following scriptures:

John 14:27 (New Living Translation)

"I am leaving you with a gift—peace of mind and heart. And the peace I give is a gift the world cannot give. So don't be troubled or afraid.

Isaiah 41:10 (New King James Version)

"Fear not, for I am with you; Be not dismayed, for I am your God. I will strengthen you, Yes, I will help you, I will uphold you with My righteous right hand."

Doctors, Tests and Surgery

We arrived home about midnight on May 31. I had a physical scheduled on June 7 so I didn't think I could see a doctor any sooner. Dr. Chamberlain examined my right breast and didn't find the lump. I had not told him that I had found one because it was almost under my arm, and I wondered if a doctor would ever have found it. The doctor did examine it after I turned on my left side and showed him where it was. Dr. Chamberlain's office set me up for a mammogram and ultrasound in two weeks on May 22, which was the first appointment available. In my opinion this was too long to wait because my mind played tricks on me during those uncertain times. I have since shared this concern with my doctor.

The mammogram didn't show the radiologist the lump. When the technician came back to me, I suggested that I show her where the growth was. She actually made an "X" on the spot. In order to get a successful mammogram, a more specific means of targeting the tumor was used. It was not pleasant, but at least it was soon over. This time the tumor was visible. I then had an ultrasound, and the radiologist answered my question when I asked if the growth was solid or liquid. I had hoped it was liquid. Since it was solid, it confirmed in my mind that this was indeed cancer.

Dr. Chamberlain had asked me to call him after the visit to Shelby Radiology. While in the parking lot of Shelby Radiology I called and left a message on his answering machine at the office. Before I drove even three miles he had returned my call. His question then hit me like a *truckload of concrete blocks.* "Who is your surgeon?" A surgeon? I didn't have a surgeon. He suggested several, and I chose Dr. Douglas Hobson about whom I had heard good things. The appointment was scheduled for two weeks later, but when my daughter-in-law Wendi heard of the plan, everything changed. She knew the Hobson's personally, so with a word from her, I saw the doctor sooner. Dr. Hobson examined the lump and proceeded to do a needle biopsy in his office--BAD NEWS! PAIN! This test was inconclusive when the report came a week later. I was scheduled as an outpatient for a biopsy to remove the mass as an outpatient on July 12th.

The biopsy was scheduled for one o'clock. About noon I left Larry in the outpatient unit and was taken upstairs to the surgery department's holding stall to wait for surgery. This room had several curtained areas where patients waited until they were taken into surgery. I was the only one at the time in this cold room. One of the surgical nurses came to me as soon as I arrived and told me that Dr. Hobson was running about an hour late. She asked if I wanted to return to the outpatient department or stay in the surgical waiting. I told her that I'd rather stay where I was and wait. The nurse started an IV and covered me with several warm blankets. The nurse who was taking care of me asked if I wanted the anesthetist to give me something to calm my nerves; I said no. I really wasn't nervous. She asked me several times, so I decided to close my eyes to reassure her that I was okay. In order to concentrate on being calm, I began to repeat the 23rd Psalm silently. It is one of my favorites. If my mind wandered from the Psalm, then I'd pray. The time passed, and I was rolled into surgery. In late afternoon, I was released from the hospital to go home.

On Sunday following the biopsy, we had a visiting speaker at morning worship, Dr. Alice Cullinan, a former professor at Gardner-Webb University. Her scripture for the morning was the Twenty-Third Psalm. I immediately knew the Lord had sent her that day to reassure me. She shared her notes with me the next week and sent me a copy of the book *A Shepherd Looks At Psalm 23* by Phillip Keller. She had referenced this book in her sermon. I will never forget the "*3 P*'s" that she mentioned: His (1) presence, (2) provision and (3) protection. I was reminded that my Good Shepherd knows my every need, He provides both protection and provisions, and He is always with me. Dr. Hobson called in a few days to give me the results of the biopsy. It showed cancer. The surgery had removed the cancer but additional surgery would be necessary to remove a wider margin. Some of the axillary lymph nodes would also need to be examined. Dr. Hobson seemed surprised at my reaction when hearing that the tumor was cancer, but it was no surprise to me. My only question was "What's next?" He said that the second surgery should not be scheduled for two weeks, so we made an appointment for July 27. I wanted to talk with several knowledgeable family members before making a decision as to what type of surgery I would have. Uncle Gene, Daddy's youngest brother, is a retired physician and he helped me interpret the report from the biopsy. I called two cousins, Linda and Ann, both of whom had had breast cancer but had made different decisions as to how to treat it. Linda chose a lumpectomy and Ann a mastectomy. Neither of them had had chemotherapy. They shared with me what stage their cancers had been. Ann said she just wanted the breast removed. She did not have any follow up radiation treatment. Linda chose a lumpectomy and then had radiation. Linda was able to tell me about the lymph node removal and helped explain what I was to expect. She also chose to take the five year pill regimen to prevent estrogen production.

With the surgery scheduled in two weeks and with my surgeon's permission, I decided to fly to San Diego, California, the site for the biannual convention of The Delta Kappa Gamma Society International. Plans were already in place for the trip. This international organization is for key women educators, and I was serving North Carolina as parliamentarian at the time. My roommates, Emily Weigel, Carmen Redding, and Betty Marshall encouraged me to go. Prior to the convention, Betty had knitted a prayer shawl for me. The knitting group at her church had passed the shawl through each member's hands and a prayer was said for me. Betty's Presbyterian Church altar had held the shawl as their pastor blessed it. The North Carolina delegation in San Diego passed the shawl among them--without my knowledge--and each prayed a blessing for me as well. My roommates presented the shawl to me in our room as I was resting one afternoon. It was so beautiful and soft. I couldn't hold back the tears brought on by this wonderful expression of love and support. Betty and I had heard about this ministry from Katherine Collins. I had bought the book Knitting into the Mystery and dreamed about starting a group in our church but had not been successful in starting one at that time. Judy Carlson arrived late to the convention but had heard about the shawl. She asked if she could hold the shawl and pray for me at the same time. This, too, was very special.

During the week in San Diego, Carmen, our state president, suggested that she call my home every week for a report on my progress and that she would then write a summary and send an email to the North Carolina leadership. This would allow everyone to hear of my progress but not everyone would need to call. It was a wonderful idea. What she didn't say was that she was going to be keeping her own weekly journal, which I didn't learn about until ten months later.

The second surgery didn't start very well. I arrived by 8 A.M. for a 12:30 P.M. surgery time only to find that I had not been scheduled in the radiology department. This was imperative in order to have the radioactive substance injected into my breast to help identify the sentinel lymph node. I was given a choice of canceling the surgery or having the surgery after lunch. I did not want to delay the surgery. This meant that the hospital had to send someone to Charlotte to pick up the medicine. Now the surgery would be at 2 P.M.

About noon the radiation department came for me. I was taken to the *torture chamber* for seven injections to be given into the right breast with the seventh one given directly into the scar of the biopsy. There was no medicine to ease the pain. The radioactive substance was a salt called technetium, which was tagged with sulfur collide, so the injections burned after the medicine was administered. This drug targets lymph nodes. Following the seventh injection the technician massaged that breast for several minutes to ease the discomfort and before long the burning stopped. The radiologist told me that surgery could not begin for two hours--that would be 2:30 P.M. This was to give the salts time to travel to the lymph nodes. A Geiger counter would be used to identify the node/nodes that were the brightest, indicating the ones that were first to receive the radioactive substance.

The sentinel node is the node that should have cancer cells if any had escaped the tumor area, since it is the first node for drainage. In addition to the injections of the radioactive substance, after I was in the operating room I was injected with a blue dye in the breast. This would be a second test to identify the sentinel node. I had agreed to the removal of two nodes. Often more than two are removed and no cancer is found. The patient then is more apt to suffer from lymphedema. My thought was that if more needed to be removed, that it could be done later.

My sister, Dianne, had driven me to the hospital and stayed with me until one o'clock at which time I was taken back to the *holding stall.* Larry had stayed home for the morning hours to check on things at the farm. I knew that I was going to be waiting more than anything else. The radioactive substance was completed at 12:30 P.M. so I kept thinking "No surgery until 2:30 P. M." Larry had arrived and was waiting with Dianne when I returned from the radiology department. At 1:30 P.M. a nurse came in and said "We're about ready for you." I told her that the radiologist did not complete the injections until 12:30 P.M. and that I was told that surgery couldn't begin until 2:30 P.M. She said "I'll check on that, honey!" When she came back she said they'd wait a little longer. I often wonder if the results of the lymph node dissection would have been different had the surgery taken place earlier than 2:30 P.M. We are all our own best advocates!

During the surgery frozen sections of the two lymph nodes were examined and the initial exams were clear of cancer. What a relief! Dianne held my prayer shawl during surgery. Larry and Dianne were joined by many family and friends as they waited for the surgery to be completed. Susie, my brother's wife, stayed with me that night. She got no rest because I couldn't get up to the bathroom without her help. My legs were wrapped with a massage wrap that I couldn't take off myself. My allergies to sticky adhesives had been noted and the surgical unit had used a non-allergic tape for my bandages. The skin under the tape began to itch and from previous experience I knew what was happening. By morning the skin had blistered. Dr. Mike, my primary care doctor, came by to check on me and confirmed that the skin under the tape had blistered. Soon Dr. Hobson came and removed the tape. He said that I could go home later in the day but I was warned not to raise my right arm above my shoulder. The way I felt at that time, I didn't know if I would ever want to raise it. I had two drainage tubes and would have to be careful with the suction device until it could be removed.

From this point until after radiation, Carmen and I will both be telling the story.

On August 3, Carmen wrote in her weekly journal:

> *I spoke with Ellen on the phone today. She conversed in a strong voice and seemed to be in good spirits. Indeed, the great love and care extended to Ellen and her family appear to be a wonderful medicine! Neighbors and her Sunday School class have prepared meals for the family and the beautiful prayer shawl envelops her with love and solace. The surgeon removed the drainage tubes which were inserted ten to twelve inches deep within her body. Ouch!! He also told her to stay away from the computer except for an occasional flick of the keys so that the arm would not overwork the incision site.*

I had a surprise call from Dr. Hobson in a few days. I'd been waiting for the other shoe to fall, so to speak. The more sophisticated tests on the lymph nodes showed 8/10 of one millimeter of disease in the sentinel node. He told me that I needed to see an oncologist soon to decide if more lymph nodes needed to be removed. I really wasn't shocked at the news; somehow I expected it.

On August 9 Larry and I visited with Dr. Warden Woodard, a Charlotte oncologist. He had been my mother's doctor for several years before her death with a blood disorder. When he came in the exam room, he said he knew me from somewhere. I reminded him that I had brought Mother to his office several times and that her name was Elizabeth Washburn. He said, "Yes, she had polycythemia, didn't she?" The answer was yes. What a good memory he has.

Dr. Woodard and Kim

Shared Decision Making

Name: ______________________________ (Breast Cancer)
Age: 64 General Health: Good

Estrogen Receptor Status: Positive Histologic Grade: 2
Tumor Size: 1.1 – 2.0 cm Nodes Involved: 1 – 3
Chemotherapy Regimen: Third Generation Regimen

Decision: No Additional Therapy

55 out of 100 women are alive and without cancer in 10 years.
35 out of 100 women relapse.
10 out of 100 women die of other causes.

Decision: Hormonal Therapy

17 out of 100 women are alive and without cancer because of therapy.

Decision: Chemotherapy

13 out of 100 women are alive and without cancer because of therapy.

Decision: Combined Therapy

24 out of 100 women are alive and without cancer because of therapy.

Dr. Woodard spent a couple of hours with us explaining the diagnostic reports, treatment options and percentages of cure with different treatments. He saw no need to remove any more nodes since his suggested treatment would be the same if one to three nodes were cancerous. Chemotherapy and radiation were his recommendations in either two or three week cycles. A decision was made to do the eight treatments in three week intervals. Since we already had plans with Friendship Force to go to Iowa and Oklahoma in September, we decided to start the cycles in October. Dr. Woodard told us that there was a window of three months from first diagnosis during which to decide when to begin treatment. That time would be close if we waited. On the way home Larry said that he was not really satisfied with my waiting and that the exchanges to Iowa and Oklahoma could wait. The next morning I called Dr. Woodard's office and was set up to begin the chemo Tuesday, August 22. With this schedule I would complete my chemotherapy before Christmas.

On August 10 Carmen wrote in her weekly journal:

This morning I had a long conversation with Ellen as she recounted the events that have transpired in her life since our talk last week. She related the experience as being like having one shoe fall and then waiting for the other to drop. Friday evening her doctor called to tell her that the last lab report revealed eight tenths of a millimeter of "something funny" in one of the lymph nodes. Such a discovery propelled a series of actions.

Yesterday Ellen and Larry met with Dr. Woodard in Charlotte. He was thorough in his responses to their questions, and he carefully explained the options lying before her. Both Ellen and Larry are grateful for the wonderful rapport they have with this physician and they place their trust and confidence in him. She will have sixteen weeks of treatment with chemo every two weeks.

To help with nausea, she will take a special $125 pill the day of the procedure, and one for the next two days. Twenty four hours following chemo, she must go to Cleveland Regional Hospital for an injection of Neulasta to help build her white blood cells. The second week of the cycle she will go to the hospital where she will have her blood checked to see if she can continue with the treatment the next week. The doctor feels this represents a ninety percent success rate for patients like Ellen. Indeed, this is heartening news.

I am happy to report that Ellen seems to be in good spirits. She is grateful for the many acts of kindness bestowed upon her and her family--her neighbors, church members, and her DKG friends have meant so much to her at this time.

Before my first chemotherapy treatment I had to have two additional tests. The first was an echocardiogram to see if my heart had any damage and second a PET scan to see if there were any hot spots or cancer in other parts of my body. The echocardiogram, administered at Cleveland Regional, involved an ultrasound and a substance being injected into my veins. This test did not show any problems. I left the hospital and went straight to Dr. Hobson's office for a final exam before chemotherapy. The technician at the hospital had about driven me crazy. Every other sentence was "honey, sweetie or darling" this or that. When I arrived at Dr. Hobson's office the nurse asked me if I was okay. I told her that the echocardiogram technician had rung my bell once too often and I was just tired. She asked me what my favorite soft drink was and soon had me a cold Sundrop to soothe my weariness. I call her my Sundrop nurse now.

On August 18 Carmen wrote in her weekly journal:

This morning Ellen answered the phone in a strong, cheerful voice. She was preparing for the PET scan in Charlotte today. She said that the incision was healing nicely and that gradually the area is less sore than just after surgery. Her doctor assured her that she would be able to move her arm with greater ease as time passed. Yea!! The two of us joked about our body scars and how these unique markings would be able to identify us if we were ever kidnapped.

Ellen reported that her family was very attentive to her. She lovingly referred to her sister, Terry, as her hovercraft since she spent most every day with her.

The PET scan was administered at Carolinas Medical Center in Charlotte. We arrived 45 minutes early because the traffic had been unusually light that day. I checked in at the reception desk. Reading upside down on the pages that the receptionist had in front of her, I read Elizabeth Watkins Gragg with a Mooresville address and a March birthday. The name Elizabeth Ellen is my legal name but not Watkins. The birth month was correct but not the address or telephone number. I told the lady that the information was not all correct. She said I'd have to see my doctor and have him resubmit the order. Upon hearing this, I immediately went into stress mode because the schedule was set for chemo. When I asked the receptionist for her help in calling Dr. Woodard's office, she said, "Find a telephone book; the phone is over there," pointing across the room. Finally, another lady behind the desk handed me a directory and offered me a phone at the desk. I explained the situation to Sharon in Dr. Woodard's office and she said she would fax a correct copy. I told her that I had already been told that my time slot was nearing and that I might have to reschedule. Lessons were learned on this day! One was to take important telephone numbers with you because you never know when you may need them. A second lesson was that you are your own best advocate. I was thankful for the second lady at the receptionist's desk and for Sharon's attention to time constraints.

Finally, the fax arrived and I was called back into the radiology department. I put on the hospital gown and had an injection. Some time needed to pass before going into the PET scan machine. I really had no idea what to expect, but that was a good thing! Once inside the room for the test I was asked to lie down on a narrow portion of the machine. My head was placed in what reminded me of a vise. I couldn't move my head, and my ears were also covered inside this device. A sheet had been placed across where I was lying. My arms were put by my sides and the sheet pulled around me from both sides like a mummy. The technician reassured me that she would be checking on me but that the test would last for 29 minutes. During the 29 minutes the "bed" rolled in and out of a circular tunnel open at both ends. Sometimes my head was completely on one side of the tunnel and my legs on the other. When my head was in the tunnel there was a tiny light, but the space was minimal and I could not see out either end. It didn't take too long for me to know that I would have to occupy my thoughts or lose my composure. Silently, I began quoting scriptures. The 23rd Psalm, one of my favorite passages, was the first. It was like a programmed recording of verses and so amazing to me that one came to mind right after another. I am so thankful that my rearing had included Bible study and scripture memorization. I have fond memories of both my parents studying their Bibles. Their Christian example is a most cherished memory. After a time, I thought of the words of hymns. All of this time, my body was on stop and go through this machine. This test completed--no hot spots. Thank you, Lord! This was another blessing for me.

Chemotherapy next and I'm ready for the challenge.

First Cancer Treatment August 22, 2006

Tuesday, August 22, 2006, arrived and I took my expensive anti-nausea pill before leaving for Charlotte. I was thankful that Larry was with me for this first treatment of chemotherapy. We stopped at Bojangles in Shelby for coffee and a country ham biscuit. I wasn't sure what to expect, although my sweet nurse, Kim, had tried to answer all my questions and had given me materials to read.

My name had been on our church prayer list for some time, and I knew of many others who were praying for me that day. I too, had prayed that I would feel the Lord's presence with me and that the procedures would go well.

I had decided not to go back to surgery to have a port placed in my upper chest so that I wouldn't have to be stuck every time that I went to have treatment. With only eight treatments, I chose the extra sticks. When someone has a port, it often gets infected, so I didn't want to take that chance.

Sharon, the receptionist, greeted me upon my arrival for the ten o'clock appointment and Adrienne took me to the lab for blood work, blood pressure and weight checks. With these tests completed, I was taken to Dr. Woodard's office. He asked if I had any questions and told me that the PET scan and echocardiogram were normal. Dr. Woodard had told me earlier that he thought I'd do well with the treatment. Larry asked how he could know that. He told us that from the beginning that I had had a positive attitude and that that was the key to success. I had not asked "Why me?" "Why not me?" if one out of eight females will have breast cancer. Examination over, he reassured me that he would be checking on me during the morning, and indeed he did.

Kim escorted Larry and me to the infusion room. This room had two walls of large windows with ten recliner chairs in front of them. Curtains made the individual areas private when needed. Each of the areas was equipped with a TV/DVD/radio. The command center was across another wall where doctors and nurses were buzzing about. The top half of this area was walled with glass so the personnel could monitor patients. Beside each recliner was an extra chair for visitors who came with patients. There was a warmer for blankets so that if you got cold, they provided you with a blanket. Kim told us that juice, soft drinks, and snacks were also available.

Kim asked me to choose my spot, and I chose a chair that was the last one of the ten across from the entrance. There was a wall on that side with a bathroom a few steps away. I sat down and Kim began to look at my left hand for a good vein. Since my surgery I had been told not to allow blood pressure checks or any pricks or sticks in my right arm. There is no conclusive information on this theory but the idea is to keep the arm on the surgery side pristine. Kim asked if I had already had my anti-nausea pill, Emend, and I answered yes. She told me that if I did okay with this first treatment, I'd do okay with all of them. This was reassuring.

With the needle in place, I was ready to begin. A saline solution was now dripping slowly into my veins. About fifteen minutes later Kim pushed an injection called Aloxi to prevent nausea. It is a drug that helps prevent nausea for several days following chemotherapy. Kim explained to me that pushing the medicine meant that it was not allowed to drip into my veins but was put directly into the tubing near the needle entrance. This way I would get the benefit of it more quickly. For the next few minutest a steroid to prevent allergies, called Decadron, took the place of the saline. A saline flush was performed after each change in medication. When Kim returned to my station she was wearing rubber gloves that reached almost to her elbows and carried three large syringes of bright red liquid. It was Doxorubicin or Adriamycin, the first of the chemo drugs I was to receive. I later learned this one was known as the Red Devil. Kim sat down beside me and told me that it was very important that I inform her if I felt any pain or discomfort during the infusion of this drug. Kim explained that she would be with me throughout the infusion because if any of this drug got outside the vein I would have to have surgery to remove it. She said that this medication had to be given in a time period of not less than fifteen minutes. She would press the plunger slowly to put the red substance into my veins and then pull back on it to check to see if she saw blood in the syringe. If so, she knew that the needle was still in the vein. As for me during this time, I felt no different than before. After the Red Devil was infused, I asked Kim to help me to the bathroom. She showed me how to unplug one of the machines and carefully push the stand holding the saline. It surely didn't take long for the Red Devil to show up in urine, but that's normal. Side effects that I had been told to expect with this drug were a decrease in white and red blood cells and platelets, hair loss, mouth sores, nail changes, discolored urine and severe sunburn if exposed. Back in place, Kim waited a few minutes before starting the next type of chemo. This one was called Cyclophosphamide or Cytoxin and it would take much longer to infuse. Kim brought me a cold Sprite and a package of crackers. So far, I felt okay. The infusion room was cold. I had not asked for a blanket today because I had my prayer shawl with me; it was so warm and it covered me from top to bottom. I could feel the prayer support from family and friends when I held it. I had my Sudoku book with me and I tried to work on one of the problems. As the time passed, my concentration was being affected. Kim had thought that I'd take a nap because many patients do, but I hadn't. Dr. Woodard came in several times to check on me and chuckled when I told him I couldn't think through my Sudoku problem. I think Kim and Dr. Woodard were surprised that I could work on the Sudoku problem at all. Treatment One complete, Kim removed the IV and reminded me to call if I had any problems. Another reminder from Kim was that I might begin to lose my hair before I returned for the second treatment. Side effects for these chemotherapy drugs are a decrease in white and red blood cells and platelets, mouth sores, decreased appetite, taste changes, hair loss or thinning, bladder infections and nasal congestion.

Larry helped me up and I definitely felt different now. My whole insides felt quivery, and my head did not feel normal either. At home

I headed for the recliner and put my feet up. My instructions had been to eat cool things and nothing heavy or spicy for that day. As the day passed, my headache got worse. I was not nauseated but just felt sick. Several folks telephoned or dropped by to see how I was. I don't remember much about who came or called; I really felt like I was somewhere else looking in.

By morning, the headache was terrible and even my eyes were sore. We called Kim and asked what to do. She suggested Tylenol but nothing helped for long. After lunch Larry drove me to Cleveland Regional Hospital for my six units of Pegfilgrastim (Neulasta) injection. The effect of Neulasta can be bone pain, particularly in the pelvis. The good thing about it is that it is a white blood cell booster. I had to wait until 24 hours had passed after the end of chemo to have it. If the injection did build my white blood cell count then I could keep on schedule with my treatments. Much to my delight, two of my former students worked in the outpatient department. It was good to know that I had played a part in their nursing careers, by teaching them high school biology and human anatomy and physiology.

As the week progressed, the headaches eased some. I felt weak and shaky when I was up for any length of time and continued to have a sick feeling without any emesis (vomiting). By the weekend, my pelvis ached most of the time. During the night I had to turn often because lying on either hip made the pain worse. Tylenol helped some with the pain. By the time for the next treatment, the hip bones were much better.

On Monday, August 28 Carmen wrote in her journal:

Good news! Ellen's PET scan showed no spread of cancer and the echocardiogram revealed that her heart could withstand the chemo.

On August22, she had her first chemo treatment in the infusion room of the suite in Dr. Woodard's office. The treatment included anti-nausea medicine, anti-allergy medicine and then the first and second chemotherapy drugs. Throughout the process, Dr. Woodard walked into the infusion room and asked how she was feeling and whether she needed anything. This personal attention was comforting and reassuring to Ellen.

The only difficulty she has experienced from the chemo is a tremendous headache. Our patient reported that her appetite is okay, and thus far, the nausea is in check. Dr. Woodard has encouraged her to eat a cold food every couple of hours. Jell-O, popsicles, and small yogurts are her food choices that are soothing to her body.

Ellen remains optimistic and in good spirits. May she keep this positive attitude throughout her treatment! She expressed again how much she has appreciated the cards and notes sent to her from family, friends, DKG sisters and even strangers.

The second week of the first cycle of chemotherapy was much better than the week of treatment. The headaches occurred only occasionally and pain was minimal or absent. By the end of this week, my only complaint was a sore mouth and uneasy stomach. It hurt to eat or drink with these blister-like sores. Our friends, Patsy and Doug, said that an old time remedy for stomach problems was blackberry wine. Patsy boiled blackberries from her freezer to make juice for me to drink and Doug brought some blackberry wine. I tried both and I think it did help. By Monday, the mouth was still a problem. I called Kim again, and she called in a mouth wash that was a lifesaver. The medicine was pink and thick and seemed to coat every sore spot in my digestive track. The pharmacists who took care of my prescriptions were Tonya and Tina; both are my friends but Tina is another of my students. What a blessing to have these wonderful friends to help in my journey to health.

On Wednesday I drove myself to the hospital for the blood test to see if my white blood count was high enough for treatment the following Tuesday. During the week my diet had been bland foods, no spicy or fried food and no uncooked fruits or vegetables. I was okay with these foods, since I wasn't really hungry much of the time. Libby, a breast cancer survivor and long time friend, had brought me ginger snaps and ginger ale. She said these things had helped her with the sick feeling that she had and that I'd had now for two weeks. She was right!

For this two week cycle I had been at home most of the time except to go to the hospital for injections and blood work. Terry, my sister, was with me every day to help Larry care for me, answer the telephone, and tend to the household things. If I thought of anything I'd like to eat, she made it for me. She was able to answer the phone and give the repeated reports of my progress so that Larry could check on the farm.

On Friday September 1 Carmen wrote in her journal:

With Ellen's second week of this first cycle, she reports that she is doing all right. Her tremendous headache has subsided and her eyes do not hurt as much. Her main symptoms now are stomach rumblings and some mouth sores. When friends of Ellen heard of her stomach problems, they suggested blackberry wine. Ellen chuckled and replied that she just might try some!

On Monday Dr. Woodard had prescribed a creamy mouth wash to give her some relief from the sores. He also told Ellen that he was going to research further her chemo medicine, so that she does not experience such a headache again after the treatment. Ellen hopes that he doesn't tinker with the anti-nausea medicine because that component has been successful so far!

The "science teacher Ellen" gave me a mini-science lesson on the purpose of chemotherapy. The chemo is designed to attack cancer cells, the fastest dividing cells in the body. Naturally occurring, fast dividing cells live in the lining of the digestive tract such as the mouth and stomach. The chemo was attacking these "good cells" too.

Her diet for this week is the same as last week, but now bland foods and cooked fruits and veggies have been suggested

In our conversation the two of us extolled the joys of teaching and seeing former students mature into responsible, productive adults. This past week Ellen, our patient and former science teacher, conversed with her young pharmacist and a staff member of the hospital lab, both former students. The two of us agreed that it is endearing to be attended by our former charges. As we talked, I asked Ellen what she had learned thus far. Quickly, she replied, "Live one day at a time." Now, that is wise advice for all of us to heed! Isn't it easy for us to become entangled in our mistakes of yesterday and stymied by the uncertainties of tomorrow?

As I reflect on this first cycle of chemotherapy, I am humbled by the actions of others. The medical staffs in Charlotte and Shelby have been wonderful. They treated me professionally but with kindness and encouragement. There had been no need to plan or prepare a dinner meal. Our Sunday school class, family and friends had provided every dinner during this time. Some brought cool salads and desserts to give me some variety with my cool foods diet. Special too were the friends who stopped by and said a prayer with me or told me that they were praying every day for my recovery. I know the "Great Physician" as my Lord and Savior and for those petitions on my behalf, I am grateful. Our mailbox has had cards in it every day since my surgery. It is amazing to be remembered this way. I am truly blessed!

Second Cancer Treatment September 5, 2006

My sister, Terry, was my driver and companion for "Round 2" of chemotherapy on September 5th. We started the day as Larry and I had on August 22--coffee, a ham biscuit, and a $125 anti-nausea pill.

Dr. Woodard wanted to know how the two weeks had been for me. He was aware of the headaches and was going to make some adjustments today with the infusions. For the most part, he was pleased with my report.

My nurse Kim started the IV and the saline solution. Dr. Woodard had asked her to allow the cytoxin a longer period of time to infuse. This was an attempt to prevent the headaches. The same procedures were used as the first treatment--saline, anti-nausea (Anzemet was used today to see if the Aloxi had caused the headaches), saline, Decadron, saline, Adriamycin, saline, Cytoxin and saline. As Kim worked with me, she asked about my hair and if I had noticed any hair coming out. I had noticed more strands of hair on my pillow and on the back of blouses or sweaters than usual but nothing too noticeable.

Terry had brought a book to read, and I had my Sudoku book. We talked some and read or worked. She had brought a light jacket, and I had the warmth of my prayer shawl given to me by my DKG sisters. Kim provided morning snacks for both of us.

After the second treatment was complete, we were ready to drive home. The quivery-inside feeling was back and I just felt strange. When I drank my Sprite that morning, I had noticed a metallic taste, but Kim assured me that this too was normal. No more of my favorite soft drink,

Sundrop, because I didn't want to mess up my taste for it later. When I got home I headed for the recliner. I just felt so tired and shaky.

On Wednesday after lunch I went to Cleveland Regional for my Neulasta. It had worked well two weeks before and I wanted to be able to continue the treatments on schedule. My white count on Tuesday was so high that Dr. Woodard told me that I could have raw fruits and vegetables through the coming weekend. I couldn't wait to have a crisp, crunchy, green salad rather than the soft, bland diet I had had. I was reminded that it would be safer to have the salad at home rather than in restaurant since salad bars are more apt to have bacteria. I experienced the same hip bone pain that weekend following the Neulasta. I would wake up during the night with the pain and turned often to try to ease it. Tylenol and Advil helped some.

On Friday, September 8 Carmen wrote in her journal:

In our phone conversation on Thursday Ellen said, "one-fourth cup chemo done." Translated this means that our dear Ellen has completed two of the eight chemotherapy treatments. The increase in her white count this week was so significant that she can eat raw fruits and vegetables for a few days.

As Ellen's story unfolds, we are learning that a patient may have some good days, followed by some fair ones. On Wednesday she felt good most of the day. That afternoon her two year old grandson Joe was visiting Larry and Ellen. When her winsome grandson asked his grandmommie to rock him to sleep, she was able to comply with Larry's help to lift him into her lap. Now that makes a good day! It should be noted that Larry picks up little Joe at the daycare center and brings him to the Gragg household. When I called on Thursday, Larry was taking little Joe for a ride on the tractor. What a gift each is to the other!

In the Thursday conversation, Ellen remarked that she did not feel as well as she had on Wednesday. While she was gratified that she did not have a headache, she felt quite weak. In her words, she was just spending the day "laying around." The previous night she had awakened around 2 A.M. feeling nauseous. To counteract this symptom she took half of an anti-nausea pill and ate a Jell-o cup. Unfortunately, the lack of estrogen makes hot flashes worse and impedes Ellen's sleep patterns.

As I reflected upon my conversation with Ellen, I was reminded once again of the simple gifts offered us each day....

- *savoring a crisp garden salad or a rosy peach, sweet and juicy*
- *tenderly embracing a loved one*
- *opening a get well card with a cheery note penned into it*
- *rocking to sleep a grandchild with innocence and trust spread across his face*

So, Ellen, with an assortment of your favorite raw fruits and veggies to savor, we SALUTE YOU! EAT YOUR FILL OF THESE RAW PLANT DELIGHTS TILL SATURDAY! Then, the limp, cooked veggies and fruits!

Ellen and grandson Joe

When I brushed my hair later in the day I could see hair, too much hair, in the brush. The next morning when I even touched my hair, a clump would come out in my hand. I called Jan, my dear friend and hair stylist, who had told me to call when I needed to have it shaved. She said to be in her shop at noon. No other customers would be there then. Larry took me and I took one of the scarf hair coverings that I had bought. Jan turned me away from the mirror and began to clip first so that I could take a sample with me. It reminded me of saving a lock of each of our sons' first hair cuts. She continued by shaving my head and then she shampooed and conditioned my scalp. She asked me if I wanted to see myself or should she just put the scarf on my head. I told her that I wanted to see myself so she turned my chair around. At first my eyes saw my deceased Dad and in another flash, my brother Beaman, but not me for a time. It was a very strange experience. At this moment bald was not beautiful to me! As time passed I accepted the look and understood that it would grow back. I called my brother and told him my experience. He later came over to see me. He agreed after I pulled the scarf off that we did have the same shaped head. We both laughed.

I bought two different wigs, and a friend, Barbara, helped me style them. They made me feel hot and with the hot flashes I was having so often, I could not wear the wigs. My friend, Libby, brought me the hats she had worn when her hair was gone. Emily, my DKG sister, sent me three reversible cotton eyelet hats in green, blue and black. They became my dress-up hats. I had to wear a crocheted hat to bed because my head got cold at night. One of my favorite hats was a pink John Deere bill hat. At first I wore a pink scarf inside the hat.

One of my journal entries that week read: "This last week has been better, but I continue to be very tired and weak. I have to be careful of strong smells and overtiring, because this can cause nausea quickly. It can hit like a flash! Ice chips and lying still seem to help the most."

On September 15 Carmen wrote in her journal:

Bald is beautiful!!! Clumps of hair filled Ellen's brush as she brushed her locks. Then, as Ellen touched her hair, handfuls fell away. Quickly, hair was everywhere except on Ellen's head.

Larry accompanied Ellen to her 12:15 appointment with her hairdresser. Due to lunch hour, only the beautician, Ellen and Larry were in the salon. Here, her hairdresser buzzed Ellen's hair, washed her scalp and gently rubbed conditioner on it to keep it moist. When she was turned to face the mirror, Ellen saw her image, but only she had quickly seen her father's face and the face of her brother. An experience such as this stirs one's emotions. For such a moment it was reassuring to have Larry by her side.

Earlier Emily had sent three cotton hats in different colors. On an outing to the grocery store Ellen donned the blue hat and jauntily turned up the brim!

For her Tuesday eye appointment, our bald-is-beautiful patient wore her wig. While the wig is a little lighter brown than her natural hair, Ellen is basically satisfied with its appearance--that is, as far as wigs go! We laughingly remarked that at least a wig gives that perfectly coiffed look!

Such is the tale of Ellen's necessary loss--the result of her chemo treatment.

When I spoke with Ellen on Thursday afternoon, she was sipping tea and nibbling some gingersnaps. Did you know that ginger soothes the stomach? Ellen reported that she was having a good week as compared to earlier ones. She recalled after her first treatment how she had experienced a huge headache, water retention, mouth eruptions, stomach pains, diarrhea, and mental confusion. This week she has been feeling okay. She did admit that in a flash she could begin to feel nauseous. Stoic Ellen reported that she usually can hold this condition at bay if she lies flat, crunches on some ice, and remains still and quiet.

Her wonderful Dr. Woodard has tried to make adjustments in her medications/treatment in order to minimize the ill effects. Changing her second chemo from forty-five minutes to one hour and fifteen minutes seems to have removed her terrible headache. Thank goodness for this improvement!!!

This illness has reminded Ellen often of the goodness of people. She is always touched and comforted when she learns that her name has been placed in a prayer group. In our conversation she continued by saying, "Usually there is something for dinner here each evening, whether it is a full family dinner, part of a meal, or two served plates." *Ellen added that her Sunday School class had been especially helpful in this area. Recently the generosity of a neighbor touched her heart. This kind soul brought sixteen quart bags of shelled field peas ready for the Gragg freezer! On some cold, blustery days of winter these peas will make a satisfying dish for supper! Of course, the sweet notes and bright cards always add cheer and encouragement to her day. Ellen paused and questioned,* "How do people make it without the support of others?" *Her oncologist remains wonderfully attentive. Recently dear Ellen gave him a bag of North Carolina apples. This thoughtful doctor immediately penned her a note to thank her for the fruit and to tell her he was sorry that her first weeks of treatment had been trying. He stated he was working to ease the negative effects of the chemotherapy. How comforting it has been for Ellen to be under the care of this caring, competent physician!*

As we ended our conversation, Ellen stressed that I share with our DKG sisters her thanks for their support. Indeed, it is our pleasure to love, comfort, and honor our friend... How fitting is this old Irish proverb, "It is in the shelter of each other that people live."

Third Cancer Treatment September 19, 2006

For the third chemotherapy treatment on Tuesday, September 19, 2006, my friend, Betty, went with me. We began this day as we had the first two chemotherapy days-- coffee, a ham biscuit and a $125 pill. The procedure for treatment always began with a visit to the lab for blood work and then an exam by Dr. Woodard. This perceptive doctor could tell that I was really tired and had no energy. My hemoglobin was down some, but I told him that I was trying to eat a beef filet or two every week. He was pleased with the white blood cell count. He did warn me that if I had to go to the emergency room to tell them that I was on Neulasta or they'd think I had leukemia. The Neulasta was doing exactly what it was supposed to do. My white cell count had been very high with every injection, so I was to skip Neulasta this next week.

After the exam, Kim took me to the infusion room. I don't know if I was a little dehydrated or not but for the first time, Kim had trouble finding a suitable vein. After three sticks, she called Billie to come and help with the IV. Billie got the vein the first time. I think Kim just got nervous when she had to stick me more than once. The medicines were given in the normal order and time restraints. This week I was again given the Aloxi for nausea as I had been during the first treatment. Nothing ever hurt, but the shaky feeling is a memory that I won't ever forget. It was almost like an out-of-body experience.

The first treatment was especially bad with the terrible headache, but thankfully, this had not happened again. My brain seemed to go on *pause* during that first cycle, as well as during the second week of treatment. I couldn't remember things as usual. I've read that this could be identified as *chemo brain.* A friend of mine who was a year ahead of me with breast cancer treatment said that she still suffered from *chemo brain.* Her oncologist told her that it may never be any better.

Larry was going to check on some new tires at a local business, and he asked if I'd like to get out of the house for a ride. I was almost stir crazy from being inside, so much that I decided to go. Arlin, one of my former students, came over and asked how I was. It is such a special feeling to be remembered by a former student. He told me that his Sunday School class was praying for me, and that my name was on his church's prayer list. I asked him the name of his Sunday School teacher and was happy to learn that it was Kim McNeilly Creswell, a former student teacher of mine. Kim is a cancer survivor herself. People never know how far their influence will travel.

As the week progressed I felt worse. I had a cough and just had no energy. I had a sick feeling I couldn't seem to shake.

Monday, September 25 Carmen wrote in her journal:

Ellen's eyes popped as she read her Shelby hospital statement recently. There in print it read...one Neulasta injection... $16,000.00! This miracle medication, designed to build white blood count, is given the day after each of Ellen's chemo treatments.

She reports that during the few days after chemo her body insides felt all quivery. She has been tired and sleepy more, and has a dry cough.

Recently, Ellen received a different but priceless medication in the form of kind, loving words. While she and Larry were at a local tire establishment, Arlin, a former student, put down his tools and walked to the car where Ellen was seated. "How are you, Mrs. Gragg?" he asked. He continued by telling his former science teacher that his church prayer group and his Sunday School class were praying for her. It should be noted that Arlin's church is located in a rather remote corner of Cleveland County, some distance from Ellen's home! How touching it is to have students grow up and become responsible adults and offer loving words to a former teacher!

As I ponder our friend's progress, the words endurance and persistence enter my mind. Her journey is an arduous one. Let us continue to support our wonderful friend as she walks with her faith into the unknown.

The second week of this cycle got worse with each day. For the first time during treatment I had nausea, emesis and diarrhea. This had been the worse week yet and my no-energy level sank even lower. Larry called Dr. Woodard's office and explained what was going on with me. New medications were called in to the drug store. The doctor suspected an intestinal infection. The gastro-intestinal tract responded well to the new medicines.

Sunday, October 1 Carmen wrote in her journal:

On Friday I telephoned Ellen in the morning, the late afternoon, and in the evening. Each time I called there was only the answering machine message with Ellen's cheery voice identifying the Gragg residence. I thought to myself, well, Ellen might be feeling well enough to be on a day's outing with Larry. My inner voice said otherwise. I sensed something was wrong.

When I called again Saturday afternoon, Larry, Ellen's steadfast and loving mate, quickly confided that our Ellen was having a rough time with nausea. He told me that new medicines were ordered to try and alleviate her incapacitating symptoms. May Ellen improve in order that she can undergo her fourth and last Red Devil treatment. I urged Larry to get our dear friend to wear her prayer shawl. He quickly responded that she always takes it with her for her treatments.

Ellen's wonderful oncologist encouraged our dear Ellen by stating that the last four chemotherapy treatments should be somewhat easier for her than the earlier ones. The only down side of the treatment is that it will take three hours to infuse her body with the chemicals! With this information Ellen can at last see the light at the end of the chemotherapy tunnel!

Special quotes for reflection:

"I've learned that no matter what happens, or how bad it seems today, life does go on and it will be better tomorrow." Maya Angelou

"Friendship is like two clocks keeping time!" Author unknown

"Piecin' a quilt's like livin' a life... The Lord sends us the pieces, but we cut'em out and put'em together... to suit ourselves, and there's a heap more in the cuttin' out and the sewin' than there is in the calico..."

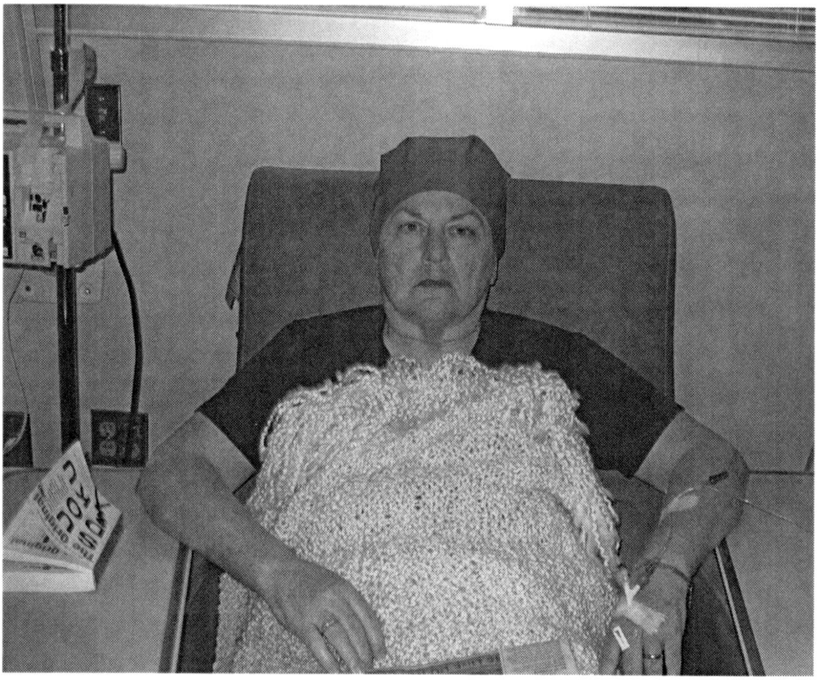

Ellen during an infusion, note the Prayer Shawl.

Fourth Cancer Treatment
October 3, 2006

Dr. Woodard could see that I was weak and not my usual perky self. He is so perceptive. He walked over to me, put his hand on my shoulder and told me, "We're going to work this out!" I appreciate so much that none of my doctors talked down to me *and* recognized that I did have a few brain cells working. One of my pet peeves with doctors has always been that they talk to most people as if the patient's lights are on, the door is open, but nobody's at home. I could not have chosen more competent, caring and perceptive physicians. Dr. Woodard and his entire staff have become part of my extended family.

Kim called on Rick, another nurse in the unit, to start the IV. I tried to encourage Kim to do it so that she could overcome this fear of hurting me if she couldn't find a suitable vein. She shook her head no. Once the IV was in place then Kim took over. The usual infusion procedures were followed. When the last drop of that Red Devil was in the vein, I wanted to jump up and down and scream. With this day's infusion complete I was half way with the chemotherapy treatments. I had the usual shaky feeling, and my head again felt like there was a band of drums playing for a time.

Although I didn't need it during the last cycle, the next day I went to the hospital for the Neulasta injection. The pelvic pain followed the injection in three to four days.

Dr. Woodard had told me that the next four treatments should not cause the nausea that I had experienced during those first four. I would continue to take the regular nausea medication and also be given additional nausea medication during infusion process. He wanted me to know about the last four treatments. The drug for these treatments is Paclitaxel or Taxol. The side effects are similar and yet different in ways from the first two drugs. White blood cells, red blood cells, and platelets might all decrease. Also, allergic-like reactions, numbness and/or tingling in fingers or toes, muscle aches, bone pain, mouth sores, hair loss and diarrhea are possibilities, plus many more. Taxol would be given over approximately three hours to try and prevent allergic reactions. Taxol is more likely to cause allergic reactions than the others that I had had. An extra anti-allergy medication was given. I did recognize it; it was Benadryl. The three hours of Taxol would, of course, follow all the preliminary infusions.

This was the best week of treatment so far. Just knowing that I was half through was encouraging. I was tired and weak but did feel some better than other weeks. The nauseous feeling that I'd had before was not so noticeable.

On Tuesday, October 10 Carmen wrote in her journal:

> *"Like night and day . . . feels like you're rolling downhill" . . . "can see the light at the end of the tunnel"... such were Ellen's words as she described her response to the fourth treatment, the halfway mark of her chemotherapy! In a strong and cheerful voice our patient related that she has experienced thus far no pain or discomfort with the fourth infusion. Indeed, Ellen recounted that she was grateful for her high white blood cell count and good hemoglobin reading of 12.6. She believes that her good genes and her positive attitude* have *helped her progress through these first four treatments*
>
> *Dr. Woodard had told her that with the next four treatments that she would feel muscle pain, particularly in her legs. During these weeks she most likely would lose her eye lashes and eye brows. And she might experience neuropathy or tingling in the soles of her feet or fingers. She will be encouraged to eat chipped ice throughout the infusion of Taxol. For some patients this ice prevents neuropathy or at least makes the symptoms milder.*
>
> *I asked Ellen what she had learned thus far. She quickly responded,* "You have to be your own advocate!" *Simply put, she stated that*

a patient should be alert, ask questions, and keep up with his or her progress.

South Mountain Tours owner, Donnie Ivester, had asked me to make the plans for a long weekend bus trip to Lancaster, Pennsylvania. Larry and I have taken several groups from our church to this area in the last few years to see the *Sight and Sound Theater* performances. Since this trip had already been planned and reservations made, I wanted to go. Dr. Woodard approved the trip if I thought I felt like it. Usually, the last weekend of a cycle is my best weekend. Everything about the trip went well, but I took advantage of every opportunity to rest.

Several years earlier I had met Rachel, an Amish-Mennonite lady, and so I arranged for her to join our group and tell us about the Amish customs, beliefs, and traditions. As the bus drove over the rolling farmland, Rachel was answering questions and explaining their weddings, dating customs and the reason that most of the houses looked as if they had "add-on" houses. The houses add-on when there is a marriage in the family so that the new couple will have their own home. As the families age, they change their part of the house to suit their needs at the time. Rachel invited the group to her Aunt Lena's for lunch. The food was delicious and Aunt Lena shared two of her pie recipes with me.

As Rachel, a breast cancer survivor herself, shared stories of her family, I was reminded of my own family. Both of us had loving parents who taught us by example, and we both enjoyed the support and encouragement of extended family. Our families, friends, neighbors and church supported each of us during our treatment journey.

Reflections:

"The way I see it, if you want the rainbow, you gotta put up with the rain."
Dolly Parton

"The best and most beautiful things in the world cannot be seen or even touched. They must be felt with the heart.
Helen Keller

Fifth Cancer Treatment
October 18, 2006

This treatment began as had the others. I had my blood drawn and then a visit with Dr. Woodard. He told me that my red blood cells and platelets were within the normal range but that the white blood cells were borderline; however, he felt that it was safe to have the fifth treatment.

Today a new preliminary drug would be given in addition to the usual ones. When Billie had the IV in place and the saline solution dripping, Kim was ready to begin the other drugs. I had taken the anti-nausea pill at home, so now I was given Aloxi, Benadryl, Decadron, and Tagamet before receiving the new chemotherapy drug, Taxol. At 11:15 A.M. the 350ml Taxol drug was begun for a three hour treatment. During this infusion, Kim asked often if I had any unusual sensations such as heart palpitations, difficulty in breathing, or feeling anxious. Such sensations could indicate an allergic reaction to the Taxol medication. I had already been told by Dr. Woodard that Taxol was a drug that was more apt to cause allergic reactions and Kim was very careful to check on me often. I asked Kim if I would get the same preliminary drugs that I had been given with the first four treatments. She told me yes, but that I would also have one additional drug, Tagament, to help prevent allergic problems. She brought me a cup of crushed ice and asked that I eat the ice during the Taxol infusion. It was believed that the ice would help to prevent some of the unusual sensations. Dr. Woodard explained that in several days I would likely feel hip, leg and muscle pains and perhaps even cramping. He advised me that Tylenol would probably relieve these discomforts.

The next day I received my Neulasta late in the afternoon. The Taxol treatment lengthens the day several hours and 24 hours must pass before the injection of Neulasta. Due to the low white count on the 18th, Dr. Woodard asked me to stay in and limit my contacts until the white count was back to normal.

On October 26 Carmen wrote in her journal:

Back safe and sound in Shelby, Ellen rested and awaited her fifth chemo treatment. She said the regimen of preliminary drugs had changed some with an additional drug given to help prevent any allergic reactions.

Throughout the three hour infusion of Taxol, our patient munched chipped ice and dined on peanut butter snack crackers. I could not help but ask Ellen what she did when she needed to go to the bathroom! She quickly and calmly replied, "I just roll the chemo stand with me." *Whee!!*

The day after her treatment on the 18th, Ellen reported that she was feeling okay. She did say that with Taxol she could lose her eyebrows and eyelashes within 18 days. Dr. Woodard did order that she be quarantined at home.

As the two of us talked, Ellen reflected a moment and replied that she was grateful to Larry who is always there for her. The three sons and their families check in often but with children, work and school they stay busy. Her sister, Terry, comes to see her almost every day. Her sister, Dianne, cares for a little grandson and is not able to come as often. Her brother's wife, Susie, often sends two plates for dinner which really has been a wonderful blessing too! She continued by saying that she views this experience as a journey. It has given her a better way to look at life. She admitted that she has always tried to live right, but that with this experience her priorities have changed. She is learning to live more fully in the moment than in the past. Now she seems keenly aware of the world... the blue sky... the earth. Yes, she said she is living fully one day at a time.

As we engaged more deeply in conversation, Ellen revealed that this event has increased her faith and has given her a sense of peace about it. Indeed, she said, I'm grateful for God's mercy. I believe that there is a master plan. I don't know what God has in store for me but at some point I hope to work with other breast cancer patients. *She admitted that the illness sort of clipped her wings. At times it was stressful to the mind, causing uncertainty, with the thought of cancer growing--and getting it out of her body.*

Ellen and I ended our free ranging talk with her saying these words, Five out of eight! I've three more treatments to go! This is a journey…. I'm going to beat this!! *"Oh, what a trooper you are, Ellen!!"*

On Wednesday, October 25, 2006, I was chilled all day. I had wrapped up in blankets to try and keep warm. That night Larry got the thermometer and had me take my temperature. The thermometer registered 102 degrees. I had been warned to go to an emergency room if my temperature went above 101.5 degrees. Larry called the oncologist's office and was told to either bring me to the emergency room at Charlotte or Shelby as soon as possible. I had no symptoms other than the fever. The tests proved that I had a UTI (urinary tract infection). Dr. Paul Munoz took care of me. I was grateful to have someone whom I knew; he attends our church. After being checked out I was able to go home with some powerful antibiotics.

The second week of this cycle was different from the first four treatments. The terrible sick feeling was gone so far. I began to notice leg aches and joint pain particularly in my thighs, knees, shins and ankles. I had some leg cramps too. Tylenol did help, but didn't take away the discomfort. I was happy that some of the other possibilities hadn't affected me yet.

Saturday, October 28 Carmen wrote in her journal:

When I called Ellen on Thursday afternoon, she answered the telephone with a strong voice. Our patient stated that she "had felt compelled to stay put." Wise Ellen heeded Dr. Woodard's orders to be housebound this past week. Actually, our star patient admitted to taking two little outings…. On Sunday afternoon Larry took her for a ride to view the fall foliage. With Shelby in the shadow of the majestic North Carolina Mountains, the brilliantly colored leaves were especially beautiful! Then on Thursday morning, October 26, a faithful Ellen visited briefly with her Aunt Emily. There she paid her respects to her deceased, ninety-four year old uncle, a former physician. This uncle was a brother to Ellen's father. Today few remain of this large brood. Ellen and I remarked as the two of us talked how sad it was to see our beloved aunts and uncles die, one by one . . . Our losses-- They just seem to accelerate with age

"As for me, I never thought of myself as being close to death during my treatment, *Ellen said.*"

As we continued to talk, Ellen described her response to the new chemo medicine. She reported that she has experienced some aching in her knees and legs. She is alternating Tylenol and Advil to try to relieve the pain.

Larry sensed that Ellen had a fever since she had been wrapped up all day. He was concerned when the thermometer was at 102 degrees since Dr. Woodard's cautionary words were to call his office if her temperature reached 101.5 degrees. A trip to the emergency room proved that she had a urinary tract infection. The hospital drew seven vials of blood and administered a chest x-ray in addition to a urinalysis. The physician prescribed an antibiotic and dismissed her.

For a moment the two of us paused to marvel at medical technology. Thursday morning Ellen's X-rays, lab results, doctor notes, and diagnosis had been encoded in the Carolina Health Care computer system so that Dr. Woodard's staff had all of Ellen's medical information from the previous night.

Ellen's determination, positive attitude, and strong faith, coupled with her superb medical care, enables her to make this demanding journey. The unswerving love of her family and friends remains also an important part of her recovery.

"Faith is the substance of things hoped for, the evidence of things not seen."
Hebrews 11:1 King James Version

Sixth Cancer Treatment October 31, 2006

My sister, Terry, accompanied me on this Halloween Day. My first stop was in the lab for the usual blood tests and then on to Dr. Woodard's office. It was good to be able to give him a good report from the past weeks. I was feeling much better except for the leg and muscle pains. I had not had any numbness in the soles of my feet or tingling in my fingers or toes; however, I remained tired and out of breath if I walked up stairs too quickly.

The infusion room was next, with the usual regimen of anti-nausea pill and Aloxi, three anti-allergy drugs, saline solution, and Taxol. The patient next to me, Frieda, happened to be a former college friend of mine. As we talked, she shared with me that she had had a recurrence of breast cancer. Her second breast cancer was in the other breast and she was told that it was not related to the first one. Most breast cancer survivors always wonder if that could happen to them. She had been allergic to Taxol and still had some of the neuropathy that I had heard about. I was sorry to hear that she had not had the support of a church or neighbors that I have had. I decided that I could pray for her and also send cards to encourage her.

We were mid-afternoon getting home, but after a good rest I hoped to feel like going to "Trunk or Treat" at church that night. Several years ago our members had decided that house-to-house trick or treating was dangerous. Members now volunteer to decorate the trunks of their cars and themselves. They park in a semi-circle in the church parking lot. The neighborhood children are fed dinner and then are able to visit each "trunk" for a treat. This was my first fun excursion in two months and it proved to be much more enjoyable than doctors' offices and needles. We didn't stay long but just enough to see most of our grandchildren dressed in Halloween costumes.

Thursday, November 2 Carmen wrote in her journal:

As I talked with Ellen on Wednesday afternoon, a day after her sixth chemo treatment, she replied, "I feel good today. I've completed three fourths of my treatments and I'm beginning to see the light at the end of the tunnel. It's getting brighter and soon I'll see the full light at the end of the tunnel." *Ellen happily reported that as of yet she had not experienced tingling in her fingers or toes. She admitted that she is weak and only does non-strenuous activities such as watching television, solving Sudoku puzzles, reading books and magazines, working some on the computer, and keeping up with her medical bills*

As we talked, I learned that Ellen enjoys taking little treats to Dr. Woodard's staff each time she goes there for a treatment. For Halloween, she had fun decorating treat bags and filling each with treats. YUM!!! She usually brings a plate of brownies or North Carolina Mountain apples. Our Ellen knows how to put a little magic in the day for others!

Reflections:

"Love comforteth like sunshine after a rain." William Shakespeare

The second week of the sixth treatment I had to shift roles. Our youngest son, Jeff, had suffered with a heart arrhythmia problem called Wolf, Parkinson, White Syndrome (WPW) since his senior year in high school. Medication had been keeping the situation in check, but in recent months he had begun to experience some problems. As a building contractor, he was often on rafters or in other dangerous situations and did not need to feel faint. The surgical procedure to correct this defect had improved greatly in the 18 years since his diagnosis, and now laser surgery was available. The latest procedure suggested for him was a freezing method. The advantage of this was that if the wrong area were frozen, it could be quickly unfrozen. I wanted to be with him for this procedure on Monday, November 6. The freezing procedure would not work because the area needing the repair was very close to a valve, and the blood was warming the area that they attempted to freeze. The surgeons decided that the laser procedure would be safe so the laser ablation procedure was then used successfully. His electrocardiogram registered normal after this procedure. How grateful we were for this blessing!

The next day, I had my blood checked. For the first time, my hemoglobin had dropped significantly. Today it was 10.7 mm/hg. When I started chemo my hemoglobin was 16 mm/hg. If my hemoglobin were not up to 11 by the next Tuesday, then I could not have the seventh treatment as scheduled. There was a possibility of a red blood cell booster, but I hoped that it would improve on its own.

Wednesday, November 8, 2006, Carmen wrote in her journal:

"It was a miracle," *replied Ellen as she described the procedure performed on her youngest son on the 6th of November. His doctor commented that on the average he performs only two ablations a year to correct this syndrome in patients like Jeff whose extra pathway is in this location. This past week in the Gragg household Jeff's miracle dominated the scene.*

Prior to the medical procedure on the 6th, our stoic Ellen admitted that she had experienced lots of aching on Thursday, Friday, Saturday, and Sunday. To help alleviate the pain in her knees, ankles, and leg and thigh muscles, our patient has been alternating Tylenol and Advil. The hip and joint discomfort from the Neulasta is also helped by these drugs.

On Thursday the two of us had another conversation. I wanted to know more about her church and family, the anchoring forces in her life. During this conversation Ellen provided me with some background information about her wonderful place of worship, Double Springs Baptist Church. In 1844 this church was founded and served as the home church of her paternal grandparents and parents. The two springs which flow through the property inspired the naming of this historic Cleveland County place.

As Ellen and I conversed further, I probed deeper; I urged, "Tell me how you have created and maintained such close family ties". Ellen attributed the family's closeness to the values her grandparents and parents placed upon the church, their love of family, and the importance of supporting one another. Ellen chuckled softly and remarked that it was understood that if she or her siblings stayed up late on Saturday night, they were nevertheless expected to be up and dressed for church Sunday morning!

Ellen's paternal grandparents, the Washburns, reared eleven sons and daughters. "The Washburns were church going people," *added Ellen. When the Washburn siblings grew to adulthood and had families of their own, it was not unusual to have as many as seventy-five at the Washburn home for a meal! Of course, with this number, the family could not have a sit down meal at the table, but no one seemed to mind eating from their laps.*

Ellen paused for a moment and then related a lovely tradition created by Grandfather Washburn. At Christmas, he presented each grandchild with a silver dollar. Later on when he was unable to obtain silver dollars, he gave each grandchild a paper dollar. In a somewhat wistful voice Ellen said that she probably still has twenty of those silver dollars. This beloved grandfather lived to the age of 92! All of the deceased Washburn siblings lived to be eighty or more with two living to 94 and 91.

Her maternal grandparents, the Martins, lived in the small town of Blacksburg in South Carolina, where Ellen's family drove to spend a weekend with her mother's parents about once a month. Ellen fondly recalled how her Grandmother Martin loved entertaining family and friends at parties and showers. After such events this grandparent liked nothing better than sitting around and reliving the occasion. Ellen believes that Grandmother inspired her love of entertaining. In the Martin household her grandmother believed in seating guests for meals even if there had to be several seatings! As a child Ellen remembers that she waited until the third seating to be served! Ellen remarked that this practice taught her self-discipline that proved useful during cancer recovery.

Yes, Ellen has many happy memories for gathering with grandparents, aunts, uncles, and cousins as the family came together to celebrate holidays and special events. Always, Ellen felt the love and the support of these endearing kinfolk.

Seventh Cancer Treatment November 14, 2006

My friend, Betty, was with me. I was concerned about the low hemoglobin the week before and hoped that it was up to at least 11.0 so that I could have the treatment. My blood was drawn and then I was taken to see Dr. Woodard. When he came in to see me he had good news. The hemoglobin today was 12.3 mg/hg. Great! This seventh treatment was now possible. We talked about my treatments thus far and made plans for me to meet Dr. Helen Maddux in mid-December. She is an oncologist/radiologist who will oversee the administration of the radiation in Shelby. Dr. Woodard was pleased with my progress and said that we'd celebrate on the 28th with the final treatment.

The infusions were given as usual and I had no noticeable side effects. I nibbled on the ice chips again. The leg muscles and joints ache, but I tried not to complain about it. Once I was up and walking the pain subsided. I have been so thankful that I have not had any tingling or numbness in my feet and hands. I realized that I had been blessed to be free at least for now from these terrible side effects.

Sunday, November 19 Carmen wrote in her journal:

Our Ellen was in good spirits when I spoke with her on Thursday afternoon, two days after her seventh treatment. She replied, "I'm feeling pretty good; I'm just tired. It seems the steroids they gave me on Tuesday got me wired so I didn't sleep well on Tuesday night. When I closed my eyes, it was like I was watching movies." *All said and done, however, Ellen declared that these two weeks had been the best weeks of her chemotherapy.*

Ellen reported that she had had a lengthy conversation with Dr. Woodard as they reviewed her case. This oncologist stated that he was pleased with the steps they had taken to tackle Ellen's cancer. In mid-December this wonderful physician will contact a radiologist who will discuss the radiation treatments.

For several weeks I had had a cough. Larry insisted that I call Dr. Woodard's office. He said he could prescribe medication but would prefer to see me. Terry agreed to take me. After a chest x-ray he diagnosed me with bronchitis and sinusitis. Several prescriptions later we were on our way home. The medicine helped and before long I was feeling good again.

The second week of this cycle included Thanksgiving Day. My siblings and their families along with our family have our celebration on the Sunday following Thanksgiving. For the last 8-10 years this meal had been in our home. All the families bring their favorite dishes and we have a bountiful table. If everyone is present, we have forty-five. The question this Thanksgiving was whether I would feel like having everyone here for the day. My sisters and sister-in-law said that they would take over my usual responsibilities if I would just take it easy. We all agreed and the meal was scheduled.

There were several things that I wanted to do for Thanksgiving, so I said that I would cook the turkey, bake pumpkin pies and make the cranberry salad. These were things that I could do over several days and this would prevent me from being too tired.

Our family has always been supportive of members having difficulties of any kind; however, we try to continue our lives with whatever would be the next thing to be done. This doesn't mean that we don't pray and talk about the situations, but we don't focus on the difficulty. For Thanksgiving that year my family insisted on my greeting the family from my recliner. Thanksgiving Day for this family was good!

As the 28th of November approached I was thankful that the ordeal of chemotherapy was about over. I felt blessed that I had withstood the treatments as well as I had.

Friday, November 24 Carmen wrote in her journal:

Can you guess what our Ellen was doing when I called her Thanksgiving afternoon? She was in the kitchen where she was removing four savory pumpkin pies from a hot oven. Our friend confessed, "I do a little each day; then, I'll be ready for Sunday." *Thanksgiving 2006 will be an especially blessed event for the members of this close, loving family!*

As Ellen and I continued our conversation, the two of us remarked that Tuesday, November 28, was her last chemo treatment . . . eight infusions and sixteen weeks of chemicals coursing through her body. I exclaimed, "Just think, you are through the worst of it!" We both marveled at this thought.

Ellen then commented that it was sort of amazing that after three Taxol infusions, she had not experienced any tingling or burning sensations in her fingers or toes. She added that Dr. Woodard had told her that many patients experienced such sensations after the first Taxol treatment. Ellen believes her good fortune is due to the many prayers said for her. Ellen said that it would take a month for all the Taxol to leave her body. Gradually, she then will regain her strength. It should be noted that Larry will accompany Ellen on Tuesday for her last treatment just as he did for her first treatment. Larry would have gone with me to every treatment but my sister and several friends had volunteered to take me. I especially wanted him there for the first one since neither of us really knew what to expect or how I would feel afterwards. The celebration following the 8th treatment was special and he didn't want to miss the celebration.

Ellen's parting comment to me was, "I feel great!" *With such words and Ellen's indomitable spirit, my heart sang! I feel great! Yes, I am grateful to be alive. Indeed, I am thrilled to be a participant in this circuitous journey of life!*

Eighth Cancer Treatment November 28, 2006

I woke up with a cautious excitement. If I've learned anything from chemotherapy, it is that it is serious business! I had been able to keep on the two-week cycles and as my breast cancer friend, Hermie, had told me, "The treatment is bad but it is doable." I confess that it has been the worse pains and feelings that I ever recall, but it was indeed "doable".

In preparation for this last treatment, Dianne and her daughter, Ginger, had prepared goodies for the office: cheesecake, cookies, brownies, and fudge. This was, of course, to be a celebration.

As we began the usual activities at the office, everyone did their usual tasks, but it seemed with greater enthusiasm than usual. The blood test complete, the visit to Dr. Woodard and the infusions were all good. I crunched ice for the three hour Taxol infusion and enjoyed the usual morning snacks offered by the staff. Dr. Woodard had explained to me that until the radiation was completed, he would not need to see me. His reassuring smile and words gave me confidence that the good times were ahead of me.

When the infusions were completed, the staff began to come together. There were hugs, kisses, and well wishes all around. I was presented with a card from the group. All the staff members had signed their names and written notes to me. I still remember Dr. Woodard's words on the card, "It has been a privilege to be your physician".

The week went well after this and still there had been no signs of tingling or numbness although the effects of Taxol might have taken a month to be completely out of my body. As for my eyebrows and eye lashes, they were almost all gone by this time--but only for a while.

Friday, December 1 Carmen wrote in her journal:

November 28th was a historic day for our Ellen!! On this date she completed her eighth and final chemo treatment! For this red letter day, Larry accompanied Ellen to Dr. Woodard's office. A scrumptious array of caloric sweets was showered on the staff. Dr. Woodard started with a seven layer cookie and then on to his favorite . . . the Gragg brownies.

The blood was drawn, followed by a visit to the doctor. Dr. Woodard told Ellen that he had her set up for an appointment on December 19th to see the radiologist. This was good news for her. From August through November, Ellen had placed her life in the hands of Dr. Woodard and his skilled staff. What a journey they have made together! Periodically, he will meet with Ellen, as he is her oncologist; in fact, she has an appointment with him in February. For three months now, Ellen had seen Dr. Woodard every two weeks and the thought of not seeing him in case there was a problem concerned her. She had not seen her primary physician during this entire episode.

Finally, Ellen asked the question that was on her heart, "Dr. Woodard, from this point on, if I have a cold, what should I do?" *Without hesitation, this caring physician replied, "You call me any time you want to. You feel free to call me any time." How comforting and reassuring these words were to our dear Ellen!*

As she prepared to say her farewells and leave, something wonderful happened. Dr. Woodard's staff presented her with a card signed by every staff member and a special note from the doctor. With a catch in her voice, Ellen described how overwhelmed she felt about this outpouring of love.

I asked her how she felt now that she had completed her chemotherapy. Her response was, "I am so relieved that I can wake up in the morning and know that I do not have to think about another treatment. It is very reassuring, like a burden has been lifted!" *Dear Ellen, we are so happy for you!!!*

> *New York, New York!! Ellen, whom I've nicknamed the pathfinder, will help lead a group of fifteen ladies from the Shelby area on a weekend jaunt to the Big Apple from December 8-10. This adventuresome group will stay at the Paramount Hotel in Times Square. The sightseers will wander the city streets and ogle the sparkling Christmas decorations and attend a performance of the Rockettes. Thank goodness for Ellen's Neulasta shot! May it boost her white blood cell count so that she and her friends can have a merry time in the Big Apple. It should be noted that Ellen planned this trip before her illness.*
>
> *As Ellen and I concluded our conversation, she once again stated how grateful she was for all the support she has received during her illness. The myriad kindnesses bestowed upon her have helped tremendously in her recovery. Indeed, Ellen knows how important these acts of kindness are in helping a person recover from an illness. Our friend remarked,* "Such acts of kindness we just need to pass on." *You've got that right, Ellen!*

The week after the eighth treatment I felt okay. I did get Neulasta and a blood test Wednesday of that week. With favorable blood test results, I was given the go ahead for New York. Judy, my friend and former coworker, and I have been to New York many times with grandchildren, co-workers, and just groups of ladies who wanted to go. We had 15 ladies for this trip. Some in the group were seasoned travelers and others had never flown. In New York we hailed two van cabs and were off to the hotel. Judy was in charge of the touring since I had to take it easy. I walked as much as any of them but took every opportunity to sit and watch the people passing. The decorations were spectacular at Macy's and at Lord and Taylor's. While the ladies shopped in Macy's I went downstairs and had a Sprite and rested. I guess my hat and scarf were perfect giveaways to my bald head because a lady across at another table pointed to my hat and then mouthed, "Are you okay?" I nodded that I was. After putting her coffee cup in the garbage, she came over to me and we talked for several minutes about the C-word. We had had so many similar experiences. She gave me some advice on what she had done about the painful muscle and joint pains. We both still suffered from these pains. I thanked her for her sensitivity to what

I had been going through. People are so amazing! As I left Macy's that day I saw the lady again at the Chanel counter. She recognized me as I waved a good-bye to her and thanked her again for her kind remarks.

The three days in New York were great but I must admit that my energy level dropped drastically. We saw the tourist sites like the Statue of Liberty, Ground Zero, Central Park and the Empire State Building. On Friday night we had tickets for the Rockettes Christmas Show at Radio City Music Hall. Our hotel was located in Time Square so it was a pleasant walk to the theater. As usual in New York, the streets were busy with yellow cabs and the sounds of cab and car horns. As we approached the last street crossing to the theater, I could hear police whistles as they halted traffic for pedestrians to cross. Crossing the street to Radio City Music Hall, I tripped and fell to my knees. I really think that my legs just folded under me because I was so tired, but I wouldn't ever have admitted that! A policeman directing traffic ran over, helped me up and asked if I was okay. I had a skinned knee but was okay except for the embarrassment.

I think it is ironic that for months I had endured the tests, needles and chemotherapy drugs with a willing determination; and, at that point, when I had perhaps stepped out of my regimen, I fell to my knees.

As I reflect, it seemed that the disease had not brought me to my knees except in prayer, but being a tourist had.

I enjoyed the trip but was glad to get back to my recliner.

L to R Sister Terry, friend Betty, Ellen, Cousin Ann
and sister Dianne in New York City!

Ellen in NYC in front of Lord and Taylor's Christmas Windows.

Wednesday, December 6 Betty (Carmen is in Hawaii) wrote:

The eighth treatment completed, Ellen says she will have an intermission from treatment during the month of December. She says that she has had some cramping in her thighs which she had not experienced before but she was doing fine.

Friday, December 15 Emily (Carmen is still in Hawaii) wrote:

Ellen continues to amaze me! She is doing well, and shared that she is finally seeing the "full light at the end of the tunnel!" She was a bit confused not to be traveling to Charlotte, having done so every other Tuesday since September, so she called Dr. Woodard's office and spoke with Kim, her kind and caring nurse, saying she was having withdrawal. They both chuckled.

Her trip to NYC was, and I quote, "cold as kraut" *but fun-filled. Many of the ladies she traveled with had either never been to the city, or hadn't been in several years. They were enthusiastic sightseers and covered much territory in a short weekend! She sounded as if they walked miles, which was more than Ellen had exercised in some time, but she kept up well. After a light lunch they traversed 5th Avenue shoulder to shoulder, admiring the store windows and joining the lines at FAO Schwarz. The ladies did some shopping in Macy's, but Ellen wisely took a break sitting downstairs with a Sprite in hand and people-watched. She would have preferred a Sundrop but they are only available in the Carolinas. While she was relaxing, she noticed a lady at another table who pointed to her hat. She moved over to Ellen's table and they mentioned the C-word: What type? Breast cancer. Me, too. Then the lady pulled her shoulder length hair hard, so Ellen could see that it was real, and said, "It'll grow back!"*

This week finds Ellen preparing for Christmas. She and Susie, her sister-in- law, had made what their family calls German hard candy. She hadn't done much shopping but had made her annual purchases of Christmas ornaments for the eight grandchildren. It is a tradition that hopefully will ensure when the children are grown, their trees will be full of memories.

Ellen asked me to once again convey her deepest gratitude for all the contacts made in her behalf, but especially for the prayers. She knows that is what has enabled her to endure the chemo regimen with minimal side effects. Dr. Woodard says her positive attitude from the beginning assured him that she would do well, but she believes that it had the intervention of family, friends, church and DKG sisters. God is good ALL THE TIME!!!

Radiation Begins

The next step in my treatment was radiation. Dr. Woodard's office had made my appointment in Shelby with Dr. Helen Maddux for December 19. Larry and I were both somewhat apprehensive about this treatment, since we really didn't know much about it. After our visit with Dr. Maddux, we felt so much better knowing what to expect. We were impressed with Dr. Maddux; she was so personable and soft-spoken. As she discussed my case, it didn't take long to know that she had studied my cancer history thoroughly. She explained that she would be using a very specialized computer program to plan my treatment. Treatment would depend on the location, size and depth of my cancer. She also went over several of the possible side effects from radiation therapy including fatigue, aches and shooting pains in the breast, sun-burn effect on the skin, discoloration of the skin, dryness, itching, swelling or heaviness in the breast, radiation pneumonia, heart damage, and years later, possibly cancer in other parts of the body.

The next day, I went to the hospital for the planning session. The procedure began with my disrobing from my waist up and lying on a CT table. A special marking pen was used to draw a line down my sternum and several reference points on both breasts. Following the marks, tiny wires were placed on designated points and then taped down. This whole process was necessary prior to marking the laser lines with tattoos so that every radiation treatment would be aimed precisely on the targeted area.

The most difficult part of this procedure was holding my position. I had to extend my arms over my head and hold onto handles above my head. This doesn't sound too hard but try it for 45 minutes without moving. During the process, the radiation therapist came to adjust my body position several times. I could hear a clicking in the machine as images were made and sent to Dr. Maddux's computer. After Dr. Maddux had all the information that she needed, I was ready for the tattoos. Three tattoos--tiny blue dots--were made, one placed under each arm and the third several inches over the incision site. These tattoos would glow in the dark and enable the therapists to align my body with the laser lines in the treatment room. This, of course, would ensure that the dosage of radiation would hit precisely on the targeted area. The tattooing itself was painless, and the dots resembled very tiny blue moles.

WOW! This was mid-December and time to decorate a tree for Christmas. I had never thought about it until now, but I had been decorated, too!

Christmas is always a special time for our family. With the help of Larry and my sisters, we continued with our annual morning coffee for Friendship Force on December 23, followed by the gathering of our Sunday School Class and neighbors on Christmas Eve. I wore my red hat for this occasion but had begun to see a few straggling hairs appearing on top of my head and kept that a secret.

There had been no signs of returning eyebrows or eyelashes either and most of them were lost during the last four treatments. I tried not to complain about my legs and knees, but they ached every day and particularly when I was on them for long periods of time.

On Christmas morning, we have always had a tradition of a family breakfast. Before our children were born, we went to my parents' home for breakfast where we opened gifts. After the children were born, my parents would come to our house or to the home of one of my other siblings. Now that our children are grown and married with children they come for brunch about mid-morning. Our middle son, Lee, and his family live an hour away and so they wait until after lunch and then come to meet with the whole family. Two of our sons, Kelly and Jeff, and their families live close to us, so they come for brunch and then return to open gifts when Lee's family arrives. At 5 P.M. on Christmas, all my siblings and their families and our family have a dinner at my sister Terry's home. When everyone comes, we have 45.

On December 26, 2006, at 8:50 A.M., my first appointment for radiation began. A male nurse, Alan, (whom both Wanda and I had taught) took me in to see the visiting radiologist. Alan usually works in the emergency department, but that day he was needed in the cancer center. A radiation assistant then came for me and took me back to meet the therapists. I was pleased to renew another friendship with a former student, Beth, who was the radiation therapist who would operate the linear accelerator. Pam, another therapist, would help with this initial treatment. This appointment actually lasted about an hour. When I entered the room for the treatment I noticed several things. The walls as I entered the room looked to be at least a foot thick, and the door moved with the push of a button on the outside of this chamber. Through a window on one wall, the therapists could view patients while the treatment was being administered. The ladies assured me that we could also communicate during the process. When CT scan images were compared to the computer program designed for me, the team realized that the field of radiation would extend to my cervical vertebrae, spinal cord and upper right lung. Adjustments had to be made to prevent the exposure to these areas. Once the adjustments were made I was ready for the first radiation treatment. The radiation room was very cold and blankets were placed to cover me except for the bare radiation sites. The therapists placed me on the table and left the room. Hearing that big, heavy door slide closed gave me a strange feeling, although I knew that I was safe. The linear accelerator stopped at four different sites: three areas on my right breast and one under my right arm. This huge arm moved to each area, hummed for a time, and then moved to another site. The actual dosage of rays took only a few minutes on each site. The most difficult part again was the position of my arms over my head. They were numb when I was finally able to move them. Since Dr. Maddux was on vacation for this first treatment, the physician from Bowman Gray Medical School in Winston-Salem directed it. She also suggested that I use corn starch several times daily on the right breast. The corn starch in her opinion was better than the Biafine cream already prescribed.

I was so pleased to be taken care of by two of my former students for this first treatment. Alan and Beth were both good students and to have them on hand to help with my treatment made it a special day. Knowing that you've played a part in the success of your students is a wonderful reward for a teacher.

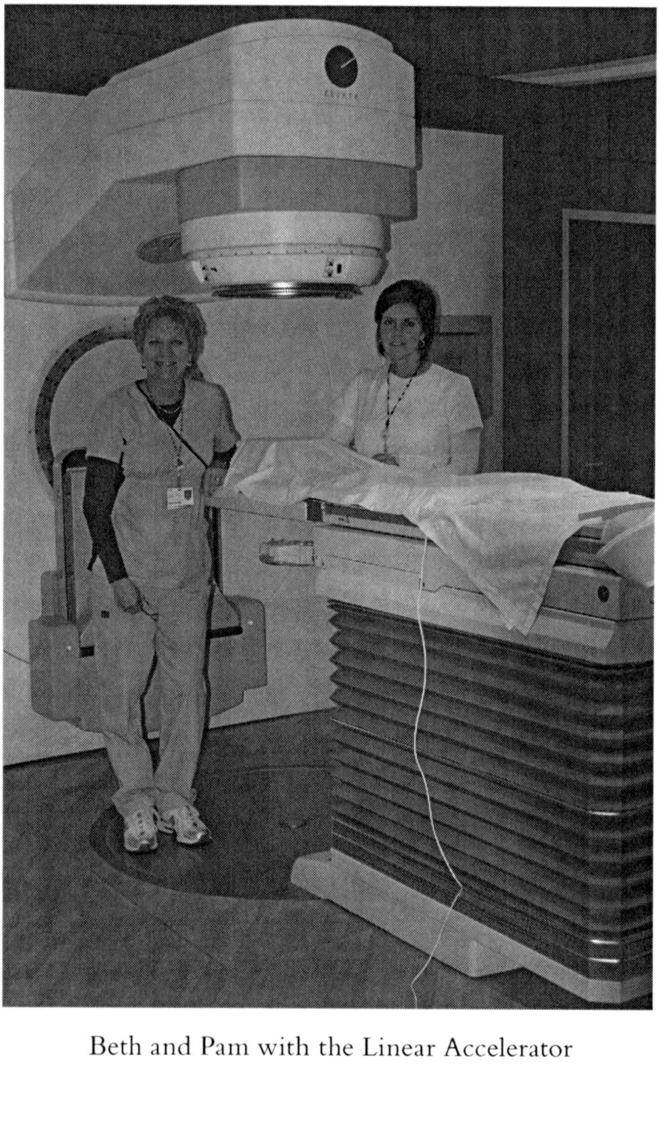

Beth and Pam with the Linear Accelerator

I asked Carmen if she would allow me to send a message to my DKG sisters in her next installment and she agreed. She included it in her December 28 report as a separate message. A copy of it is included here.

Wednesday, December 27, 2006
Dear Friends,

I wanted to send all of you a message directly from me. My report will not be as eloquently written as those of your previous reporters, Carmen, Betty and Emily. I have not read them but have heard about them from some of you. I do appreciate their dedication to keep you informed about my journey.

Tuesday the 26th was my first radiation treatment. The first hour was checking to see that the tattoo markings lined up correctly with the laser lines. They took many images to see that the computer program planned for me was positioned correctly for internal structures. Again my arms were over my head for all this time. I could hardly move them when the time was up. I was told that a small area of my cervical vertebrae was in the radiation zone so adjustments were made to block that area. The treatment itself was quick and painless. The machine is amazing! It is a linear accelerator. I've read about them but had never seen one. They are designed to give superior precision treatment and are very reliable. Once I was positioned correctly I was not to move but the machine did. My treatment focuses on four areas and the machine moves to those positions according to the computer plan for me. The universal plan for breast cancer radiation is full affected breast and underarm. I was given an opportunity to go to Charlotte for an experimental program with three options. I would not have had a choice in the options. I was not interested in going for this experimental program because I wanted to follow the recommendations of my doctor. Since I might not have the chance to have the program that she thought was best, I chose to decline the opportunity.

Today was treatment number two of 33. I will have treatments every Monday through Friday except holidays unless there is a problem. The list of possible problems was long and included everything from cancer to rib breakage.

When the radiation oncologist asked if I had concerns about the treatment or the cancer, I said no. She was amazed. I told her that I settled those concerns months ago. I explained to her that I found the cancer while in Japan and that I felt that it was divine intervention. I know that the Lord has been in this all the way. He has worked through all of you with calls, cards, gifts and prayers. Our family and friends provided food for months when I felt the worst. Also, I had family or friends to go to every chemotherapy treatment with me. People from all over the country sent cards, people whom I didn't know but whose church had my name on their prayer list. My students have been such a blessing to me--from nurses to my pharmacist to the fellow who takes care of the tires on my car.

I am doing all my usual workload. I rest more than normal but am anxious to get back to the YMCA. I hope to start tomorrow morning. I have been walking but have not done any weight resistance since my surgery, and won't until but my surgeon has given his approval. During this holiday season I have reflected on many things but particularly the last seven months. From the discovery of the mass until now I can see the Lord's hand in it all. Recently I read the phrase "great is Thy faithfulness" and remembered the hymn from which it came, "Great is Thy Faithfulness." For a day or so this phrase just rang in my ears and I was singing what I could remember of the hymn. I looked up the hymn. It seemed to be written especially for me, to reassure me of God's presence and to remind me that He is *compassionate* and does provide *forgiveness* and *peace.* He does *cheer* and *guide* and is the *hope of tomorrow.* All of this and more *He provided* during my life, but especially during the last months... and yes, *morning by morning new mercies.*

May we all enjoy 2007!

My love to all of you and my sincere thanks for your unwavering support.

Ellen

Since chemotherapy I had been able to attend church again on most Sundays with a reasonable amount of energy. On a Sunday in January, one of the morning hymns was "Great is Thy Faithfulness," I couldn't sing a word. The tears just flowed down my cheeks as I was reminded of the words and how meaningful they had been to me. Even now, when I hear this hymn I am unable to sing the full song. The phrases that seem to ring in my ears are "morning by morning new mercies" and "great is Thy faithfulness to me".

Realizing how faithful the Lord had been to me encouraged me to reach out to Kelly's wife, Wendi. From my own experience I know that sometimes you need to just talk with someone about a situation. Her mom had been treated for bone cancer for several years. I tried to keep a check on her mother's condition and help out with meals occasionally.

Since Wendi is an only child she has had many decisions to make on her mother's behalf. Larry and I have tried to help out with school pickups for two of her children, Jane and Jacob, to relieve Wendi of some responsibilities. I have always believed that there is great joy in helping others because you are blessed as well.

On December 28 Carmen wrote in her journal.

On Thursday evening Ellen and I shared an animated conversation. In a strong, cheerful voice our friend replied, "I'm doing well." *She described the lengthy, initial meeting with Dr. Maddux, her oncologist radiologist, on December 19. Larry also went with her since they feel that two sets of ears are better than one. They were pleased to meet the doctor and were impressed with her knowledge of Ellen's records. Dr. Maddux explained the radiation process and asked for any questions that Ellen or Larry had. Being a thoughtful patient, Ellen asked of any dangers associated with the treatments and made notes. While she learned a whole list of possible ramifications, she noted these four:*

1. *One out of 125,000 patients could get a form of cancer from the radiation.*
2. *Some individuals could contract pneumonia.*
3. *Some patients may obtain permanent "sunburn" on the radiated skin.*

4. *Some individuals may develop a thickening of the skin with radiation.*

The planning session was scheduled for the next day. Special marks were placed on both of her breasts. After the pen markings, tiny, thin wires were placed on designated spots and then secured with tape. After Ellen was marked and wired, she was rolled under an open CAT scanner. The task of the CAT scan was to help Dr. Maddux line up the laser lines with the metallic reference points on Ellen's chest. During this 45 minute procedure, our friend could hear the click of the machine as it made images of her upper body. It should be noted that as Ellen reclined on the table, her greatest challenge was to hold her position without any movement. To accomplish this, Ellen had to extend her arms straight behind her head and had to grip a bar. In this position Ellen probably resembled a trapeze artist suspended in air! Can you imagine holding such a position for 45 minutes?!

On January 1, 2007, Carmen wrote in her journal:

On Wednesday evening, December 26, Ellen and I once again happily conversed about her week. Deep in the conversation our friend replied in a cheerful voice, "Every day I feel so much better. By 7 P.M., however, I am tired and on the sofa to rest my aching legs. Since my last chemo treatment, I have had some swelling in my fingers and hands and can't wear any rings. I am thankful that I've not had neuropathy, the tingling and burning sensation in the extremities."

On December 26, an eager Ellen arrived at the hospital for her first treatment. Our gal was ready and anxious to plough ahead with the next phase of her cancer treatment, radiation. Remember that radiation treatments are specific in nature, whereas chemo treatments are systemic, flooding the whole body to eradicate cancer cells. The linear accelerator buzzed as it shot calibrated rays into the four areas. After administering the prescribed radiation at each of the sites, the great machine fell silent, moving automatically in a resting position. Then, this amazing robot-like device once again assumed the correct position for the next targeted site and dispersed the prescribed rays. According to Ellen, the actual radiation procedure took no more than ten minutes!

To Ellen's surprise and delight, two former students were also part of the medical team that day. A 1990 female graduate operated the linear accelerator while a former male student, who normally works as a nurse in the Emergency Room, assisted in the cancer center that Tuesday. Ellen confided that she felt fortunate to have played a part in the lives of these two responsible students.

As the year 2007 eclipses the old year, I asked Ellen to reflect upon 2006. Without hesitation, she answered that this year presented new challenges. No one in her immediate family had had to deal with breast cancer. Ellen calmly replied, "We learned a lot. I think I've been a miracle." *Upon hearing this response, I asked our friend to elaborate upon these statements. Ellen responded by saying that if she had not gone to Japan seven months ago, she probably would never have discovered the lump in her breast until it was much larger. She believes that the Japan experience was divine intervention. Since her visit to Japan, Ellen has focused on her journey to health. Her faith and positive attitude have helped sustain her with this challenge.*

On Thursday, the 28th my siblings, our spouses, and Trudy and Troy Washburn had dinner together at Terry and Tommy's home. Troy is a cousin of ours and Trudy is his Austrian-born wife. They live close to our parents' home, and our family considers them part of our family too. We treat Trudy as an unofficially adopted sister. She was unable to see her parents often, so she considered our parents like her own. Tommy had gotten a new grill for Christmas, so he grilled steaks for all of us. The meal and the fellowship were great! Everyone seemed well and in good spirits.

The next morning the phone rang about 6 A.M. It was Terry asking us to "come quick". She thought Tommy was having a heart attack. The rescue squad rushed him to the local hospital and then he was airlifted to Charlotte. He had had a massive hemorrhagic stroke and died on the following Sunday morning with the family in attendance when life support was removed. The next days were filled with helping Terry and her family with plans for the funeral, greeting visitors and doing whatever else needed to be done. The entire family was on hand at different times. I continued my radiation every weekday first thing in the morning as planned. I turned my focus from healing myself to helping Terry during this time. I was doing okay and at this point there were no problems with my treatments. I am thankful that I felt well enough to help.

January 2, 2007, Carmen wrote in her journal

It is with sadness that I inform you of the death of Ellen's brother-in-law Tommy. On the 28th the siblings and spouses had met for dinner at the Royster home. Delicious food, relaxation, laughter, and, most of all, loving fellowship made the evening special. Such an event is a reminder to us to embrace each day fully.

January 14, 2007, Carmen wrote in her journal:

Last week Ellen and her family lived an adrenalin-laden marathon as they attended to, prayed for, mourned, and buried their beloved Tommy Royster. Ellen stoically replied, "You do what you need to do. We'll have time to rest." *Throughout this heart wrenching time, Ellen and her family stood at the side of Terry and their three sons, ever ready to embrace, console, and to assist them*

Tommy's funeral service was held Wednesday afternoon, January 3, at the steepled Double Springs Baptist Church. As mourners filled the sanctuary and spilled into the balcony, the rays of the late afternoon sun shone through the stained glass windows, creating a kaleidoscope of jewel colors. Beneath the pulpit was the large coffin draped in the American flag. To the hymn, "A Mighty Fortress," the family members proceeded to the front pews.

The family nephews were pall bearers. Following the funeral, outside the church, they picked up the coffin and in lockstep, walked to the gravesite. Usually the coffin would have been placed back into the hearse for delivery to the grave. The pall bearers out of respect and honor for a family member, carried the coffin to the cemetery that was adjacent to the church property. Quiet permeated the air of this pastoral setting. Fencing separated one side of the cemetery from a pasture filled with grazing cows. In the distance the ancient Blue Ridge Mountains stood guard, for in this very graveyard are buried Ellen's parents, grandparents and great-grandparents.

The flag was folded and given to Terry. The silence was broken by echoing gunfire and the pure notes of a lone bugler, playing his horn under a great oak with spreading branches.

We all knew that Tommy's health was not good, but there were no signs that death was imminent. As the eldest of the siblings and with the fact that our family had already lost Dianne's husband to heart disease and cancer, I was compelled to pause.

I had a surprise on another of the radiation treatment days. Latonya McKissack Hopper, who works in the cancer center, recognized me as I was waiting for my treatment. She told me about an experience that she had while in my class in high school. She was denied a place in the band because of my record of her tardies to my class. She transferred to another school in rebellion but later realized that she had to settle down and make better grades and be punctual to class. After high school, she became a social worker and worked for twelve years, and then she earned a nursing degree. She told me that my influence had made the difference in her life.

January 14, 2007, Carmen's journal continued:

As Ellen makes her journey to health, it is interesting how she continues to meet former students in various medical settings. She met another former student in the cancer center, Latonya McKissack Hopper. Latonya reminded Ellen that she had not qualified for a band position while in her class, due to tardies and below average grades. This made her settle down and work to make better grades. She became a social worker and later a cancer nurse. As educators we work with an attitude of faith, often never knowing the effect we have on our students. How gratifying it is for a teacher to hear a testimonial such as Latonya's!

Throughout this shocking, somber week, Ellen faithfully continued her radiation treatments and applications of cornstarch on the radiated areas of her body. Our patient admitted to some aching in her legs because of standing on them for long periods each day. Ellen relieves this aching by propping herself up in the recliner and taking Tylenol.

As Ellen and I closed our conversation, she summed up her feelings with these words; "This experience is a reminder of the importance of faith, family, neighbors, and friends. I treasure them, and I feel blessed that all my siblings live within two miles and see each other often."

A New Year, A New Goal

In mid-January I decided to register again for my quilting class that I had enjoyed for several years. Our instructor allowed us to choose our own projects. Two years earlier, in 2005, I had attended the National Quilt Show in Paducah, Kentucky. In addition to hundreds of beautiful quilts, the show had vendors selling all kinds of sewing machines, materials and notions. As I walked though, I noticed a yellow and blue quilt hanging in a vendor's area. They were selling chances on a raffle quilt for a dollar, so I bought one. The last day of the show when I checked to see if I had been the lucky winner, the answer was "Not this time." I did however, buy a quilt kit with identical fabrics and pattern so that I could make it myself. Many quilters have a STASH of patterns and fabrics on hand at any time so that they are always ready for a new project. In the two years since that purchase, I had not looked at the kit again and had not ever seen the pattern. When I opened the pattern book and saw the picture of the quilt, I was reminded again of the quilt's beauty. With further observation of the page, I noticed the title of the quilt—"Lady of Hope"—and next to the title I could also see the pink breast cancer ribbon. *The McCall's Quilting Magazine* presents annually a finished quilt to be raffled at the Show. This quilt was designed by a McCall's staff member. Tears just filled my eyes as I read the article and realized that the Paducah quilt had been a money making project for breast cancer research. I saw this as a sign that this was to be my next project. The traditional pattern block featured is *Lady of the Lake.* This pattern had 1152 small pieced triangle squares and 72 large pieced triangles. When I unfolded the fabrics and was preparing them for washing I noticed another "tear jerking" sign—every selvage was labeled with "quilt for a cure". Can you believe that more than a year before my diagnosis, the Lord was preparing the way to remind me that He was in control? So my first quilting project following cancer was to be "Lady of Hope"! Members of my quilting class were so supportive and with their encouragement I was able to keep to the task. It is completed now and is a reminder to me that life is good--every day.

Radiation continued Monday through Friday every week in January. I never had any pain from the radiation, but I had shooting pains in that breast and even some strange feeling like a worm was on the loose under my skin. There were doses of cream and corn starch at different times during the day. I had had two different doctors and two different recommendations for treatment of the breast during radiation. To this point I had not noticed any blisters or severe redness in the radiation area. Holding my arms over my head seemed to cause a fold or crease of my arm tissue and upper chest tissue, which caused that tissue to get a double dose of radiation. Dr. Maddux prescribed Benadryl cream to help soothe the discomfort.

January 18th Carmen wrote in her journal:

Do you remember that silly, little rhyme, "Fuzzy Wuzzy was a bear-- Fuzzy Wuzzy had no hair?" I'm happy to tell you that our star patient proclaims a little fuzz atop her head and a few minute eyelashes sprouting from her eyelids. YEA!

Ellen reports that the radiation treatments are going well. As of Friday, January 12, she had completed 13 of the 33 treatments. Several times a day our patient continues to rub cornstarch on the radiated areas of her body and is very pleased that there is no blistering or "sun tanning" of her skin thus far. She is also pleased that she has been able to move her 8:50 A.M. appointment to 8:00 A.M. Ellen, an early bird, loves being the first patient of the day to receive her radiation treatment and the first to leave the radiation area of the cancer center at the hospital!

Ellen reports that she has not recouped the high energy level that she had prior to her illness. In the morning her sustained energy level enables her to accomplish many tasks. However, Ellen commented, "As the day rolls on, I hit the recliner to rest!" *Our friend has wonderful memories of December when she was off chemo, and was feeling spunky! She is grateful she's not worse and understands that with patience she is making progress.*

Ellen broached to her doctor her desire to resume her walking and strength-building exercises at the YMCA; this physician advised her to wait until she had completed all of her treatments for she did not want her to place extra stress on her right arm. Continue to be patient, Ellen. It won't be long before you lift the bar bells once again! Recently Ellen received a telephone call from the Assistant Principal at Shelby High School, who just happens to be the daughter of one of Ellen's best friends in high school. This educator called Ellen with an offer to fill an eleven week interim position in the computer lab to assist students preparing for the SAT exam. Our friend would be on duty two days a week from 8 o'clock in the morning to three. Fortunately, she would have a free period each day from 11 A.M. until 1 P.M. so that she could continue with radiation. The offer is attractive enough that Ellen is giving it consideration.

Saturday, January 27 Carmen wrote in her journal

When I close my eyes and think of Ellen, I see these images.

I can see her with a spunky smile on her
face and a soft hat capping her bald head.

I can see a confident soul in the kitchen,
Bending over the oven door to remove a
pan of her from-scratch biscuits.

I can see a composed individual, sitting
tall, asking her physician serious questions
about her condition and her cancer treatments.

I can see a gentle grandmother, rocking
her joyful, two-year old, Joe, to sleep.

I can see a symbolic image of our dear
friend with slow, labored movements, pushing
a gigantic boulder up a steep hill with the summit inches away.

What an arduous medical journey this is for Ellen! In a pleased voice our patient replied, "I have only three more five day weeks left! I have only 15 more treatments!" *As of Friday, January 19, our girl has completed 18 of her 33 radiation treatments. If all goes well, our star patient will have her last treatment on Friday, February 9. With Ellen's great personal strength and courage and with the excellent medical care, she will reach the finish line of her cancer treatments. Ellen, we are cheering you on for this great achievement!!!*

Since straps or tight clothing irritate Ellen's radiated skin, she cleverly devised a new fashion look for around-the-house garb. She wears what I nicknamed the "floating bra", a creation made from a bra extender.

Floating Bra

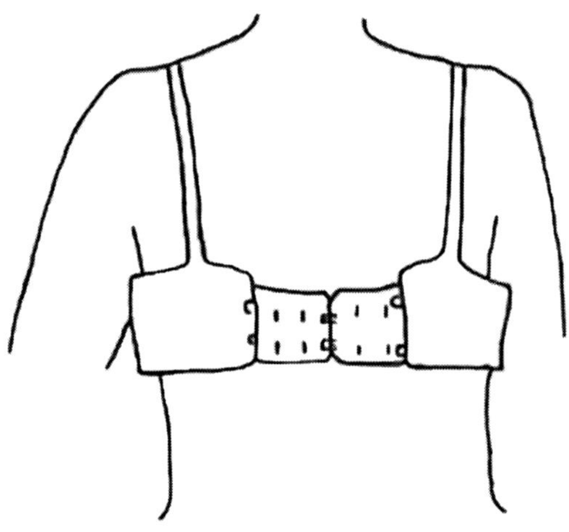

Floating Bra

Over her chest a large, roomy tee shirt provides coverage and comfort. To add some zing to her "get-up", she dons a specially ordered, pink bill cap, emblazoned with the letters of John Deere.

Did you know that Ellen loves to quilt? Recently she returned to her advanced quilting class, which is held at the Shelby Senior Center. At this level of quilting, each class member can select her own project or work on patterns introduced by the instructor. The instructor serves as a teacher and troubleshooter to the students.

What sparked Ellen's interest in quilting? I asked her to describe the genesis of this great love. Members of her family modeled this craft, and this whetted her curiosity about quilting. Our friend recounted that as a child, she had good memories of visiting her grandmother and playing with her cousins at the home place. Here little Ellen saw quilt frames holding quilts positioned on the backs of straight chairs. Her grandmother, aunt and mother often quilted together. From time to time, these kind and patient quilters invited the little ones to try their hand with the quilting needles. Ellen softly chuckled, "I don't know if they took our stitches out when we left, but they let us think we were good." *In later years her father helped her mother by making templates for various patterns.*

Farm animals--figures in nursery rhymes—bears--Noah's Ark—Butterflies- these are some of the theme quilts lovingly stitched by Ellen for her grandchildren. Prior to the birth of each grandchildren, she presented a baby quilt to the proud parents to be! Ellen simply stated "I wanted to give each of my grandchildren something made by their grandmother something especially for them." *Ah, what unique and dear gifts these are!*

As Ellen assumes a part time teaching position and resumes her advanced quilting class, one can tell that she is feeling much better than in the fall. Indeed, our dear Ellen is anxious to join the fray of everyday life... to be NORMAL once again! You are just about there, Ellen!

February 1 Carmen wrote in her journal

Twenty-four down and nine treatments to go! That was Ellen's good news on the January 29. Day by day, she is working her way to the finish line of her radiation treatments. Indeed, our patient is excited about completing this regimen soon!

Last week, Larry and Ellen provided support and comfort to their daughter-in-law, Wendi, who is married to their son, Kelly. Wendi, an only child, whose mom, Mrs. Starnes, is battling bone cancer, is a dutiful and caring daughter who visits her at least once a day. Last week her ill mom fell and was taken to a Charlotte hospital. Doctors there took x-rays and discovered that she had broken several neck vertebrae sometime in the past. Now Mrs. Starnes is in a neck brace and is undergoing radiation. Wendi is trying to honor her mother's wishes to be somewhat independent and to remain in her home. Each school day last week, Ellen and Larry helped Wendi with the grandchildren, Jane and Jacob, by picking them up from school. What loving and helpful support this was for Wendi, a busy wife, mother, and noted interior designer!

As our conversation came to a close, I asked Ellen to reflect upon the week and share with me what had impressed her most. She replied that she had read a quote by Eleanor Roosevelt that she wanted to keep. Our friend paraphrased the quote by saying, "God's promises are greater than life's problems." *Ellen continued by adding,* "I believe this to be true. God never gives us more than we can bear. God never leaves us. He is always present. Without feeling His presence, I could not have gotten through this ordeal." *Ellen then stated that she could think of a number of scriptures that illuminate this quote. Upon my request, Ellen emailed three meaningful passages that appear as a part of REFLECTIONS.*

Deuteronomy 31:6 (New Living Translation)

"So be strong and courageous! Do not be afraid and do not panic before them. For the LORD your God will personally go ahead of you. He will neither fail you nor abandon you."

Hebrews 13:5 (King James Version)

"Let your conversation be without covetousness; and be content with such things as ye have: for he hath said, I will never leave thee, nor forsake thee."

Matthew 11:29-30 (New King James Version)

29 Take My yoke upon you and learn from Me, for I am gentle and lowly in heart, and you will find rest for your souls. 30 For My yoke is easy and My burden is light."

We don't receive wisdom; we must discover it for ourselves after a journey that no one can take for us or spare us."
Marcel Proust

*"How good is man's life, the mere living!
How fit to employ all the heart and the soul
and the senses in joy!"
Robert Browning*

Most of January was uneventful as far as problems. The radiation treatments were easy and took very little time in the mornings. The days were tiring, and I found myself sitting quite often. My legs and knees continued to ache when I was on them too much. This hasn't changed in the years since 2007. The lack of energy had increased as the radiation progressed. During that time, however, I had met several other patients who were in much worse condition than I. One I recall had radiation on her skull due to a brain cancer that could not be removed. Another had been diagnosed with lung cancer following a routine physical exam and no surgery was possible. Comparatively I was in good shape, and I was thankful for it. The experience did give me an opportunity to give them some encouragement and words of support. Surely, cancer is no respecter of persons.

I had decided to take the temporary teaching position at Shelby High School for two days a week. I had asked for permission to wear a hat because I knew that students were not allowed to wear them. The students didn't seem to notice that I was wearing contraband (a hat) or if they did, they never mentioned it. The students were upperclassmen and wanted to prepare for the SAT exam, so I assumed my work would be easy. The first day on the job, I arrived early and--would you believe it?--another of my former students, Omar, worked with at-risk/special needs students. He recognized me as he was speaking to the assistant principal in the hall. After a hug and a few questions about his life, I was off to the computer lab in the rear room of the student library. These classes were filled with sophomores, juniors, and a few seniors, mostly male athletes. Some classes had as few as four, and one was filled with sixteen males. WOW! Did I really sign up for this?! There were only 18 computer stations and I would need one of these so that I could monitor their work. I had to give a practice test to all of them so we would know where to start with each student. The computer program was a good one and had tests for every section. I could see each student's test scores and know who needed remediation and in what area(s) they were weak. I miss teaching and this part-time experience gave me an opportunity to test my wings, so to speak. I was able to sit some of the time and there were no lesson plans to prepare, so it was a good opportunity to give my weakened body an endurance test.

During January I had an appointment with my surgeon. He was pleased with the healing of my incision. I asked him about the occasional shooting pains and the worm-like crawling feeling that I experienced. He reassured me that the regrowth of nerves could cause some strange feelings. I had been using the exercises that he recommended with my right arm to allow me to raise my arm to the heights that I had before the surgery. These were simple exercise in which I let my fingers walk up the wall several times a day from two different positions. I stood facing the wall at first and also with my right side to the wall. The only name I have heard for these exercises is *wall walking* exercises.

I continued with the cream and corn starch daily. I used the Benadryl (chemical name Diphenhydramine hydrochloride) cream on the reddened area. So far, it hadn't blistered and that area would only be targeted through the January 28 treatment. Dr. Maddux was pleased with the way my skin had cooperated with the radiation, even though I was still experiencing the shooting pains and the worm-like crawling feeling. The only relief from either of these was to cross my right arm over that breast and press. The light pressure seemed to do the trick.

For Boost Week, which for me was February 5-9, a special cone-shaped device, the length and shape of the scar over the tumor incision, was made for each patient. The rays would no longer focus on the underarm lymph node area. As I understand, this boost treatment on the incision ensures that if any minute cancer cells have been left after all the other treatments, then this boost should eliminate them.

During this time our family was involved in another family medical issue. Wendi, our daughter-in-law, was spending much of her time now at Hospice Care with her dying mother. Her doctor had told Wendi that her mother needed to be at Hospice where they could help control the pain. It was sad to think that I was on the last of my treatments but Wendi's mom was weaker and in more pain.

February 2 Carmen wrote in her journal

"Now, she was a tough one. She didn't put up with any junk!" said a smiling Omar Porter, a former student of Ellen's. On our school marm's first day at Shelby High, Ellen met handsome Omar and the assistant principal in one of the corridors of the school. Omar now works with at-risk students.

Following the first class period, Ellen heard a commotion in the hall. While two students were engaged in a brawl, students encircled the pair. To break up the fight, the resource officer, a woman policeman, sprayed mace on the culprits. Ellen learned that resource officers now are not allowed to grab or pull students from a fracas. Welcome back to school, Mrs. Gragg!!! Even with the melee in the hallway and some of the rowdy, immature males, Ellen simply said, "I loved the day!" *The teaching and the interaction with the students, along with the camaraderie of colleagues, are what our friend misses from teaching. We both heartily agreed that we did not miss the numerous meetings and the stacks of papers to grade!*

Yea! Our dear Ellen completed her 28th standard radiation treatment on Friday, February 2! Our patient explained that standard radiation treatments involve the use of protons in atoms which allow for a deep penetration of tissue. The right arm pit, sites involving the tumor, and the incision itself received this type of radiation. After these treatments, she will have a Boost Week. She will receive radiation with electrons only on the scarred areas of her right breast. I learned that the electrons can be better controlled for depth than protons. The scarred breast tissue does not need the depth of penetration offered by the proton radiation treatment. After the 28th radiation, a stoic Ellen confided that she felt thankful and relieved! Knowing that she had only five more treatments, called the Boost Week, she quickly interjected, "I can make it!"

Radiation Over, Ring the Bell

The Boost Week began on February 5, 2007. Since I was teaching, my last treatments had been scheduled between 11 and 12 noon. The only differences that I noticed with these treatments were that the cone-shaped device was used on the gantry, and it came closer to the scar and focused only on that area of my skin. This was the only position that administered radiation. The time involved in these treatments was much less. I was very careful to use the cream and corn starch because these treatments can cause the sunburn redness. For many patients this redness is permanent.

The five day Boost Week continued and I was told that we would celebrate on Friday, February 9, when I had my last treatment. My sisters, Dianne and Terry, came in time for the celebration. Larry had come in with me for an early appointment since school was closed due to a teacher work day. Following the last treatment, Larry was allowed to view the treatment room and linear accelerator. This was a big treat for Larry, since he loves machines. The therapists followed us to the reception area where we were joined by my sisters, the nurse and the receptionist. A bell hangs in the reception area, and I was told that the bell ringing indicated that a patient had completed the treatments. They told me that the bell can be heard all over the cancer center. WHAT A GREAT TRADITION! After ringing the bell and getting hugs all around, we left for a family breakfast

Oddly, I wanted to take a sigh of relief, but yet I found myself at the point of tears. I had been determined to go through the treatments without any delays and had not allowed myself to have a pity-party. Now, with the last radiation treatment complete, I wanted to let go. Looking back at the last ten months I realized how blessed I had been and how thankful I was.

As I reflect on the surgery, chemo, and radiation I can truthfully say it was the worst experience of my life. No one who has not been through this experience could ever appreciate the pain and horrible feelings that cancer patients experience.

Larry and a group from our church had planned to go to Gulfport, Mississippi, for a week with the North Carolina Baptist Men. The purpose of this trip was to help with the cleanup and repairs to homes damaged by Hurricane Katrina. Dianne and several ladies also were going to do the cooking. I was trained in disaster relief with the American Red Cross and North Carolina Baptist Men but didn't think I could do them any good this time. I wished that I had felt like going, but I didn't think they would have a recliner for me. Larry was concerned about leaving me for a week, but I reassured him that I'd be okay and I was.

February 14 Carmen wrote in her journal:

Let's hear a drum roll, please! On Friday, February 9, 2007, our girl completed her 33rd and last radiation treatment! For the moment let us imagine ourselves encircling our friend and hugging her. Ellen, we are happy for you and proud of you for completing this great challenge.

The hospital has a wonderful tradition of conducting a simple but meaningful ceremony for its patients completing the radiation regimen. This event is referred to as the Bell Ringing. In a special area of the cancer center, the graduate patient reads aloud a special poem about the journey and rings a bell. Those in the center who have attended the bell ringer try to come to the little commencement.

During Emily's tenure as Eta State President, she became friends with Hermie Gaston, the president of the South Carolina DKG organization. A year prior to Ellen's illness, Hermie was diagnosed with breast cancer. When Ellen learned about her breast cancer, our wonderful Emily connected Hermie and Ellen while in San Diego in 2006. Indeed Hermie's friendship has helped to sustain Ellen through this difficult time. Throughout this ordeal Hermie has telephoned or emailed Ellen, offering her love, support, and first-hand experience with surviving breast cancer. This friend, who had the same chemo regimen as our Ellen, had this to say, "It is bad, but it is doable."

Ellen remarked that it had meant so much to her to have someone who had undergone something that she had been going through. As Ellen's voice trailed off, she replied, "You just can't imagine how horrible it is until you're there."

I had appointments with two of my doctors in the next weeks of February. I saw Dr. Chamberlain and Dr. Woodard. Dr. Chamberlain gave me a good report and wanted to make sure that I had another mammogram scheduled for summer. Dr. Woodard wanted to know if I had any new pains or problems. I had had some headaches and a lingering cough, so he scheduled me for a CT scan of my head and an echocardiogram. He explained that any new complaints would need to be checked out since there is no blood test to check for the return of breast cancer. There was no problem with either of these tests. Dr. Woodard told me that since my cancer was sensitive to estrogen I needed to take one of three drugs available for at least a five year period. He prescribed one tiny 25 mg Arimidex (chemical name Anastrozole) pill a day. This would block the production of estrogen. The theory is that if any cancer cells had escaped everything so far and if there were no estrogen for five years, they would starve and die. I surely hope that this theory can be proved in my experience. Dr. Woodard warned me that many patients on Arimidex had joint pain, particularly in their hands and fingers. I will see Dr. Woodard every three months for a time. My next mammogram was scheduled in Charlotte at the Charlotte Breast Radiology Center. The advantage of this is that a radiologist is on duty and will speak to patients following their tests. They also have the latest equipment for the test. If anything questionable is found, the radiologist can do a needle biopsy during that visit. It would certainly speed up the process of diagnosis. For the first year I had mammograms twice a year, and when everything was okay, then annually.

New Challenges

March brought some new challenges. My friend, Marietta, and I spent several days in Atlanta with the International Friendship Force meeting. At these meetings we can always make good contacts for future exchanges or invitations to people of other countries to visit with us. The days were filled with activities, and I soon realized that three full days of activities with little rest was too much for me. I was no longer ready for all-day activities with little rest.

The position in DKG of North Carolina (Eta) State Executive Secretary had been announced, and I had applied for the position to begin work July 1, 2007. I had filled positions of Region VIII Director, various committee chairmanships, the offices of secretary, second and first vice president and president. I was currently serving a second two-year term as parliamentarian. The Personnel Committee chose me for the position. I was to shadow the current secretary until her term was over June 30, 2007. This position is only part-time, and can be done from home for the most part. I accepted this challenge.

As the month progressed, I began to notice that my fingers ached and the joints were swollen, so that I could no longer wear any ring that I had. That has never changed! Every person who I know who takes this drug has had the same problems. Several have had their rings resized so that they can be worn. My leg muscles and knees continued to ache. After sitting for long periods of time I could hardly get up without pulling up. After I was up and moving, I didn't notice the pain. I guess this is a small price to pay to be cancer-free.

My hair by now was like a very short crew cut and on warm days I went without any head covering. My eyelashes and eyebrows had not begun to regrow. I didn't have to shave my legs or underarms. There was nothing to shave! This mammal had been hairless for a long time!

Friday, March 16 Carmen wrote in her journal:

March days with sunny skies of blue, camellia bushes with blood-red blossoms and dancing daffodils of yellow sing spring, a verdant season of hope and rebirth. Such a landscape mirrored my conversation with Ellen on March 10. With a strong, confident voice laced with cheer and optimism, she gaily recounted her recent weeks since our last conversation prior to my vacation to Egypt.

With our free--ranging animated conversation, our friend gave an update on her medical condition, quilting project, new role with Eta State, her interim teaching experience, plans to travel to Sweden, and wisdom gleaned from her recent journey to health. Wow! What a productive and rich life our Ellen leads!

Ellen will be under the care of Dr. Woodard for at least the next five years. Every three months she will see him for checkups. Of course, she knows that she can always call him in between appointments if a need arises. This, indeed, is very assuring for our friend. This amazing doctor remains Ellen's lifeline, her anchor.

During the five year period, Ellen will take Arimedix daily. This medication counteracts the estrogen produced in her body. The major side effects of the drug are dry skin, hot flashes, and joint pain. "When I wake up, my hands are a little stiff. I try to continue to use my hands such as with quilting. But I can manage this."

When I spoke with Ellen on Saturday morning, she was absorbed in her quilting. Tiny fabric squares of sunshine yellow and vibrant blue were scattered about her as she stitched on her "Lady of Hope" quilt. As you may recall, quilting is one of Ellen's loves. Now, quilting affords her an opportunity to use her hands to work out some of the stiffness in her fingers that she feels at the beginning of the day.

Piece by piece, our quilting friend is giving shape to her "Lady of Hope" creation. When this quilt is completed, it will be composed of seventy-two 9¼" squares! In turn, each of these squares will contain a large square in the middle of the block with sixteen smaller blue and yellow squares surrounding it. This cheery field of seventy-two blocks of yellow and blue will be bordered by strips of white and deep blue.

Let's hear a cheer for Ellen! On July 1, 2007, she will assume the position of Eta State Secretary. In our conversation, our friend remarked that she is excited about serving our wonderful state organization in this position. When I congratulated her on her new assignment, she chuckled and replied, "I think I know all the questions. Now, I'll work on the answers!"

The Gragg family will take on the Big Apple the first week in June! Larry and Ellen, along with three grandchildren, her daughter-in-law, Lea, and her mother will see the sights in New York. Years before, Ellen had already taken her eldest granddaughter, Lucy, and her mother to New York. This time it will be the next three in age--Jane, Jacob and Kate. This grandmother had already purchased tickets to see Mary Poppins. *Honking yellow cabs, swishing limos, throngs of New Yorkers marching purposefully down city sidewalks—wow. What fun the grandchildren will have soaking in the energy of this international city as they lean back and peer up at the skyscrapers! Of course, they will visit the landmarks, the Empire State Building, The Statue of Liberty, Central Park, and F. A. O. Swartz.*

As we talked Ellen stressed, "I feel it is important to have time with the grandchildren. Travel will give them some sense of the world. We have four other grandchildren that I hope to take to New York as soon as they are old enough."

When I spoke with Ellen on Saturday, she and Larry had just returned from a big breakfast prepared by an octogenarian friend and cancer survivor at his glorious country getaway cabin. As their friend fried country ham, he remarked that he had "good, better, and best days." For him there were no bad days. What simple but powerful wisdom this is.

With her friend's insight, Ellen reflected upon her own illness. She replied, "I didn't really know what was in store for me but I knew there was a purpose. My family has been phenomenal!! I know how important it is to have faith. I did not see my illness as a doomsday. I knew I would get through it. I had peace with it.

I just knew that things would work out for the best." *Yes, dear Ellen, faith, family, and friends give meaning to our lives and sustain us in challenging times.*

As we continued to talk, Ellen stated that she knows that in some capacity she will be an advocate for breast cancer. She considers the spring cancer walk, "Relay for Life," as a possible avenue.

Ellen, we are grateful to you for allowing us to be part of your life these past months. You've enriched us as human beings as you allowed us a glimpse into your life as a cancer survivor.

Yes, Ellen, your DKG friends have been cheering you on for a full recovery! You made it through surgery, sixteen weeks of chemo, a month interlude without any treatment, and 33 blasts of radiation!

Throughout this ordeal, you exhibited deep faith in God, great optimism and determination, and strong courage. May we each remember that life is a gift and we should live each day fully and joyfully. May we always encircle you with our tender love and care.

REFLECTIONS:
"Love is the river of life in the world." Henry Ward Beecher

"Be willing to relinquish the life you've planned, so as to have the life that is waiting for you." Joseph Campbell

"Begin at once to live, and count each day as a separate life." Seneca

Old Irish Blessing
"I do not wish you joy without sorrow
Nor endless day without the healing dark
Nor brilliant sun without the restful shadow
Nor tides that turn against your bark
I wish you faith and love and strength a wisdom but
Goods, gold enough to help each needy one
I wish you songs also blessed silence
And God's sweet peace when every day is done."
Unknown

What a friend Carmen is! As president of Eta State during my treatment, she volunteered to call and check on me every week or so and report to the other officers, past presidents and many others in Eta State. She was wonderful in her reporting although I was not allowed to read any of it until she completed the task. Thank you Carmen! And to Emily and Betty, who filled in a week for her, thank you as well.

More Side Effects

The next months were busy with school, family and plans for a Friendship Force exchange to Sweden. As the exchange director, I had the responsibility of making travel arrangements for the exchange and also for a trip extension to Finland, Denmark and Norway that the group wanted to take.

The Floyds, Larry, and I decided to go a week ahead of the group of ambassadors and visit the Normandy Coast of France. Friends of ours in Middleburg, Netherlands, were going to join us and do the driving, so we flew to Belgium where they picked us up. Our bags took another route from ours and for five days neither of us had luggage. Luckily, we had packed an extra set of clothes in our carry-on luggage. We bought a few items that we had to have and decided to try and enjoy the French coast. Larry was the "tour guide" for our daily visits to the sites along the way. We started at the southernmost part and continued northward until we had covered all the landing sites for the *Operation Overlord* maneuvers of World War II. *Operation Overlord* was the code name for the invasion of the coast of Normandy, which General Montgomery commanded until Supreme Commander Eisenhower took over. Luckily, one of the Floyds' bags and both of ours had finally arrived after five days. Our bags had had a full tour of France before arriving in Caen.

This was a great experience but a very tiring one for me. I did, however, walk down the hill to Omaha Beach and also onto Utah Beach. Our daughter-in-law Wendi's dad had served in the army and landed on Omaha Beach on D--Day plus one. He had never wanted to speak of the experience very much. His memories were of the beaches strewn with the bodies of his comrades. Walking on Omaha Beach where he had walked and seen the many lives lost for our freedom was sobering.

We left France and drove back to Brussels where we boarded a flight to Copenhagen in order to meet our ambassadors. The Swedish Friendship Force Exchange Director met us and took us by train to Helsingborg, Sweden to meet our hosts. Our Swedish hosts were wonderful and we enjoyed the experiences they had planned for us. My legs got a real workout on this trip, but I kept up with the group. I did take every opportunity to rest.

During the month of June, as we enjoyed our European experiences, I noticed that my hair seemed thinner and thinner. It was so short that I had not taken a curling iron or rollers to help with styling. Actually, the hair that I had was much like my mother had said it was as a baby--fine and curly. The hair problem was really beginning to bother me, but I knew I had an appointment with Dr. Woodard in August.

July was a busy month. Larry always plants a big vegetable garden full of sweet corn, tomatoes, peppers, green beans, sweet potatoes, okra, cantaloupes, watermelons, beets, and peas. There was freezing and canning to do since I was not able to help much the summer before. With my aching knees unable to stoop to pick beans I became the "bean snapper," which suited me okay.

My first mammogram was scheduled for the last of July. I really dreaded this appointment because the breast tissue was still very tender. I had to go by the local hospital and pick up all the mammograms that I had ever had to take with me to Charlotte. The Charlotte Breast Radiology Center, which Dr. Woodard recommended to me as the best place to go, does mammograms all day every day and a radiologist is on duty to speak to every patient following the tests. Mammogram complete, I asked the technician if I could also have ultrasound since the last mammogram that I had did not show the cancer until I had been marked with an "X." The radiologist came in to talk with me and agreed to do the ultrasound that I had suggested. He could see that I was apprehensive about the whole situation and wanted to reassure me that there was no problem, no signs of cancers! It was reassuring to me to have both types of tests and for the doctor to say that everything was clear of tumors.

In August I had a three month appointment with Dr. Woodard. My first question to him was, "Should I be losing my hair again?" I bent my head over so that he could see my whole head and he seemed really shocked at what he saw. He said that I shouldn't have lost most of it again. He then said no more Arimidex and prescribed Aromasin, another of the three drugs (Arimidex, Femara, and Aromasin) used for women who are post-menopausal to block the production of estrogen. He recommended that I see my dermatologist.

Dr. Pearson, my dermatologist, took a biopsy of my scalp. The results indicated the hair follicles were alive but were being traumatized by the drug. He then made an appointment for me to see a dermatologist who specializes in hair problems at the Bowman Gray School of Medicine in Winston-Salem, North Carolina. She was not very helpful, although she was sympathetic to my problem. She suggested the foam-style, male formula of Rogaine, once a day. She also prescribed half the oral dose that is prescribed for men who have hair loss. I was reluctant to try the pill so I called Dr. Woodard for his opinion. He asked me to wait until he could research it for a few days. With his approval a few days later, I tried both the suggestions for a year. I saw little improvement. I kept my remaining hair as short as I thought I could stand it while I dreamed of a full head of hair. Can you imagine this? Little hair, almost no eyebrows or eyelashes--but at least cancer free! I can't remember the times that I was told not to worry about the hair, since it was better than the cancer. Did they really think I didn't know that?

Have you ever heard of trigger finger? This results when you bend a finger and it won't straighten by itself or if it does it has a clicking sound. "Murphy's Law" (if something bad can happen, it will happen to me) always gets me! My left thumb began to click occasionally and then every time I bent the joint. It was getting worse and causing pain when it did click. I made an appointment with an orthopedic doctor who recommended that it be surgically repaired since it had gotten worse. I was curious about the reason for this, so I went again online to the side effects of Arimidex since it had already caused me so much grief. On two different sites, I read about other breast cancer patients who had had the same experience either with a finger or thumb. Several reputable sites confirm the possibility of trigger finger from taking the drug. This was considered an unusual or rare side effect of the drug. At this point in my life, this type of drug had caused: hair loss, extreme hot flashes, trigger thumb, increased blood pressure, weight gain, weakness and fatigue, increase in my lipid panel, dry skin and dryness in almost all orifices, and joint and muscle pain. These symptoms had required the addition of a pill for blood pressure, an increase in cholesterol-lowering dosage, a pill for hot flashes, a pill for joint pain, a pill for hair loss, and surgery on my thumb. By the way, the drug also causes bone loss, so I must have a bone density scan every year.

There have been two other problems as a result of the five year pill! The purpose of the medication is to prevent estrogen production in my body. This is good as far as my cancer is concerned, since no estrogen for any possible straggling cancer cell would mean death to the cell. But no estrogen means you dry up like a prune inside and out. Lotions and creams help with skin and conditioner for the hair. My gynecologist suggested an E-string for vaginal dryness. It is a flexible ring that emits a tiny amount of estrogen over a three month period of time and then it is replaced. For about a year this worked successfully.

In October of 2008 I noticed some vaginal spotting and called the doctor. An examination identified a tiny spot of granulation tissue which my doctor explained was healing tissue. We discussed the E-string and I told him that it had recently been difficult to remove. The consensus of three doctors was that the E-string could be the culprit. Over the course of nine months, I made one or more visits monthly to see my doctor for a cauterizing procedure using silver nitrate with no healing success. In July of 2009, I underwent major surgery to remove this small piece of stubborn tissue.

I have mentioned before that within months of beginning the five year pill, I had enlarged finger joints. These have caused some of my worst pains. These joints have been the second biggest visible change in my treatment, my loss of hair being the first. The fingers have ached for years, but recently they have become worse. My left ring finger will barely bend and looks much larger than normal. I can't make a tight fist with my left hand. At a recent physical with Dr. Mike, I told him of the hand pain. He examined the hand and the finger in particular, and said he felt a growth on top of the bone. He ordered an x-ray and then asked me to see a hand specialist. Growth or not, just the suggestion that there might be one sent me into a spin.

Larry had hand surgery a year ago in Charlotte, so I called his Dr. Gaston for an appointment. Dr. Gaston ordered additional x-rays and found that the finger joint in question had dark streaks in it, as well as arthritis like all the other fingers. He felt it was just a bad case of arthritis, but with my history he wanted to check out all the possibilities. These possibilities included a bone biopsy. He wanted to consult with the colleagues in his practice as well as radiologists and oncologists. He did agree that I possibly had a cyst on the finger.

Dr. Gaston gave me a copy of an article that he coauthored with Dr. Bryan J. Loeffler. *"Aromatase Inhibitors and Their Side Effects: What Hand Surgeons Should Know."* Gaston and Loeffler found that "Aromatase inhibitors include the trade names Arimidex, Aromasin and Femara. The generic names are Anastrozole, Exemestane, and Letrozole in the same order as trade names."

'In it, the doctors note "growing evidence associating aromastase inhibitors with carpal tunnel syndrome and trigger finger as well as tendon, muscle and joint problems. Musculoskeletal side effects can be severe and incapacitating symptoms requiring hospitalization. Severe early morning stiffness and hand/wrist pain are the most commonly reported symptoms affecting activities of daily living. In addition to the musculoskeletal system pains and problems the estrogen deprivation causes may also lead to decreased bone mineral density and fragility fractures."[12]

HELLO!!! What have I been saying for years?!

I saw my oncologist Dr. Woodard that day also. He assured me that he had never had a breast cancer patient who had the cancer metastasize in the bones of the hand. I was again given the wonderful words *cancer free*!

---

12 Loeffler, MD, Bryan J., and R. Glenn Gaston, MD. "Aromatase Inhibitors and Their Side Effects: What Hand Surgeons Should Know." *American Society for Surgery of the Hand* (2010)

With my second visit to Dr. Gaston, he told me that he had seen breast cancer metastasize in bones of the hand, but he didn't think that was my problem. He thinks that my hands are severe cases of arthritis, but he will check them again in four months. He offered to prescribe an additional drug to help relieve the pain but I declined. The pain and aching can be soothed with Advil, but nothing ever takes the pain completely away.

I am happy to have been invited recently to speak at the local Cancer Center to a group of ladies who had been diagnosed with breast cancer in the last six months. I spoke with them about my experiences and journaling. As I shared my experiences, I could see heads nodding in agreement with many of the side effects and experiences that I had shared with them. When the meeting was over, many of the ladies wanted to tell me how much my experience had been like their own. Two of the ladies asked for my telephone number in case they thought of something else that they wanted to ask. Rita Wortman, the cancer center nurse who had invited me, sent me a thank you note following the meeting. She said that the evaluations were all positive and that we both probably could read their minds that "they were feeling what I had been through." Mrs. Wortman concluded the note by saying that "sometimes she meets a person and is never quite the same—thank you for touching my heart." I hope that in the future I will be invited to share my story again. It reminds me of Proverbs 13:19 (KJV) "A desire accomplished is sweet to the soul."

"It is Doable!"

As you can see, the familiar phrase, "It's not a sprint but a marathon," is true after breast cancer. I really am not bitter over the lingering side effects, but, do want others to know that it doesn't end with the surgery! As Hermie told me, "It is doable!" Now, four years out from the cancer, I still have many of the side effects, but, for the most part, I am doing great. An extra handful of pills, thin hair, joint pains, few eyebrows and eyelashes compared to a meaningful life don't amount to much. Life is good!

My goal in writing this book was to tell my story so that others might learn what to expect either as the patient or as the care-giver. I want to reiterate several things that I think are most important. Know your own body. Do self-breast exams regularly! Have mammograms when recommended by your physician. Be your own advocate when you are diagnosed with breast cancer or if you suspect a problem and the process is moving too slowly. Talk with someone who has been through the process and read about it. Don't automatically accept what is recommended until you know the pros and cons of your decisions. Ask questions.

Another important part of my story was the human network of support. How could you deal with tragedies, deaths, illnesses, and other bad things without support? My family surrounded me with encouragement, love, food, and prayers. Our church, neighbors, friends, and even strangers sent cards of encouragement and promises of prayer. Many showed their love with food. My DKG *sisters* kept up-to-date by

Carmen's journal, sent cards and gifts and offered prayers on my behalf. The medical staff at every institution was exceptionally competent and caring. And what blessings to be taken care of and/or remembered by my former students.

I would be remiss if I did not share with you my greatest support. As a young teenager I gave my heart to God. My salvation I know was a gift from God as promised in His word.

Ephesians 2:8 (New King James Version)
For by grace you have been saved through faith, and that not of yourselves; *it is* the gift of God.

Dr. Richard Blackaby, in Putting A Face On Grace, states that "Grace looks beyond a person's misguided attitude and sees the beautiful potential of a life freed from sin's grasp."[13] Our salvation does not mean that we are perfect but takes time and lots of God's grace. Grace is produced when we allow the Holy Spirit to work in our lives.

As a Christian, I know that God owes me nothing and I deserve nothing. My salvation is totally unmerited from a loving, merciful God. God's Son, who was crucified and arose from the dead, bridges the gap from God to me. What a blessing it is to wake every morning knowing that God is in control of my life. It is so reassuring to know that His presence is with me in good times and bad. In difficult times, He surrounds me with His love and peace and this gives me hope. I have been strengthened through the difficulties I experienced with breast cancer because of His faithfulness to me. **May God be glorified!** My prayer for those who read this book is that they will have the same support that comes only through faith in God.

---

13 Blackaby, Richard. Putting a Face on Grace. Multnomah. *Master Work* summer (2009): 28.

Appendix A: From My Experience

FROM MY EXPERIENCE:

WHAT YOU MAY EXPERIENCE WITH BREAST CANCER DIAGNOSIS, SURGERY, CHEMOTHERAPY, RADIATION AND FOLLOWING.

THE SCIENCE OF THE EXPERIENCE

1. It is important to do self-breast exams, and have clinical exams and mammograms.
2. Know your body's own lumps and bumps.
3. If you find a lump, see a doctor; get a mammogram--and surgery if needed, all as soon as possible.
4. Choose surgical options with your doctor after determining the stage of your cancer. The results of the biopsy will identify the size, type and stage of cancer With explanations from your surgeon you can agree on the surgery needed.
5. Expect seven radioactive salts injections in the affected breast prior to sentinel node surgery. These injections, plus a dye added in surgery, can help identify the sentinel node. The pain is a stinging feeling and then burning, but at least it doesn't last too long.
6. Consider the number of lymph nodes that will be removed. My theory is that two or three can identify whether cancer has spread. If it has and more are needed, then you can have more removed, but why take most or all of them only to find that the cancer has not spread? Lymphodema is a serious

problem and removing more lymph nodes increases your risk for that problem.

7. After the breast heals, you will need some rehab on that arm. I found that stretching my arm above my head and Wall *Walking* with my fingers several times a day was helpful. I still cannot reach into the back of high, deep cabinets with that arm like I once did.
8. The Affected Arm is to be considered pristine--no pricks, sticks or blood pressures in that arm.
9. Ask questions about procedures, side effects and the pros/cons.
10. Keep a list of your medications and take it with you always.
11. CHEMOTHERAPY
    - ❖ If chemotherapy is necessary, you may have a choice of two or three week intervals.
    - ❖ Adriamycin and Cytoxin chemotherapy
        - ➢ With chemotherapy you probably will lose your hair by the second treatment, feel sick and be exhausted!
        - ➢ If you are given Neulasta 24 hours following treatment to build your white blood cells, expect good results but also hip pain for several days after having the injections.
        - ➢ You may be given a choice to have surgery to place a port into your chest where the chemotherapy would be administered. I chose not to have it and to be stuck for each chemo treatment, because there is a significant infection risk with a port.
        - ➢ Ginger ale and ginger snaps help with the nausea.
        - ➢ Cool foods in small amounts taken more often help during chemo.
        - ➢ No spicy foods during the first days after chemotherapy.
    - ❖ You will need a variety of HATS even if you wear a wig at times.

- ❖ Protect yourself from the dangers of infection and avoid crowds.
- ❖ Taxol chemotherapy
  - ➢ You may possibly have neuropathy.
  - ➢ Eating ice chips are recommended during Taxol infusion.
  - ➢ Eyebrows and eyelashes may come out or at least thin during this treatment.
  - ➢ Expect joint and muscle pains.
  - ➢ Extra preliminary drugs may be given to counteract any allergic reactions.
  - ➢ The infusion of Taxol is given over a longer time period.

12. RADIATION THERAPY
    - ❖ Tattoos are made to provide precise targeting of the radiation following a planning session.
    - ❖ The radiation session is short and painless, five days a week for approximately six or seven weeks.
    - ❖ You will experience a loss of energy.
    - ❖ You may experience a sunburn look or even blisters and peeling.
    - ❖ You may experience shooting pains or a crawling feeling in the affected breast. This results from nerves regrowing.
    - ❖ Following radiation the breast tissue may feel like it has thickened. I have this thickening and am told that it will always be that way.
    - ❖ Buy bra extenders if you choose to wear a bra that becomes too tight to be comfortable on tender skin.
    - ❖ Corn starch and prescription creams help keep the breast in good condition so that radiation can continue on schedule.

13. If your cancer was hormone sensitive then you will be given one of three or four available drugs to block estrogen

production depending on whether you are pre-- or post--menopausal.

14. With any new pain or difference, you will wonder if it is the return of cancer. Tell your oncologist and check it out, if you feel it is necessary.

THE HEART OF THE MATTER

1. Your initial reaction to breast cancer diagnosis may be fear but if so, get rid of it quickly. New research is in your favor.
2. The longer you have to wait to confirm cancer, the more your brain will play tricks on you. So, don't waste any time and be your own advocate to get an appointment as soon as possible.
3. Stay focused on only the next step in the process.
4. Live one day at a time--that's all you can handle at once.
5. Talk to someone who has been there.
6. Take someone with you to doctors' appointment; two sets of ears are better than one.
7. Keep your mind busy with reading, games, and puzzles if you feel okay.
8. Keep a positive attitude.
9. Wear loose, comfortable clothing to chemotherapy treatments.
10. Buy a wig and have it styled before you lose your hair.
11. Have a supply of hats to wear and remember to have one for nighttime. Your head gets cold when you have no hair.
12. Keep a daily journal if you feel like it or have someone help on days that you don't feel well.
13. No pity-parties.
14. Join a support group, if you don't have one.
15. Be your own advocate!
16. You will need a good caregiver.
17. This experience strengthened my faith in God.

Appendix B: Glossary

1. ADRIAMYCIN... (Doxorubicin) A drug given intravenously to treat cancer.
2. ALOXI... (Palonsetron) A drug given intravenously or orally to control delayed nausea and vomiting that appears 24 hours or more after chemotherapy.
3. ANZEMET... (Dolasetron) A drug given to reduce nausea and vomiting following chemotherapy.
4. ARIMIDEX... (Anastrozole) A drug used to treat breast cancer following surgery of post-menopausal women. It interrupts the body's synthesis of estrogen.
5. AROMASIN... (Exemestane) A drug used to treat breast cancer following surgery of post-menopausal women. It helps lower estrogen by preventing the production of estrogen.
6. ARRHYTHMIA... (Cardiac Dysrhythmia) Abnormal electrical activity in the heart. The heart beat may be too fast or too slow.
7. AXILLARY LYMPH NODES... Large lymph nodes found in the armpit or axilla
8. BIAFINE CREAM... a topical emulsion for use in radiation dermatitis as well as other dermatologic wounds.
9. BENADRYL...(Diphenhydromine Hydrochloride) An antihistamine mainly used to treat allergies.
10. CNA... In the USA an acronym for Certified Nursing Assistant.

11. CT SCAN… (Computed Tomography) A medical imaging machine used to support diagnosis and treatment of diseases.
12. CHEMOTHERAPY… The treatment of diseases especially by killing cells that divide rapidly. The fast dividing cells can be cancerous or normal such as bone marrow, digestive tract or hair follicles.
13. CYTOXIN… (Cycloposphamide)A drug used to treat various types of cancer and some autoimmune disorders. It slows or stops cell growth.
14. CHEMO BRAIN…Following chemotherapy the inability to concentrate or to have cognitive impairment.
15. CAUTERIZE… Electrocautery or chemical cautery is a medical practice or technique of burning a part of a body to remove or closeoff a part of it.
16. DOSIMETRIST… a professional who is responsible for detailed treatment calculations and quality control.
17. DECADRON… (Dexamethasome) A synthetic steroid that acts as an anti-inflammatory and immunosuppressants that is often given to cancer patients to counteract the side effects of chemotherapy.
18. EBRT ...(External Beam Radiation Therapy) A beam of radiation from outside the body is directed onto the cancerous organ or tissue within the body.
19. ECHOCARDIOGRAM… a three dimensional ultrasound to view the heart muscle and valves and to determine blood flow, velocity of blood, etc.
20. EMESIS… vomiting or throwing up
21. FEMORA… (Letrozole) an oral non-steroidal treatment given after surgery for breast cancer that is hormone sensitive.
22. ESTRING… a flexible, silicon ring with a low-dose of estradiol (estrogen) released slowly over a three month period to treat hot flashes and vaginal atropy associated with menopause.

23. HDR ... (Brachytherapy) a high intensity radiation delivered with precision into the tumor site or next to the area requiring treatment
24. HEMORRHAGIC STROKE... (cerebral hemorrhage, CVA or cerebrovascular accident) The rapid loss of brain function due to a disturbance in blood supply.
25. HEMOGLOBIN...in vertebrates, the red iron-containing pigment that increases the oxygen-carrying capacity of blood.
26. HORMONE THERAPY... the use of hormones in medical treatment
27. *IN SITU*... a Latin phrase meaning in the place or location; it is pre-cancer or the early stage of unusual breast cells.
28. INFUSION...the administration of fluids, medicines or nutrients, into a patient's circulatory system
29. LEUKEMIA... cancer of the white blood cells.
30. LINEAR ACCELERATOR... a device using microwave technology to greatly accelerate subatomic particles or ions. The high energy X-rays then are directed to patients tumor sites.
31. LUMPECTOMY... (Tylectomy) a common procedure to remove a benign tumor or breast cancer considered a breast conserving method of surgery.
32. LYMPH NODE... small, round structure that traps bacteria, cancer cells or other harmful pathogens.
33. LYMPHATIC SYSTEM... a body system that is a network of conduits that carry clear fluid called lymph. This system is important in the body's defense against disease.
34. LYMPHEDEMA... Fluid retention and tissue swelling caused by a compromised lymphatic system
35. MAMMOGRAM...A diagnostic and screening technique using low dose amplitude X-rays to examine human breasts.
36. MASTECTOMY... the surgical removal of one or both breasts either partially or completely.

37. NEEDLE BIOPSY… (needle aspiration biopsy) a diagnostic procedure used to investigate superficial lumps or masses. A hollow needle used to extract fluid or solid cells for examination.
38. NEULASTA (Pegfilgrastim)…an immunostimulator which is used to stimulate bone marrow to produce Neutrophils (white blood cells to fight infection in patients undergoing chemotherapy.
39. NEUROPATHY… a term for damage to nerves of the peripheral nervous system caused either by diseases of the nerve or from side effects of systemic illnesses.
40. ONCOLOGY…branch of medicine that deals with tumors/cancer
41. PARTIAL MASTECTOMY…a breast conserving method of surgery that removed about one fourth of the breast tissue.
42. PET SCAN (Positive Emission Tomography)… a nuclear medicine imaging technique which produces a three-dimensional image or picture.
43. POLYCYTHEMIA…bone marrow produces too many red blood cells but it may also result in the overproduction of white blood cells and platelets.
44. PORT (Medical port or portacath)… a small medical appliance that is installed beneath the skin under the clavicle or collar bone where a catheter connects the port to a vein.
45. QUANDRANTECTOMY (Partial Mastectomy)…a breast conserving surgery that removes about one-fourth of the breast.
46. RADIATION THERAPY… the medical use of ionizing radiation as part of cancer treatment to control malignant cells.
47. RADIATION ONCOLOGIST… a doctor who specializes in the treatment of cancer.
48. RADIATION PHYSICIST…… a medical specialist in imaging and radiotherapy

49. RECONSTRUCTIVE BREAST SURGERY...surgery to restore form and function of the body following breast cancer
50. *RED DEVIL,* RED KILLER, ADRIAMYCIN, DOXORUBICIN...a red chemotherapy drug used often in breast cancer treatment.
51. SALINE SOLUTION...A sterile solution of sodium chloride in water but it is sterile only if given intravenously, otherwise it is simply a salt water solution.
52. SENTINEL LYMPH NODE... the hypothetical first lymph node or group of nodes reached by metastasizing cancer cells from a primary tumor.
53. SURGICAL BIOPSY ... The removal of an entire lesion during a surgical procedure with a negative or clear margin if possible.
54. TAGAMENT (CIMETIDINE)... an H2 (histamine) receptor antagonist that inhibits the production and decreases the amount of acid in the stomach.
55. TATTOO (RADIATION TATTOO)... a tiny round and blue mark that resembles a mole that is used for positioning a patient for irradiating a breast
56. TAXOL (PACLITAXEL)... a natural product from the bark of the Pacific Yew Tree that adversely affects the process of cell division by preventing restructuring of cells. The fast-dividing cancer cells are more susceptible to Paclitaxel treatment than normal cells. Decadron (Dexamethasone) is given prior to infusion to help with some of the side effects.
57. TECHNETIUM TAGGED WITH SULFUR COLLIDE...... a nuclear medicine that is used in preparation for a sentinel lymph node dissection.
58. TNM SYSTEM... a classification system for identifying malignant tumors; a staging system that describes the extent of cancer in a patients body.

59. *TRIGGER FINGER*...this occurs when the motion of a tendon that opens or closes the finger is limited, causing the finger to lock or catch as the finger is extended.
60. WOLF PARKINSON WHITE SYNDROME (WPW)... the electrical signals of the heart normally use only one path when they move from the top to the bottom of the heart. If an extra pathway is present, the electrical signal may arrive at the ventricles too soon.

Appendix C: Index of Names

Delta Kappa Gamma Friends

Betty Marshall
Carmen Redding
Emily Weigel
Hermie Gaston
Katherine Collins
Judy Carlson

Double Springs Baptist Church

Gragg Family

Ella .... granddaughter
Izora .... granddaughter
Jane .... granddaughter
Jacob .... grandson
Jeff .... son
Joe .... grandson
Kate .... granddaughter
Kelly .... son
Kim .... daughter-in-law
Larry .... husband
Lea .... daughter-in-law
Lee .... son
Lucy Pope .... granddaughter
Troy .... grandson
Wendi .... daughter-in-law

Martin Family
William Jefferson............Grandfather
Anne Elizabeth (Bessie)...Grandmother

Japanese Hosts
Goto Family.... Azu, Chie, Kayo, Joshi, Saho, Taki
Kawai Family... Shinya Kawai, MD, Ikuko

Medical Professionals
Carolinas Hematology/Oncology Associates
101 W.T. Harris Blvd. Building 1000 Suite 1214
Charlotte, NC 28262 704-863-6160
Warden L. Woodard, MD
Adrienne Washington
Billie Rhymes...nurse
Kim Rippy.......nurse
Rick Davis.......nurse
Sharon Holder...receptionist

Cleveland Dermatology PA
700 N. Lafayette Street
Shelby, NC 28150 704-484-0464
Lawrence H. Pearson, MD

Cleveland Regional Medical Center
201 East Grover Street
Shelby, NC 28150 704-480-1921
Paul Munoz, MD

CRMC Cancer Center
Radiology............980-487-3144
Helen Maddux, MD
Alan Sanders
Beth Allison Condrey
Latonya McKissick Hopper
Pam Helms
Rita Wortman

CVS Pharmacy
212 Main Street
Boiling Springs, NC 28089 704-434-6560
Tonya Gantt................pharmacist/friend
Tina Hawkins ....pharmacist/friend/former student

Kings Mountain Women's Care
821 E. King Street
Kings Mountain, NC 28086 704-734-0304
Steven Chamberlain, MD

OrthoCarolina
1915 Randolph Road
Charlotte, NC 28207 704-323-2426
R. Glenn Gaston, MD
Orthopaedic Surgery
Hand and Upper Extremity

Shelby Medical Associates PA
711 N. Dekalb Street
Shelby, NC 28150   704-482-1482
Michael Ribadeneyra, MD

Shelby Surgical Associates PA
200 W. Grover Street
Shelby, NC 28150 704-487-8591
Douglas Hobson, MD

H. Gene Washburn, MD retired

New Life Sunday School Class

Washburn Family
Ann W. McSwain........cousin
Beaman.......................brother
Dianne W. Garner.......sister and sketch artist of *Lady of Hope*

Dietz ....Daddy
Emily ....Aunt
Elizabeth ....Mother
Estilla (Tillie ....Grandmother
H. Gene, MD..............uncle
Ginger G. Orient ....niece
Gordon, Rev...............uncle
Joe Chauncey ....Grandfather
Linda L. Wilson ....cousin
Susie.............................sister-in-law
Terry W. Royster ....sister
Tommy Royster ....brother-in-law
Troy ....cousin
Trudy ....“adopted” sister

Others mentioned by name:
Arlin Bush...................Friend and former student
Alice Cullinan, PHD ..University professor
Betty Lockridge ....Friend
Barbara Lail.................Lea’s mom and friend
Donnie Iveste ....Friend and To Company owner
Douglas Cabiness ....Friend
Jan Cabiness Jenks ......Friend and hairdresser
Jerry Floyd ....Friend and travel mate
Judy McSwain ....Friend and former coworker
Lena Ish ....Pennsylvania Mennonite Caterer
Libby Sarazen ....Friend and breast cancer survivor
Linda Lee ....Friend
Marietta Floyd ....Friend and travel mate
Omar Porter ....Former student
Patsy Cabiness ....Friend
Paul Stacy ....College Professor
Rachel Smucker ....Amish-Mennonite Tour Guide
Wanda Scruggs............Friend and former coworker

RESOURCES

American Cancer Society, Inc.
250 Williams Street
Atlanta, GA 30303
1-800-227-2345
www.cancer.org

Blackaby, Richard. "Putting a Face on Grace." Multnomah. *Master Work* summer (2009):28.

Loeffler, MD, Bryan J., and R. Glenn Gaston, MD
"Aromatase Inhibitors and Their Side Effects:
What Hand Surgeons Should Know." J Hand Surgery.
2010;(A):1206-1208.

National Cancer Institute
NCL Office of Communications and Education
Public Inquires Office
6116 Executive Blvd. Suite 300
Bethesda, MD 20892-8322
www.cancer.gov

1-800-422-6237
LiveHelp Online Chat
Monday through Friday 8 A.M.-11 P.M. Eastern Time

National Cancer Institute Footnotes by Number

1. NCI: Breast Cancer. Bethesda, MD
   Available at cancer.gov/cancertopics/types/breast
   On our site. Accessed January 1, 2011
2. NCI: Cancer Staging. Bethesda, MD
   Date Last Modified: 09/22/2010
   Available at cancer.gov/cancertopics/factsheet/detection/staging
   On our site. Accessed January 1, 2011
3. NCI: Computed Tomography (CT) Questions/Answers Bethesda, MD
   Date Last Modified: 09/08/2003
   Available at cancer.gov/cancertopics/factsheet/detection/ct
   On our site. Accessed January 1, 2011
4. NCI: Prognosis and Predictive Factors. Bethesda, MD
   Date Last Modified: 12/23/2010
   Available at cancer.gov/cancertopics/pdq/treatment/breast/healthprofessional
   On our site. Accessed January 1, 2011
5. NCI: Sentinel Lymph Node Biopsy. Bethesda, MD
   Date Last Modified: 04.27/2005
   Available at cancer.gov/factsheet/therapy/sentinel-node-biopsy
   On our site. Accessed January 1, 2011
6. NCI: Dictionary of Cancer Terms. Bethesda MD
   Available at the following sites:
   EBRT cancer.gov /dictionary/?cdrID=46751
   Dosimetrist cancer.gov/dictionary/?cdrID=44665

RadiationOncologist.cancer.gov/dictionary/?cdrID=46546
Radiation Physicist cancer.gov/dictionary/?cdrID=44718
Radiation Therapist cancer.gov/dictionary/?cdrID=44719
On our site January 1, 2011

7. NCI: How is Radiation Therapy Given to Patients. Bethesda. MD
   Date Last Modified: 06/30/2010

Available at cancer.gov/cancertopics/factsheet/therapy/radiation
On our site January 1, 2011
8. NCI: Chemotherapy. Bethesda, MD
Date Last Modified: 06/29/2007
Available at
cancer.gov/cancertopics/coping/chemotherapy and you/page2
On our site January 1, 2011
9. NCI: Targeted Therapy. Bethesda, MD
Date Last Modified: 06/21/2010
Available at cancer.gov/factsheet/therapy/targeted/question4
On our site January 1, 2011
10. NCI: HER2/neu. Bethesda, MD
Available at cancer.gov/dictionary/?cdrID=44945
On our site January 1, 2011
11. 11.NCI: Monoclonal Antibody. Bethesda, Md
Available at cancer.gov/dictionary/?cdrID=46066
On our site January 1, 2011